Law in Light

Law in Light

Priestesses, Priests, and the Revitalization of Akan Spirituality in the United States and Ghana

Lauren Coyle Rosen

UNIVERSITY OF CALIFORNIA PRESS

University of California Press
Oakland, California

© 2024 by Lauren Coyle Rosen

Cataloging-in-Publication data is on file at the Library of
Congress.

ISBN 978-0-520-39706-4 (cloth)

ISBN 978-0-520-39708-8 (pbk.)

ISBN 978-0-520-39709-5 (ebook)

33 32 31 30 29 28 27 26 25 24
10 9 8 7 6 5 4 3 2 1

For Jeffrey Rosen,
and for the Light.

CONTENTS

Introduction

1

1. Okomfohema Nana Akua Amoabaa Botwe I,
Queen Mother and Chief Priestess

15

2. Ankobeahema Nana Amoabaa Atei Asiedu,
Elder and High Priestess

55

3. Several Young Priestesses of the House: Call,
Initiation, Graduation, and Pathfinders

83

4. Nana Osofo Yaw Nkrumah: Law, Order, Vitality,
and Health in Shrine Governance

105

5. Okomfohene Nana Yaw Yirenkyi Opare Gyebi I, Chief Priest
at the Asuo Gyebi Shrine in Larteh, Kubease

116

6. Okomfopanyin Nana Afoah Baakang, Eldest Priestess
at the Asuo Gyebi Shrine in Larteh, Kubease
139

7. Okomfokese Nana Baakan Okukuranpon
Yirenkyiwa, Chief Priestess
146

Conclusion: Revitalized Visions and Transatlantic
Copresence in Akan Spirituality
160

Acknowledgments 169

Notes 171

Bibliography 189

Index 215

Introduction

In January 2019, Akan path priestesses and priests from Ghana and the United States joined together for the inaugural Freedom Friday, celebrating the great return of African Americans and other African diasporans to the shores of one of their ancestral homelands. Then-President Akufo-Addo had welcomed all from across the world to come home to Ghana. In honor of the occasion, a sacred Akom ceremony to summon key *Abosom* (exalted divine spirits, often referred to as deities, deified ancestors, saints, or angelic beings) and ancestors from inside the notorious Elmina Castle, with its horrific dungeon and door of no return, was held. Portuguese traders built the castle for trading purposes in 1482, with the Dutch seizing it in 1637. By the seventeenth century, it had become a central part of the Atlantic slave trade.[1]

Okomfopanyin Nana Afoah Baakang (Nana Afoah Baakang), the Ghanaian eldest priestess of the legendary Asuo Gyebi shrine complex at the bottom in the mountain in a Ghanaian town called Larteh, was among those who led the Akom.[2] It was her first visit to the castle. Other priestesses, priests, and spiritual authorities from the Akan shrine culture in Larteh and the United States also took part on this historic occasion.

The Akom, a central part of Akan spirituality, involves the pouring of libations and sacred music and dancing, to call forth the named spirits, including those ancestors who had been brutally stolen and forced through the door of no return. The spirits often will possess the priestesses and priests (*akomfo;* sing., *okomfo*), speaking, prophesying, singing, dancing, and celebrating through the human vessels.[3] This was a call to the spirits to invite them to join in a celebration of the ancestors' descendants returning to the land, and their living in freedom while working to help heal and liberate people still enslaved, whether spiritually or physically.

One of the key orchestrators for Freedom Friday was an African American priestess, Okomfohema Nana Akua Amoabaa Botwe I (Okomfohema Botwe I), who is a leader in the Akan shrine culture and a queen mother and chief priestess of two prominent shrines—the Akan Spiritual United Order (ASUO) in Maryland and the Asuo Gyebi shrine in Larteh.

I asked Okomfohema Botwe I what this Freedom Friday ceremony, in its essence, meant to her and the shrine community.

"The Elmina Castle Akom is an example of the resilience of African people. We were forced through the doors of no return. And four hundred years later, the *return*," she replied.

It is not just the people who are returning. It is the spirits of the ancestors who were forced from the lands as well. They have returned, joining the spiritual and physical realms in this profound statement of aspiration toward healing, restitution, and liberation—or, at least, a fuller reckoning.[4]

Okomfohema Botwe I is one of the leaders of the second-generation priestesses who have been helping to guide and drive the revitalization of Akan shrine culture in the United States and its flourishing ties with the source shrine in Larteh. She has been a member of the Akan shrine culture since her teacher, Okomfohene Nana Yao Opare Dinizulu I (Nana Yao Opare Dinizulu I) and the family of Bosum Dzemawodzi (the spiritual house he founded and led), went to Ghana and received permission to set up the first Akan shrine house in the United States, in New York City. He received this spiritual charge and official authorization from the then-chief priestess of the Larteh Akonnedi shrine, Okomfohene Nana Akua Oparebea (Nana Oparebea). Nana Oparebea had been a close religious adviser and personal healer of Ghana's first president, Dr. Kwame Nkrumah, in the years around 1957, as the anticolonial resistance movement first achieved the nation's formal independence from the British.

Nana Dinizulu established the first Akan shrine house in New York City in 1967.[5] Okomfohema Botwe I was a member of Nana Dinizulu's second graduating class of priestesses and priests in the United States. She initiated as an *okomfowaa* to the *Obosom* Nana Asuo Gyebi in 1973 when she was twenty years old, and she graduated from training to become an *okomfo* (a graduate priestess) in 1976. She has been integral to the growth and expansion of the Akan shrine culture and its ties to Ghana ever since. The shrine elders, *Abosom,* and ancestors chose Okomfohema Botwe I to serve as one of the leaders, as queen mother, at the Asuo Gyebi shrine in Larteh in 2003. Nana Oparebea transcended to spirit in 1995.

Law in Light is an ethnography of the multisensorial worlds of Akan path priestesses and priests in the United States and Ghana. Through detailed and collaborative ethnographic portraits of spiritualists based in Maryland, Washington, DC, New York City, and Ghana, the book explores their journeys of spiritual governance, ancestral reconnection, and innovative pursuits of social and racial justice. The Akan sacred culture is currently undergoing an expansion and revitalization in its shrine house communities in the United States, as well as in its transatlantic interconnections with the shrine family in Larteh, Ghana. Many of the American priestesses and priests graduate at the famous Larteh shrine houses—the Akonnedi (also named Nana Panyin) shrine, the geographically upper shrine, and the Asuo Gyebi shrine, the geographically lower shrine that is part of the broader Akonnedi shrine family.

All of the American Akan path spiritualists featured in this book identify as African American, and all are of African or African diasporic descent. Many long for deeper relationships with ancestors and other spirits, as well as new paths of self-knowing and spiritual evolution. They also seek novel avenues for justice and healing alongside the established modes of state governance or religion. In the Akan sacred culture, many find new approaches to personal flourishing and spaces for true identification and social belonging. These spiritualists are increasingly turning to Akan shrine communities that are governed through spiritual laws and principles that operate through the elders, Abosom, ancestors, spiritual authorities, and other members of the sacred culture.

In the Akan system, spiritual pathways are guided and governed under spiritual laws and ethical principles, which are taught through proverbs, some passed down since ancient times, and transmitted through the community. These are aligned with the Light—that is, what is considered to be just, true, liberated, proper, and fair, according to enlightened spirits as well as human spiritualists. Their shrine expansion efforts also bring to light a sacred path of healing and the pursuit of justice that has long been misunderstood and not fully recognized in American society. While Akan spirituality had been practiced since the time of enslavement in the United States, it was mostly practiced under the auspices of historical ancestral traditional culture.[6] Other forms of African or African-related traditional spirituality—such as Santería, Voudun, Orisha, and Candomblé—have been more prominent and well-known.[7]

In their sacred realms of lawcraft and soulcraft, these Akan path spiritualists confront and reckon with legacies of violence and enduring patterns of injustice in novel cosmopolitical forms of spiritual governance. In tracing and theorizing their myriad spiritual journeys, this book builds on key anthropological debates concerning spiritual jurisdictions and diasporic copresences, cosmopolitical and pluriversal politics, racial justice and liberation movements, and legal anthropologies of belonging and governance in increasingly postsecular and, in many ways, post-state-based forms of justice.

When the first official Akan shrine houses were set up in the United States, they joined broader efforts to strengthen connections to African cultural roots and ancestral ties within the wider civil rights and other empowerment movements. The shrine houses have been more formally recognized and spiritually accepted, in part owing to the growing and simultaneous public presences of churches, lodges, synagogues, meditation centers, temples, and other kindred establishments. There are now an estimated three thousand Akan path priestesses and priests in the United States.

This current expansion of the Akan shrine house system resonates with the growth of other African or African-related spiritual paths in the United States. These Akan path spiritualists often join forces with a spiritually plural national association called the African Traditional Spiritual Coalition, headquartered in Washington, DC. The shrine culture is also growing alongside broader national trends, including the increasing search for alternative practices, spiritual principles, and forms of consciousness and mindfulness.

This book is based on extensive ethnographic research that I have conducted with priestesses, priests, and other interlocutors at the prominent Akan Spiritual United Order (ASUO) house in Maryland and the Asuo Gyebi source shrine house in Aburi, Larteh, Kubease, in the Eastern Region of Ghana. This book is based on research that began for me in 2018 and continued into 2023. Okomfohema Botwe I, queen mother and chief priestess for both shrine houses featured in the book, is the first African American ever to be chosen by the spirits for the historic stool, or throne, at the Asuo Gyebi shrine in Larteh.

I explore many aspects of the Akan path spiritualists' deep and multifaceted modes of knowing, expanding, and navigating the worlds through their philosophies and dynamic assemblages of energies. The spiritual and physical realms are ultimately interwoven as one. There is no meaningful separation in an absolute sense, though people speak of them as distinct (yet intertwined) as a form of interpretive or descriptive shorthand. I also consider how these forms of spiritual-physical interweaving are intimately tied to their efforts to adhere to the spiritual laws of their lineages and to formulate novel versions of their spiritual laws that can fashion pathways to new realms of social belonging, justice, and community.

The spiritualists live, and perpetually become, in dynamic interrelation with key ancestors, Abosom, and other spirits. For these circulations of spiritualists, Abosom, cherished ancestors, and other spirits, I utilize the term *copresence*. In doing so, I draw on Aisha Beliso-de Jesús's deployment of the concept in her recent work on transnational Santería, in which she also works with theories of affective charges, resonances, and assemblages.[8] Beliso-de Jesús defines copresences as "the spirits, deities (*oricha*), priests, video technology, and religious travelers that operate in contemporary transnational networks as active spiritual agents."[9] My usage of *copresence* differs in the realm of the electronic devices and audiovisual media, which I, following my Akan path interlocutors, conceive as potential conduits for copresences rather than as the actual spiritual agents themselves.

As with copresences in Beliso-de Jesús's work, the Akan path copresences course through multiple spatiotemporalities. Many of the spirits that come to interlace with the subjectivities of Akan priestesses, priests, and other spiritualists have ready access to information and wisdom from different past or future times, with many of these spirits able to simultaneously be in different physical spaces. In other words, there are multiplex and varying spatiotemporal registers within which the spirits move—and through which the spiritualists interface with them—to carry out their work. These exchanges and interrelations can happen in conscious waking hours but also in other states like dreams, visions, trances, sacred possessions, or other modes of channeling and divination.

Through intricate ethnographic engagement with key spiritualists—and their modes of spiritual governance in the Akan path communities—I advance two central theoretical arguments.

First, I argue that the Akan path spiritualists' practices and ways of life unsettle and expand conventional understandings and theorizations of subjectivity. They do so through their approaches to becoming spiritually interconnected and interlaced through their varieties of spiritual modes of knowing, performing, discoursing, and governing. These priestesses and priests seek justice, truth, and healing through knowing themselves more deeply as singular souls, on the one hand, and through existing as evermore entwined and enmeshed with copresences such as Abosom, ancestors, related spirits, and fellow spiritualists, on the other. These expansive forms of subjectivity, in turn, render possible their various spiritual pursuits for healing, social justice, and alternative registers of knowledge production.

Second, I argue that the growth and flourishing of Akan spirituality is a prime domain for new anthropological explorations of novel assemblages of politics and power beyond, alongside, or in the interstices of state and other legal forms of politics. In this way, Akan path spiritual culture builds on what Carlota McAllister and Valentina Napolitano recently have theorized as "theopolitics," or "sovereignty from below" (2021, 7.1). As mobilized in this book's theorizations, *theopolitics* refer to spaces in which we can observe novel assemblages of politics that work alongside—or in the interstices of, or outside of, or in resistance to—state-based secular legal systems as privileged sites of politics.

In a related fashion, the Akan path spiritual communities participate in a broader global shift that legal anthropologists Mark Goodale, Olaf Zenker, and others recently have theorized as the "after law" moment, or the "post-juristocratic transition.[10] The post-juristocratic transition addresses the marked turning away from the post–Cold War privileging of formal domains of juridification for contemporary contests over rights, politics, and justice, not least for people who often feel marginalized in contemporary societies. In these same ways, Akan path spiritualists also participate in "thinking justice beyond law," as Diana Bocarejo has recently formulated it in her writing about spatiotemporal aspects of environmental justice as process in the context of Colombia.[11]

The contemporary secular liberal democratic settlement is under siege on many fronts. Both theopolitics and the post-juristocratic transition offer compelling new theoretical frameworks for analyzing social responses to the precarity of legal and political legitimacy in the United States, in Ghana, and elsewhere throughout the neoliberal world.[12] These ethnographic worlds of Akan spirituality help to expand these emerging bodies of theoretical literature in anthropology.

In order to establish these two central theoretical arguments for Akan spiritual communities in the United States and Ghana, I propose and argue for the centrality of two novel theoretical concepts that have emerged from this collaborative ethnographic research but of course carry generalized revelatory power for theorizing spaces and phenomena far beyond the spiritual worlds that this book spotlights. They frame my ethnographic analyses and theoretical interventions, and they run throughout the book: *constellations of subjectivity* and *copresent jurisdictions.*

First, I define *constellations of subjectivity* as the fluid and dynamic ways in which priestesses and priests come to exist as interwoven—not only as interrelated—with key ancestors, Abosom, and other spirits. These fragmented-yet-whole dynamic assemblages of priestly subjectivity and spiritual copresence can be productively apprehended through the lens of a constellation, with multiple forces, temporalities, spatialities, and consciousnesses at play. The copresent forces and figurations of spirits come evermore into view, variously fusing with priestesses and priests to rebirth or regenerate their ways of life and their ever-expanding constellations of subjectivities.[13]

Second, I define *copresent jurisdictions* as the ways in which the Akan spiritual systems—with their Abosom, ancestors, spiritualists, practitioners, and other spirits—operate with their own spiritual laws and forms of governance that, in the current moment, supplement, collide with, or otherwise interact with state-based realms of law, politics, and justice in innovative and expansive ways. On the one hand, copresent jurisdictions denote the authorities and governance of the shrine houses, with their elders and the key spirits within the spiritual community. On the other hand, copresent jurisdictions refer to the ways in which the Akan spiritual communities work with, alongside, outside of, or in tension with formal state institutions, such as courts, police, prisons, youth detention centers, schools, or social services. These copresent jurisdictions offer alternative pathways of law, politics, and governance from within the broader contexts of neoliberal democratic orders, which many find inadequate for true redress and holistic justice.

Copresent jurisdictions add multiplex, multidimensional forms of spiritual governance to formulations of the "after law" era, and they help to reveal the roles that alternative faith orders are playing in this moving away from formal law as the center of political life and resistance struggles. These Akan path priestesses and priests alternately support *and* seek to reframe and resist existing state-based institutions, such as courts, police, prisons, youth detention programs, and social systems. They also seek to work alongside and, at times, assist those who are part of more mainstream forms of spiritual belonging, such as Christian churches.

The Akan spiritualists at times provide informal spiritual advice as they assess evidence and engage in fact-finding, adjudication, and other determinations.[14] They also work to provide alternative modes of healing and deeper forms of historical and cultural understanding within these communities of governing forces. It is not that they are for, say, the police departments. Rather, they seek to try to change the mentality of those involved in these institutions for the growth and empowerment of people in the communities. They strive to facilitate higher understandings in order to encourage a move away from patterns of violence, aggression, or structural oppressions. They also help people to resist injustices and to heal from various traumas, including those caused or exacerbated by aspects of the state legal systems.[15]

In these ways, copresent jurisdictions evince powerful new forms of cosmopolitical assemblages and pluriversal futures-making that strive to move beyond the apparent political impasses of contemporary societies, aiming always to lessen or eradicate the deep-seated forms of structural violence that run through them.[16] To take one example, Okomfohema Botwe I has created a specific tool to advance these aims, which is called Soul Journey, Inc. At times, Akan spiritual governance supports and enhances the healing and spiritual governing activities of Christian pastors, who increasingly are adopting elements of Akan and other African values and protocols in formalized spiritual systems.

In this book, I focus on copresent jurisdictions as they perpetually emerge and bring together communities in the United States and Ghana. These jurisdictions operate within vital spaces in both the spiritual and physical realms, and they do so in ways that constantly transcend the conventional liberal conceptual divisions of spirit and matter, inner and outer, interior and exterior. In their philosophies and their practices, everything is interconnected.

The Akan spiritualists, in their everyday lives and pathways, as well as in their spiritual governance worlds, expand productive conceptualizations of theopolitical phenomena in contemporary times. Part of their power derives from what is not said or shared in a wholly public way. What is most central and sacred cannot necessarily be uttered or shown but may be *experienced* in different ways for different people. Copresent jurisdictions resonate with how theopolitical forms often operate in ways that center on the power of what is not said or shown or revealed, rather than privileging what is stated directly in, for example, legal settings or political institutions. Also, Akan priestesses and priests are working within state institutions but also alongside of them, pursuing their own paths toward justice and redress—"from below," so to speak—and not from the center or head of the state. These theopolitics of copresent jurisdictions involve collaborative and performative jurisdictions that partake in a variation on what Justin Richland has innovatively theorized as "cooperation without submission."[17] In their entwinements with expansive constellations of subjectivity, the theopolitics of copresent jurisdictions bring to light significant avenues of what Kamari Maxine Clarke, in her powerful book called *Affective Justice,* refers to as the "affective registers" central to legal knowledge production, performative jurisdictions, and pursuits of justice.[18]

Copresent jurisdictions also illuminate additional numinous or sublime aspects of the post-juristocratic transition, which addresses the marked turning away from the focus on formal domains of juridification.[19] Copresent jurisdictions add multidimensional forms of spiritual governance to these "after law" conversations. This helps to reveal or highlight the roles that alternative faith orders are playing in this moving away from formal law as the center of political life, as well as in healing and resistance struggles. These Akan path priestesses and priests both support and productively offer alternatives to extant legal institutions.

These copresent jurisdictions and constellations of subjectivity are *vital affective assemblages* with cosmopolitics that are interlaced with—yet irreducible to—secular liberal forms of subjectivity, law, and politics. In this way, copresent jurisdictions and constellations of subjectivity build on current anthropological debates concerning multiple, interconnected, and polymorphous networks of copresences in plural cosmopolitical worlds, as well as in transnational assemblages of spiritual copresences.[20] The copresent jurisdictions are powered, in part, by the Akan spiritualists' constellations of subjectivity. The copresent jurisdictions are nonlinear networks of energies, intensities, affects, and perpetual emergences that both diffuse and coalesce at varying moments.[21] They are fluid realms of differentially empowered *Abosom,* ancestors, other spirits, and spiritualists that cocreate and otherwise co-interact with the cosmopolitical worlds of other governance structures in the United States and Ghana. This means that liberal democratic law, often depicted as a bastion of secularism, is sometimes suffused by spiritual copresences.

In emphasizing a jurisdictional dimension with the use of copresences, I bring into focus spiritual laws and ethical principles that govern the many dynamic assemblages of spiritual copresences. In these ways, copresent jurisdictions are very similar both to the adjudicatory principles found in J. Brent Crosson's work on Obeah justice in Trinidad and N. Fadeke Castor's work on "the vision and experience of spiritual citizenship" in Trinidad.[22] Copresent jurisdictions also are akin to what Mark Goodale has called an "unstable assemblage of law," if law here is construed to encompass the Akan path's spiritual laws as well as state-based legal domains.[23] Jurisdiction as a specific analytic allows for a more rule- or law-oriented focus than would a more generalized, though fascinating, analytic of governance. In contrast to an analytical frame of sovereignty, jurisdiction allows for more analyses of the interstitial, overlapping, and lateralized features of political, legal, and spiritual life.[24]

PATHWAYS OF THE TEXT

The structure and movement of this book, cast through the prisms of the intricate experiences of Akan path priestesses and priests, illuminate the conceptual power of constellations of subjectivity and copresent jurisdictions, as well as the wider implications for theopolitical, cosmopolitical, and post-juristocratic worlds. I foreground the voices, experiences, and philosophies of the priestesses and priests, rather than my own. They are the adepts with the wisdom about and understanding of these matters. I find this collaborative type of ethnographic writing and theorizing—one that seeks to prioritize the voices and interpretations of interlocutors through forms of narrative and dialogical renderings—to be one promising modality in broader current efforts toward genuinely equitable anthropology and decolonial knowledge practices.

The chapters that follow focus on the paths, practices, spiritual relationships, and everyday lives of various key priestesses, priests, and shrine elders at different ages and levels of rank. They also examine the ways in which priestesses, priests, and spirits creatively participate in various overlapping forms of authority and governance—or copresent jurisdictions—within their communities, along with when and how they interface with secular state-based and other societal institutions. Throughout each of the chapters, I explore how the spiritual calls, sacred paths, theopolitical engagements, and everyday lives of the priestesses, priests, elders, and other shrine family members can be productively theorized through the central concepts of copresent jurisdictions and constellations of subjectivity. The revelatory power of these two theoretical concepts is best demonstrated through the ways in which they illuminate the life-worlds of these spiritualists and spirits, along with their vital transnational assemblages.

It also bears clearly noting that these theoretical concepts have emerged from the research with my interlocutors, all of whom have helped to cocreate and refine my thinking and writing with these novel terms of analysis. In this way, the theoretical work of this book truly has emerged through collaborative conversations and engaged ethnographic practice—not only prior to the subsequent writing, but throughout the writing, editing, and final approvals process, which has involved all of the named living interlocutors throughout the book. They each have participated in refining this work and in correcting any misstatements about their lives, paths, and engagements. I have aimed to incorporate all their edits and to put forth the most accurate and collaborative version of this book possible. My aspiration is for this work to resonate with broader anthropological efforts to decolonize ethnographic research and writing, including the processes of formulating conceptual contributions and theoretical engagements. If our academic concepts and theories cannot be clearly explained in conversations with our interlocutors or others who may be working outside anthropology or its disciplinary neighbors, I feel that it is important to question our investments in including them in our ethnographic writing and theorizing.

I conclude *Law in Light* by considering its conceptual and theoretical interventions alongside multiple potential future trajectories of Akan spirituality in the United States and Ghana, in light of recent expansions of shrine houses and the rise of virtual ceremonial spaces. While the pandemic closed many collective physical gatherings, the COVID-19 era also has given birth to new virtual explorations of a global Akan spiritual community. Parts of significant sacred festivals, commemorative conferences, and other gatherings began to take place or grow in online spaces, with priestesses, priests, and others from the community copresent through digital interfaces.

The pandemic lockdown provided an opportunity for Akan spiritualists to explore how to do their healing and to provide readings and spiritual guidance through electronic media platforms in digital spheres. The ancestors and Abosom with whom the spiritualists work are in the production phase of a new possible virtual expansion, considering their options and potential avenues for future growth in the transnational healing community. This virtual realm is yet another vista of their potential expansion in their interrelations with spiritual copresences and multiple spatiotemporalities. These possible horizons offer fruitful insights for anthropological inquiry into constellations of subjectivity, copresent jurisdictions, cosmopolitics, and theopolitics within the digital worlds and beyond them. These emergent virtual spaces of vital assemblages also point toward new broader potential avenues for envisioning the contours of future world-making projects within the Akan spiritual cultures in the United States, Ghana, and beyond.

ONE

Okomfohema Nana Akua Amoabaa Botwe I, Queen Mother and Chief Priestess

"The unification of the people comes from the understanding of the oneness of God."

Okomfohema Botwe I, a leading African American Akan path queen mother and chief priestess, often voices this maxim. She created it from her everyday life, both as a social worker and cogovernor of key shrine houses in Maryland and Larteh, Kubease, Ghana.

Okomfohema Botwe I, now seventy years of age, emphasized that she draws inspiration from Martin Luther King Jr.'s words in his "I Have a Dream" speech in her unification declaration, which she also sees as a call for inclusiveness and universal order.[1] She is part of the second generation of the rise and spread of Akan shrine culture in the United States and is a central force in maintaining and expanding ties between African American priestesses and priests and their counterparts at source shrines in Larteh. She is the chief priestess of the ASUO house in Maryland and of the Asuo Gyebi shrine house in Larteh.

Okomfohema Botwe I is particularly concerned with dispelling misconceptions and the attendant fears that outsiders often have about medical conditions that have unresolved spiritual dimensions.

"Many times, in the hospitals, many people have major surgery and then afterward, ministers are called to pray for their upliftment on the backend," she explained. "We are recommending that the spiritual explorations be done on the front end, in the beginning of the situation, a condition, or a procedure."

She maintained that so much of the fear about what they do in Akan spirituality comes from false understandings about the Abosom (sing., Obosom), the Akan exalted spirits. Many do not understand who they are and what they do, as beings of the light, akin to angels or saints in the Christian religious traditions. They are not gods in and of themselves, as many will say as a shorthand translation or a quick language marker, calling them gods or deities. They are messengers and helpers to God—Nyame in the Akan system—the ultimate and absolute creator who is only ever of, and unto, itself or himself.[2]

"Rather than gods, fetishes, or deities, which are limited formulations that often lead to negative perceptions of universal principles, the Abosom are divine spirits who help and assist the Creator," Okomfohema Botwe I said. "We are at a time of a new spiritual world order, and older concepts are moot. We need new definitions and understandings, and that begins with the *word*."

She explained that so many people, especially Christians or members of other monotheistic faiths, often get hung up on words like *gods* or *deities*, as if Akan path priestesses and priests are worshipping false idols or spiritual entities that are evil and will do harm. This is incorrect and misses the point that the Abosom serve God and humanity by helping to provide divine interventions, protection, and healing. The Abosom work against the spiritual forces of destruction, negativity, chaos, or evil. The Abosom are light forces, and they only work with other energies that are harmoniously aligned with their spiritual frequencies and the tasks they receive from Nyame to aid humans in learning to become more elevated in their consciousness, to become more spiritually liberated, and to pursue authentic justice for all. The Abosom only cocreate with intentions and tasks that are aligned with the laws of light. They clear negative spirits and illnesses that are caused by negativity. They protect people from evil attacks on their physical persons, their spirits, their dwellings, their livelihoods, or their families. They also teach humans about the spiritual laws of reciprocity and the ways of resetting what went wrong and restoring moral equilibrium. The Abosom help humans to learn how to rise on their spiritual paths and in their spiritual frequencies so that they better protect and serve their own soul purposes on their journey in this incarnation.

The Abosom are forces for positivity, healing, purity, truth, and light. They are vibrations that may help to transmit knowledge, wisdom, and healing energy from God to humans, assist in the collective advancement of human consciousness and right action, and bring awareness of more inclusive avenues for the pursuits of true social justice. They help to fortify people with connections to their past lives and ancestors. They also guide humans who are seeking to discover their true soul purposes in this life. In short, a great deal of fear-based demonizing and maligning of their tradition have skewed popular consciousness about Akan spirituality in both the United States and Ghana.[3]

"So much of what people say about us, what they think they know about what we do, is rooted in a misunderstanding about what we believe. There is only one God. And then there are the Abosom, the ancestors, and other life forces. It's the same universally in every system. God is the underlying truth that permeates throughout all that is, was, and shall be. We Akan priests, we have our own systems of counselors, rituals, and protocols correcting and justifying law and order. But we are working towards a unified paradigm of life force to help free and heal people, just like all true spiritualists working with God. The *Abosom* get their directives from Nyame. Nothing can happen but by the grace of God."[4]

Okomfohema Botwe I has been a trailblazer and freedom fighter throughout her life, uplifting and redefining generations of people with African American heritage and identity in the United States. She has also collaborated for decades with transnationalists. She lives in intimate entwinement and spiritual union as the queen mother of the Obosom Nana Asuo Gyebi. She also works very closely in interrelation and co-creation with the Obosom Nana Esi, as well as other Abosom and ancestral spirits who run through her realms as copresences, in her dynamic constellation of subjectivity.

Through her spiritual governance, social work as a healer, and shrine expansion efforts, she has earned her current role of enstooled (that is, enthroned) chief priestess and queen mother at the Asuo Gyebi shrine in Larteh. She has served in this capacity since 2003. She is the first African American ever enstooled as queen mother at the shrine officially known as the Asuo Gyebi shrine. This sacred place has been well known for many years as the training grounds for higher education spiritual ordination of priests, priestesses, and family and friend organizers through the Akan order for culture and traditional living. Okomfohema Botwe I was chosen by the Abosom and elders of the Asuo Gyebi shrine to help and enrich the traditions, customs, and culture in Ghanaian spirituality.

Dreams played a central role in the spirits' transmission of knowledge to the relevant shrine elders that Okomfohema Botwe I was to assume this prominent and historic position. In this appointment, the priests, Abosom, and ancestors were performing a sort of suturing of past and present, a reinstatement of the lines of priestesses and priests in spirit that had been violently severed on earth centuries prior owing to the brutal transatlantic slave trade.

The spirits also were revealing to Okomfohema Botwe I and others that she had been so destined and appointed—that the queen mother, in fact, was her soul's role—before she knew this herself. However, she had had a deep relationship to spirituality since childhood. She had grown up with a strong connection to spirit, as her mother and father were custodians in the Baptist church. Her mother was an organist and singer, and her father was a gospel choir director. They were always in the church, rehearsing, worshipping, and playing. Most of her family was from the South of the United States. Her father and mother later migrated from the South to the North, where they resided in Long Island City, New York, in the projects.

When she was sixteen, in 1969, she became part of the Yoruba spiritual house that Nana Yao Opare Dinizulu I had founded in 1967. His house, Bosum Dzemawodzi, initially foregrounded the Yoruba spiritual tradition and several years later became more of an Akan spiritual house.[5] This house was also in the projects of Long Island City. She became involved with the group through African dance. After Nana Yao Opare Dinizulu I visited his ancestral land in Ghana, he found himself enthralled by the Akan spiritual system and developed that part of spiritualism in his house and teachings. As his trainee, Okomfohema Botwe I was formally initiated to the Obosom Nana Asuo Gyebi in 1973.

"What I want people to understand is that spirit is omnipotent, meaning that no matter where you go or are in the world, if you are a spiritualist, you will be ID'ed at a certain time—when you are needed, they will choose you to do whatever work is necessary to be performed. It's not like I chose them. They chose me. This is just how spirit moves," Okomfohema Botwe I explained.

As queen mother, she has gained even further spiritual capacities and responsibilities, extending her energetic bandwidth with copresences. This role has further integrated her with relevant beings in spirit, in effect reconstituting and expanding her subjectivity as such. The assumption of the role of high priestess is not only titular. It also involves the reconstitution of self, an even deeper interlacing and dynamic interrelation with the spirits that continuously run through her on various levels of consciousness and assist in the governing of the shrine and its family.

After she joined Nana Dinizulu's house in 1969, she took part in the second chartered flight that he organized that brought around three hundred African Americans to Ghana. Soon after, in 1973, she went under (a phrase used to denote the beginning of training as an *okomfowaa*) to become an *okomfo* (graduate priestess). Before she was initiated, there was a week-long debate between the Yoruba and Akan spirits, and the spirits decided Akan would be most appropriate in that moment. Nana Yao Opare Dinizulu I initiated her to the Obosom Nana Asuo Gyebi, under his supervision. In 1976, she graduated as an okomfo in the Akan order, as part of Nana Yao Opare I's second graduating class. This made Okomfohema Botwe I one of the forerunners in the revitalization and growth of Akan spirituality for African Americans, since Ghanaian chief priestess Nana Oparebea had named Nana Yao Opare Dinizulu I the chief priest of Akan path priestesses and priests in the United States.

A decade after Okomfohema Botwe I's own graduation as a priestess, she graduated her first trainee as an okomfo. In the same year, 1986, she also founded her own shrine house, the Akan Spiritual United Order (ASUO) in Maryland, which Nana Oparebea officially approved in 1992. The ASUO house, over which Okomfohema Botwe I presides as queen mother and chief priestess, remains one of the prominent Akan shrine houses in the United States. She plays key roles in collaborating with the wider Akan shrine family cultures in New York, Washington, DC, Philadelphia, and throughout the United States. She helps to plan regional, national, and transnational festivals, conferences, ceremonies, graduations, enstoolments, and other matters of shrine governance and expansion. Okomfohema Botwe I has trained and graduated a total of sixty-four priestesses and priests to date, all Africans and African Americans. Okomfohema has six birth children, and they are now seasoned priestesses, *abrafo* (sacred warriors), and drummers on the Akan path.

Okomfohema Botwe I also works full-time as a licensed clinical social worker, holding both a bachelor's and a master's in the field, and she regularly incorporates her vast spiritual expertise and mastery into her healing work as a social worker. Through these interchanges, she navigates and participates in copresent jurisdictions, including those of state institutions. She also now goes into churches, agencies, and foster care systems, many of which have adopted African rites of passage and naming ceremonies, after they started doing DNA tests in order to clearly determine precise ancestral origins. She has done a lot of work over the years to promote social and racial justice and healing. This has included her working to help educate African American (and at times, other) police forces about traumas and sensitivities that may be intergenerational or inherited from past lives. She has also worked with incarcerated youth and others who are seeking to find alternate paths, different life purposes, and forms of restorative healing. She helped to change the punitive approach to one that focuses on the restorative perspective of justice, with spiritual and holistic components.

Okomfohema Botwe I spearheaded the creation of Soul Journey, Inc., based in Washington, DC, in 2001. She is the founder and CEO, and she runs the nonprofit with other spiritualists from the house and broader community. According to the official description, it is "a nonprofit social services organization designed to provide youths, families, and communities with physical, mental, and spiritual resources that will enhance lives and promote growth and development." Through Soul Journey, Inc., she and other spiritualists from the ASUO house periodically run a yearlong program, also called Soul Journey, in which I participated as part of my research during the years 2018 and 2019. Okomfohema Botwe I and the team of experts had asked me to join the monthly sessions for one year so that I could better understand the incorporation of spiritual principles, understandings, and experiences.

"Soul Journey incorporates the 'it takes a village' concept into modern everyday philosophies," Okomfohema Botwe I explained.

My participation in Soul Journey was an extraordinary experience that illuminated new pathways of perceptual and affective domains for me, and it allowed me to go even deeper in conversations and other fieldwork that I conducted for this book.

In general, the Soul Journey program is for people who are interested in learning more about Akan spirituality, their souls' purpose, and forms of spiritual healing and knowing using selected modalities that Akan spiritualists deploy in their work, some of which have been lost or forgotten in contemporary societies. At the end of the yearlong program, there is a graduation ceremony that denotes the evolution process that has been utilized and the enhanced enlightenment that has been acquired. It can be repeated at any time in one's life, but the cycle ends after one year. A day name is given during the journey in order to reveal to participants the spiritual significance of the day on which every person was born.

As Okomfohema Botwe I is also the queen mother and chief priestess of the Asuo Gyebi shrine in Larteh, she remains a vital transatlantic link, cogoverning with other elders, Abosom, and ancestors on a perpetual basis. She helped raise funds and orchestrate a majestic, towering commemorative statue of Nana Oparebea within the Asuo Gyebi shrine compound. The representation of Nana Oparebea now stands very tall, with her powerful gaze over the mountain and beyond symbolizing her watching over the Akan priestesses and priests, both the Larteh lineages in Ghana and the akomfo and other Akan shrine family members that carry the Akan sacred culture forward in the United States.

Okomfohema Botwe I also helped compile a full songbook, *Whisper from the Mountains,* which includes the sacred lyrics and chants that spiritualists sing in the mountains in Larteh. This took two decades and came to full fruition in 2002, and it included the creation of an accompanying CD that recorded Larteh shrine members' performances of the sacred songs.

Okomfohema Botwe I also worked closely with Nana Oparebea while she was alive in human form. During Nana Oparebea's visits to the United States from 1971 through 1995, she supported and helped move the culture to where it is now. Okomfohema Botwe I established the Akan Spiritual United Order shrine house with official permission from Nana Oparebea in 1991 with a certificate of acknowledgement. Okomfohema Botwe I also worked with Nana Oparebea for many years at the shrine in Larteh.

Nana Oparebea's spiritual guides included Nana Asuo Gyebi, who was the forerunner of Akan spiritual governance in America. He continues to guide the priestesses and priests on governance matters from the spirit realm, along with the Akonnedi shrine at the geographical top in Larteh.

"I could not do this work without the numerous people who sacrificed their life, time, and energy in establishing the Akan culture in Ghana and America," Okomfohema Botwe I said.

In a dream, Nana Oparebea instructed Okomfohema Botwe I that one of Nana Oparebea's spiritual children, an Akan priest who trained under her, would be stationed in Washington, DC. She instructed Okomfohema to request that that particular individual assist her in the Asuo Gybei shrine house works in Larteh, Ghana, and in the United States. When Okomfohema Botwe I told the dream to the elders, they requested that the person sit as the chief priest to the Asuo Gyebi shrine in Larteh. In 2013, several rituals were performed, and Okomfohene Nana Yaw Yirenkyi Opare Gyebi I (Okomfohene Yirenkyi I) was enstooled to this position.

Okomfohema Botwe I and Okomfohene Yirenkyi I had first met in the early 1990s while both were in Larteh performing spiritual rites for the annual Nana Asuo Gyebi yam festival in January. He now resides in Ghana and in DC, where he lives with his African American Akan priestess wife. Okomfohene Yirenkyi I shared with me that he had likewise received messages from the Abosom in dreams that he was to become okomfohene of the Asuo Gyebi shrine in Larteh.

Additionally, Okomfohema Botwe I helped to initiate the central installation of another leader at the Asuo Gyebi Larteh shrine—the African diasporic Caribbean Akan priestess Nana Atei, who was enstooled as *ankobeahema* (meaning "one who always stays") in 2016. She also resides in Maryland and makes regular trips to Ghana.

In order to strengthen these transnational bonds and the copresent jurisdictions between akomfo in the United States and Ghana, the Ghanaian family that owns the Asuo Gyebi shrine gave Okomfohema Botwe I an enstooled (enthroned) husband, Nana Adu Richardson, who is an elder of the family. The family designated him as an enstooled husband to help Okomfohema Botwe I to rule and to understand Akan culture and tradition as an African American.

Nana Adu Richardson is the grandson of the late great chief high priestess Okomfohene Nana Oparebea, and he is the eldest son of the late Nana Kwasi Agyiri Richardson (Nana Agyiri), elder of the Asuo Gyebi shrine in Aburi, Larteh, Kubease. After his father, Nana Agyiri passed in 2018, he assumed more leadership and governance responsibilities among the elders in the family that owns and runs the business management for the Asuo Gyebi shrine. He delivered a formal presentation of the late Nana Oparebea at his father's memorial service at Mount Rainier, Maryland, in 2019. A successful businessman, Nana Adu Richardson currently resides in Accra and Kumasi in Ghana, as well as in Maryland. He regularly shares his deep wisdom and guidance with the shrine families on both sides of the Atlantic.

When I asked Nana Adu Richardson about his vision for the future of such enstooled marriages and transnational alliances in the Akan spiritual families, he replied as follows: "Future generations will continue to do it, and they will do it even better. People have seen the light and the strength that this spiritual path provides for them. The communities in the United States and Ghana will continue to grow, and they will become even stronger in their relations."

When the global COVID-19 pandemic began in 2020, Okomfohema Botwe I worked with the family to organize the first virtual Nana Asuo Gyebi fundraising day, which was held in January 2021 in a virtual Zoom space, for registered attendees from all over the world to join and be a part of this expansive healing perspective. I attended both the first and the second of these virtual festivals, bearing witness to the palpable healing and uplifting copresence that could be felt even in the virtual space.

The event included inspired and inspiring talks and commentaries by elder priestesses and priests, Akom ceremonies where the Abosom would come with sacred dancing and music, and an open dialogue forum with attendees and elders to speak and share from wherever their physical locations were. The contributions and donations from the event went to help support the Akan spiritual cultural order in

Larteh and in the United States, enhancing the transnational assemblages of copresent jurisdictions.

These emergent virtual spaces facilitate new forms of flows of energy, presences, affective charges, and knowledge for the copresent jurisdictions of spirits and spiritualists. The virtual zones are also additional spaces for ritual assemblages that expand the constellations of subjectivity of priestesses and priests. Much virtual gathering, while it may be documented for later viewing, is done in real time within the shrine house communities. This means that the effects of the virtual mediation on the communications, interactions, and other interrelations through the devices are light. Many times, it can feel as though people are copresent in a physical space as well.

Okomfohema Botwe I and Soul Journey tours recently appointed an official historian for the Akonnedi and Asuo Gyebi shrine family. His name is Kwabena (Alex) Boamah.

"My job is hospitality and tours based in Ghana. I got to know Nana Ansah through my American guests. I was beginning to be part of the shrines. I didn't have the opportunity to go there, to Larteh, since COVID. This year, I had the opportunity to go there again with Okomfohema Botwe I," he explained, in early 2024. "The ceremony was so moving and healing. There were a lot of powerful priestesses and priests who came to perform rituals and protocols acknowledging the spirits. It was so dynamic, and I had never seen it before."

These are only the most recent developments in Okomfohema's life-long spiritual quests. I once asked Okomfohema Botwe I if she ever looked into her past lives and whether she had been a priestess or priest in many of them, or if she knew if she had done other forms of healing and lightwork.

"I never went into that too much. I was so busy, you see. I started very young. I was sixteen when I got into the culture," she said. "From that age, I really was at a fast pace. There has been so much to keep me moving. I have to keep cleaning up my family line, and that's work because they don't know what they're doing. I didn't have time to look into who I was in the past and what I did there. I was busy, keeping connected, going to family reunions, checking out everybody, seeing where there are problems. It's a lot of work."

I asked whether any in her immediate family line from the past were healers, to her knowledge.

"No, I think my family members were traders. My grandmother was a very prominent businesswoman. Even right before she passed, she had property," she answered. "I don't know much of my ancestry. I do know that my grandmother married a Ghanaian, and that's how my mother was born, but I don't know where or other details."

Okomfohema Botwe I, though destined for these high spiritual leadership roles, had no idea when she was a younger teenager that she would become a priestess.

"I wasn't thinking anything like that. My family was in the church. Religion was always a part of my life as a child. So, it just unfolded as I grew older, and then my powers or my spiritual gifts were able to manifest as I grew older," she said.

"So, when you were a teenager, you started seeing things differently?" I asked.

"No, I went under, or began training, when I was twenty," she replied. "I was in the culture around sixteen. Then, when I started to train at twenty, I learned about more of my gifts and my spiritual powers."

"When you got called, were people surprised? Or were they excited?"

"They were absolutely shocked," she said, laughing. "They were so shocked, it was crazy. That's all how you learn, you never know *who* has those powers or those spiritual gifts. You have to really be careful and not surmise with people, 'Oh no, they don't have anything.' So, the spirits talk to you."

"Before you went under, did you start seeing apparitions? Or did you hear spirit talk to you?" I asked.

"I didn't worry about that. The way my spirit governs is not to worry about spiritualism. I let spirit do its thing, and I do mine. I never had any issues about spiritualism, because I was in it so young. I came into the culture when I was sixteen, so I was already protected. I was always praying. I would do all the things, the rituals."

Okomfohema Botwe I said the spirits keep her on a fast track.

"Do they talk to you about it that way?" I asked.

"No, they just say keep moving," she said, laughing.

Early in my research, Okomfohema Botwe I clearly communicated some of the Obosom Nana Asuo Gyebi's wishes for the book. For example, she offered some profound reflections on the centrality of positive thinking and consciousness, and how mental and spiritual positivity is mirrored, or can be mirrored, in exterior realities.

"Nana Asuo Gyebi is a healer and an *abrafo* [warrior]. He gives people hope in their struggles. What's so difficult right now is the respect that people often do not have for each other. Everybody comes with culture," she said. "When Obama was president, he showed us a way to respect the world. It's that hope. It has a lot to do with your DNA, your brain cells, your heart chakras. If you're down, things go down. If you're up, things go up. Just keeping that optimism going is an *everyday process.* Nana Asuo Gyebi helps us because he tells us, 'You'll get through it. You'll see.' Or he will say, 'This is just a time passing. Good things are coming down the way.' And he demonstrates it in small benchmarks, just giving us small benchmarks to overcome."

I asked about the Obosom's incremental revelation of the path, the reasons for this temporality of unfoldment in the spiritual knowledge production in copresent jurisdictions. How and why does it work in those ways?

"If Nana Asuo Gyebi was going to show us a whole picture—let's say, a whole dwelling of water, and he said there was a pot of gold on the other side, we wouldn't necessarily fully believe it. He'll give us bits and pieces, but he's not going to say how it all will be laid out. He'll give us hope and say we'll get through it, but the majority of the work is spiritual. That work is for the spirits to do, to outlay in the spiritual realm."

She also spoke of the responsibility that people in families and broader communities have to help each other as they navigate the spiritual processes and their mirrored aspects in the earthly realm, as they walk their human paths. There is a collective responsibility to help others and, in particular, to help elders who are no longer able to work in the ways they once did. This obligation applies not only to spiritualists but to anyone in families or communities.

I asked Okomfohema Botwe I how she relates to Nana Asuo Gyebi in intimate and familiar terms. Is he more like a husband or a father, or just a guiding presence?

"Definitely like a husband," she replied. "He does immediate processes for me to continue to understand, right away. He doesn't linger, like I'm kept wondering. Things happen so fast. When he finds out about it, he starts putting things into place."

Nana Asuo Gyebi will take swift action to address issues that emerge, and he will not necessarily even bother Okomfohema Botwe I with all the particular details regarding the spiritual dimensions of what is happening or how he is working—often, with other Abosom and copresences—to address issues or accomplish aims. She shared that, now that she is an elder, she does not debate or question things as much anymore.

Okomfohema practices nonattachment or tries not to return to things, perhaps ruminating on or replaying things in her conscious mind. Even though she is a governing elder in the spiritual adjudication and protection of the Akan spiritual order, she often does not need to follow all the spiritual aspects of a problem or situation.

"Now that I'm older, I kind of just ride it out and try not to get too down on the things that I cannot change," she said.

She added that all things may be by design, but the Abosom do not need to trouble her with all the details. They deal with the total suites of technical spiritual knowledge and information that they have on their spiritual plane of existence, and they only share knowledge and directives that are beneficial to Okomfohema Botwe I as she cocreates and cogoverns with the spiritual realm through her physical human body and life. Things will fall into place for her without her having a full understanding of how or why they are happening.

"As human beings, we are God's hands on earth. Things happen through me, and I can't know when, where, or how," she said.

I once asked Okomfohema Botwe I to explain more about her spiritual kinship within the Akan spiritual order. What is the nature of rank, authority, and interrelation among humans and spirits?

"It's so complex because there are elders involved, and rituals come through elders. They come through elders because there are certain things that we are limited to do on earth, but the spirits are not limited in the same ways, and the elders know the best ways to proceed," Okomfohema Botwe I explained. "The elders who pass down those vital traditions, a lot of people like to dismiss them. They may want to talk directly with spirit, or they want to get information directly from spirit, and, unfortunately, it doesn't take them down a good path, all because, in the world, we're limited."

She then turned to explaining profound aspects of the limitations that come from our spirits' being born into a human form. The imprints on human consciousness come not only from our families but also from the physical environments and the cosmological—or even cosmopolitical—aspects of the times and spaces in which people are born and raised.

"When you're first in spirit, you're in the heavens, and you're with God. Then, your spirit is born through the woman's womb, and you become a human being. Wherever you land, that limitation is what you have to overcome," Okomfohema Botwe I explained. "You have to overcome the limitation in order to be that divine person, vehicle, or entity."

I asked whether she meant lessons but also a kind of spiritual purification process, as she often would describe things in terms of purifying the spiritual vibration or frequency of a person or space.

"Yes, and to get to that frequency, you have to learn from what the elders are telling you from the very, very beginning. If I had dismissed them, I probably wouldn't be here today, because I would be breaking too many rules," she said, emphasizing that the elders must serve as the gateway for the Akan sacred wisdom path.

"If the youth understand more of the importance of the elders, they will understand more about where they are going wrong," she continued. "They sometimes think they only need to be directed by their money, or by the relationships they have with peers. They tend to ignore what the elders have to say, thinking that that's old, and it's not true. There is nothing you could do these days that the elders have not known about before."

In the case of spiritual offenses or violations of Akan protocols and sacred laws, the Abosom will sometimes involve the priestesses and priests who are elders, or even peers of the accused or offending spiritualists. Sometimes, they will deliver the means for justice directly from the spiritual realm. Whether there is a formal adjudication process with the priestesses, priests, and other elders in human form depends on the circumstances. At times, warnings or premonitions will be delivered by the spirits through dreams and visions. If the elders warn the person three times and the person does not heed the admonition, then misfortune or spiritual recompense may befall the person or even their family or spiritual house.

"Sometimes, the spirits will tell us that it's going to happen, to warn the person," Okomfohema Botwe I explained. "We may see the person in a dream, and there will be tragedy or problems, and then we'll know. That's a warning. Then, we'll tell the person, and we warn them three times. Then, when they hit the tragedy, they know."

Once people receive a warning, they always have opportunities to atone, correct their ways, and come back into alignment with the Akan order's laws of light, truth, and justice. People do receive grace from the divine. The spiritual consequences that result from wrongdoing or spiritually unlawful actions are always opportunities for learning and growth for those who committed the offenses—if the experiences are taken as such. Okomfohema likened the Akan spiritual philosophy of grace to the concept of grace as taught in Christian churches she has attended.

"Usually at church, when they're talking about grace, that's what they're talking about. They always give people chances. Your life cycle is about learning and learning," Okomfohema Botwe I clarified.

I then asked her about the interrelations and spiritual kinship between the Abosom and the exalted spirits from other orders, including the Yoruba *orishas*. She said that she did not know for certain whether the Abosom circulate in the same spiritual plane with the Yoruba exalted spirits, but she sensed that they all cohabitate in the spiritual realm and work together in many regards.

"I don't know for sure how they do it, but Nana Oparebea [now a revered ancestor] told me she speaks all languages, and the only way she can do that is to interrelate," Okomfohema Botwe I said.

"I see. So, they connect to the same network, so to speak?"

"Yes, yes. It's like I was telling you, it depends on the person's tradition, how they see it. In one tradition, it might be Saint Michael [a Catholic angel]. In another person's tradition, it might be Ogun [a Yoruba orisha]. In another tradition, it might be Nana Adade Kofi [an Akan Obosom]. In another tradition, it might be a leprechaun [an Irish spirit]. You see? Everybody will see it in their own way, how they're used to."

At times, wandering spirits will spontaneously possess open vessels if they have a message to deliver. Okomfohema Botwe I offered an example.

"I remember I had one goddaughter, and there was a lady who died in Ghana in a traffic accident, and they possessed my goddaughter, and she was crying," she shared. "I asked, 'Why are you crying?' She said, 'Oh, I just died in the accident.' The spirit was wandering. They wander, and they do speak."

Okomfohema Botwe I's goddaughter had not even been physically present at the accident, but the wandering spirit entered her to speak a message to someone who could understand her plight as a spirit, speaking. Her goddaughter served as a vessel and a voice box for this spirit.

Bodies can serve as vessels at any time, if the person is open and if the spirits of the vessel, or the spirit's guides in spirit, allow another spirit to use it. If a spirit were to use the body of a person without proper protocols of spiritual permission, that would be a spiritual violation.

There are also certain objects charged with spiritual energies that can amplify or fortify the spiritual presence. In this way, ritual objects are animate and course with lifeforce, or *sasa* in Twi, as do plants, animals, and other nonhuman beings.[6]

"I know there are certain objects that will amplify your power. Certain ritual objects, certain jewelry, things like that. But how do you think of them? Do you think of them like spiritual microphones that amplify the connection between the akomfo and the spirits?" I asked.

"Yes, they are amplifiers," Okomfohema Botwe I said. "It depends on different types of crystals. Everybody has them. Herbs. Everybody has them, those herbs, those crystals, those ways of communicating and highlighting what they need. Remember, I was talking about hope in the very beginning? That's what it's all for. It's just like the cross is used to shy away the devil. There has been much folklore generated through stories and movies about the power of the cross to get rid of evil."

Okomfohema Botwe I also gave many examples of types of physical operations on the body that are familiar—for example, with medical doctors. She likened spiritual operations and processes to these medical procedures on the physical body. Within every spiritual process, even tragic ones, there are lessons and new perspectives—if people are open to receiving and learning them.

In the United States, when the Akan priestesses and priests have *odwira* festivals to spiritually purify themselves and honor and strengthen their ties with the cherished ancestors, there is communication with their family members. These ancestors recall what their lives were like, and give those currently in human form their wisdom, love, guidance, and support.

"With the odwira, that's the speaking of the dead, the chiefs, the whole thing is to praise the predecessors in order to get hope. You can see this in the Wakanda movement in the blockbuster film *Black Panther* [released in 2018]. You know, when the guy had to go under and talk to his father to get hope, to learn how to be a chief, or how to run the nation?" Okomfohema Botwe I asked. "That work of getting your ancestors to support you is real. That was true. That does happen. You have to go under and believe in the ancestors and your ability to function through what they have gone through and the strife that they have gone through."

Drumming, songs, and music in general are important parts of formally invoking or calling forth the ancestral spirits and the Abosom. Okomfohema shared how instruments, during festivals and at other times, work to call the spirits, to summon them, when vocal calls alone do not. Certain patterns and vibrations created with instruments are also pleasing when they are harmonious with the vibrations of particular spirits. In this way, the instruments act as portals and invocation devices, and the spirits who respond often will be drawn into the ritually charged space.

"The drum is a way of communicating when your voice is not loud enough. You have the drum, you have the bell, you have the shaker, you have musical instruments. You have clapping, too. Those kinds of things are essential tools for communication," Okomfohema Botwe I said. "The tree is a living thing. It gets watered, and it gets sunlight. It is fed naturally. The spiritual drum is cut, and it is made of the wood, and you're able to use it so that the tonations are spiritual."

Many people will bear their burdens to the spirits of the drums or will pour libations to them. Okomfohema Botwe I explained that, in their group, those who craft the drums usually are purified before they embark on these spiritual tasks.

"Everybody has their forte. Everybody has their responsibility and abilities. The drum makers make sure the drum talks and does right," Okomfohema Botwe I said.

One day, I asked Okomfohema if she felt that people ever feared her, as she had mastered her craft and held the position of queen mother and chief priestess.

"Yes," she replied.

"Do you find that certain people avoid coming into your energy because they are afraid?"

"Yes. Once you represent that entity of what is good, and once they find out what you're able to do, and what you do not do, yes, they attack. You have to be strong enough to rise above it somehow."

I replied that I thought negativity would not even be able to enter her field, as she is fortified and protected by being in alignment with her immortal soul flame (*kra*) and the protective forcefield that the Abosom create around her.

"Well, that's not it. The thing about it is . . . Let's say, for instance, I'm supposed to stay in the village, and I go outside the village. They say, 'Stay in your village. Then, you won't have to worry that you'll get hit by a car.' But I'm going outside the village, all the time. The high Nanas don't move, because they want you to pray and stay safe," she said. "However, we in America have to get outside of our homes because we have jobs. We have to make this thing match up to be able to function. That's the difference."

She explained that lower vibrations sometimes can press up against her field as she has to move around in the world beyond her home and protected spaces.

We then spoke about the processes of self-emptying or stepping aside so that the spiritual divine forces, such as the Abosom, can work through her.

"You have to step aside. You have to stick to your laws and principles. You have to eat healthy. There are different things to do or not do, in order to keep centered. It's hard because society doesn't lend to that."

"When the Abosom actually come and speak through you, when they're possessing, is your consciousness still there? Do you remember what they say? Or do you go blank so they can speak clearly?" I asked.

"No, it depends. It all depends. Sometimes, they'll possess you completely. Sometimes, they'll possess you partially. Sometimes, they'll possess you where you can talk with the person and for the person to understand. It all depends. It's not just one way. It's all in the communication," Okomfohema Botwe I replied. "A priest can possess the Obosom, and the Obosom will speak through them. It depends on whatever the Obosom or another spirit will say to do."

"And sometimes they'll take over? It all depends?" I asked.

"Yes, it's hard to put it into writing. Their energy is just free-flowing. You're trying to put this into a word. But if it's not a word, how can you put it into one, you know?" Okomfohema Botwe I said. "We can just describe it in all its different forms, if you will. It takes different forms."

Although some people describe a feeling of floating outside their body and observing their body while an Obosom or another spirit is flowing through them as a vessel, Okomfohema Botwe I does not bear witness to herself in this way when she is possessed.

She recalled how, when she was young and started getting possessed, she did experience fear. She said that it continues today, after all these years.

"I didn't ever overcome the fear," Okomfohema Botwe I said, laughing. "It's like always going on stage for Michael Jackson. He never got over it. Every time, he was scared."

I then told her how I had recently seen a new documentary on Pavarotti, the Italian opera singer, which showed how he was terrified every time before walking onto the stage.

"Every time before he would go onstage, he would get so nervous, and he would say, 'I go to die,'" I said, laughing.

"Right!" Okomfohema Botwe I agreed, laughing.

Okomfohema Botwe I shared her wisdom about how she keeps her ego in check, despite her great success and her high rank in the Akan spiritual system.

"I think it's because of the downfalls. Not the what-ares, but the what-ifs. The experiences in life that you can't control," she said. "These challenges of just being spiritual yet you've got to communicate to people where they are. You have to reroute and relate. It keeps you grounded. It *keeps you grounded,* I tell you. All those life experiences keep you in check."

Okomfohema Botwe I said there are many things people ask her to do that she will not do. For example, some people will come wanting to try to bind the spirit of someone they desire to them, or they will ask Okomfohema Botwe I to do something else that spiritually attacks someone or that attempts to override another person's free will to make them do something. Okomfohema Botwe I will not do these things because they are not ethical, just, or in alignment with the truth and lawfulness of her path. The Abosom do not allow it, and she does not participate in those rituals.

Attempting to exercise power over another's free will is a deep violation of the spiritual laws and their code of conduct as Akan priestesses and priests. A lot of the misunderstanding that surrounds the Akan sacred path concerns matters such as these. Many people think that the priestesses and priests regularly engage in such rituals, when in fact they are forbidden by the spiritual laws of the Abosom that, in turn, the Abosom bring from Nyame, or God.[7]

"A lot of people in the world are hurt, and the job of a spiritualist is to repair the damage, as much as possible, from the hurt the person experienced," she explained. "Self-awareness, self-consciousness, and insight are the ultimate goals of the healing process. When you take a covenant, just like a doctor, some doctors won't abide by that. It's a shield, you know, of what you're supposed to do. It's called ethical values, and for akomfo, those are the values you learn. You can't go into the order of spiritualism without knowing the ethical values that you have to maintain. There are some people who break that. There are some who don't even care."

"But the people who break that ethical code, they're governed by the spirits, right? They'll meet their fate at some point?" I asked.

"The Creator, or God, has the answers to that," Okomfohema clarified.

"You probably can't really associate with those people anymore, right, once they start breaking the ethical codes?"

"It takes a village, and everyone in that village is addressed. People who commit crimes in a village are dealt with in a different way. Repenting is something that is an acceptable behavior," Okomfohema Botwe I continued. "Even in training, once they stop doing right, you have to keep yourself available for them to come, and you have to help them as much as you can. But even in training, if people have trouble breaking the evil bonds that they have themselves created, you have to allow them to go through that. If they don't make it this time, they'll come back around and make it another time in life. A lot of people come around later on in life, when they've learned, and say, 'Oh my gosh, this is no good.'"

"People end up haunting themselves, generating all kinds of problems for themselves?"

"The mind is an incredible organ, and we are not positively sure of all its potential," she said.

Okomfohema Botwe I and other shrine elders' main responsibilities with such matters involve efforts to educate and ensure that those who ask them to carry out unethical rituals at the very least understand why it is wrong to do so according to the protocols and traditions. In that way, they help to further the spiritual laws of the light and to promote healing, or at least to offer a path that people who may be spiritually lost can choose to seek and follow.

· · ·

Okomfohema Botwe I travels frequently for her work, which further amplifies the increasingly global presence of Akan sacred culture. For example, during these past several years of research, I had long conversations with her by phone while she was in Japan, Hawai'i, and Ghana.

While she was in Hawai'i to help a longtime friend, a famous musician and artist, I spoke with her at length. The musician is a longtime freedom fighter who retreated to Hawai'i to continue his creative edge of documenting historical insights. His son is a priest in Okomfohema Botwe I's ASUO house in Maryland.

I asked her how she communicates with the spirits of the lands, whether she communicates directly with the spirits in Hawai'i, or if she goes through the Abosom.

"Well, this is a vacation. Not that I'm shutting down, but I'm taking time to do some little things that I want to do. My daughter is actually setting the stage for me," she said. "This is beautiful here, nice restaurants. We're going to meet up for a dance before we go. I went snorkeling and that was the first experience I had like that."

Okomfohema is so often completely occupied by her spiritual work, social work, and family obligations that she has little time to bask in the peace of stillness and attend to family matters.

"I just want to know: what does total peace look like? Just no thoughts, no actions. Being able to be here in Hawai'i—of course, there's disruption. Of course, wherever you go, there is something going on. And a lot of people come here as a retreat from the world, to take their money and just live in peace and tranquility," Okomfohema said. "I realize from coming to Hawai'i that this is a lot like Africa. The Hawai'ians were telling me that a lot of their dances and movements are African. We went to the cultural center, and they did a whole performance. It's called *The Circle of Life*, a play they performed. The fire was part of the performance. It was symbolic of the purifications."

A lot of Okomfohema Botwe I's spiritual work is done through water, and Nana Asuo Gyebi is a water Obosom. That is his primary element. But the akomfo also use fire as a spiritual element. They work with whatever is required and called for by the spirits.

She quickly shifted gears to broaden the scope of the discussion to the fundamental purpose of spiritualists, which is to bring hope and justice to the world, however they do their spiritual work. They discern what is true, right, and just through their forms of spiritual knowledge production. They offer these discernments to people to try to bring order and justice to the worlds around them.

"Basically, our job as spiritualists, I think all over the world, is to give hope, as I've said before. Provide the world with hope, and in the midst of all kinds of disorder, we step in to settle out confusion to reset harmony. Some people like it, and some people don't," she said. "Most people, when they're found wrong, they will act out in protest, just being identified. It's a hard position to be in, as a spiritualist. You have to have compassion, as spiritual people, in all different quarters."

"Because a lot of people, they're not comfortable hearing the truth?" I asked.

"Right, that's it, exactly," Okomfohema Botwe I said.

"Do you think that a lot of times when people come to you, and they're suffering, they've been brought to you because there's some sort of spiritual basis? Either they've done something, or someone close to them has done something, that needs to be healed?"

"Yes. Usually, it's just like doctors. When you go to the doctor, and you're out of balance, their job is to put you back in balance. They don't care what happened," she said. "What we do is, we ask the spirits to identify the origin of the issue. We ask the spirits, the ancestors, and we also include conventional medical information when diagnosing situations. And the origin could be, for instance, the diet, which was something that was out of balance."

Okomfohema Botwe I explained that there are also atmospheric spiritual imprints that are made on people when they are born, owing to environmental conditions, that have nothing to do with any wrongdoing on the part of that person. These environmental spiritual imprints themselves can be the sources of imbalances, illnesses, and the like. The spiritualists can work to help people clear these from themselves so that the energetic imprints or presences do not continue to impede their path. The akomfo can teach people how to free themselves from the circumstances they were born into that may be affecting them in negative ways later in life.

"So, the geography and the energetic constellation impact the newborns?"

"Right. That will also cause that person, out of no fault of their own, to go through something. For example, the person may have been born in a place where there's already grief and suffering, and how you come out of that, and what you do as you come out of it, all of it is a process of liberation," she explained.

"So, the birthplace gets encoded in the person somehow?"

"I'm not able to answer that question," Okomfohema Botwe I said. "The ultimate goal for the spiritualists is to figure out how to set people back in balance. It's all so, so different. When you find out the origins, sometimes you can change it, and go to center, and sometimes you can't."

The spirits will deliver the information that is needed or requested in many different ways.

"Sometimes, the spirits will tell you that a person is not going to live because of the situation, or the person will become sick, or the person may stay in the situation. They will have a lot of turmoil. It all depends. The solution would be that it all depends on them now. Some people will deal with the fact that they have to make changes, and some people won't," she answered.

"Why do you think that some people choose to do nothing about it? Do you think it's because they are attached to the dysfunctional pattern because it's what they know?"

"They're attached to a dysfunctional pattern, and they're so used to a habit of disownership that they will not change," she said.

"So, a lot of times, people want to blame other people, but they won't do the work to go within?"

"The answer to that question comes from within the problem. Everybody is looking for, where do I go to be peaceful? Where do I go to ultimately know spirit? Where do I go to really have self-proclaimed freedom? And I always—well, over time—I've come to understand that it's from within," she said. "The people who are in the Soul Journey classes are guided to come to understand that. And with that understanding comes an epiphany and life-changing actions. With this wisdom, comes a shift in accountability and in the meaning of reciprocity at that particular time of that person's life."

MY ENTRANCE INTO THE JOURNEY OF
EXPLORING AKAN SPIRITUALITY

I later asked Okomfohema how these healing systems and paths for possible enlightenment for a greater number of people may have related to her openness to collaborate for this book project. She spoke with me about how spiritual orders around the world are at a particular juncture, where the spiritualists or mediums are guided to actions that may not be understood in the present but are carried forth for futuristic reasons understood by spirit. As elders within the Akan spiritual system, they had decided to further document their life journeys and spiritual principles in order to try to prevent misinterpretations, false portrayals, and the further demonization of African traditional spirituality in general and Akan spirituality in particular. Okomfohema shared that *Akan*, properly interpreted, means pure.

I first learned about Okomfohema's presence in Maryland through a mutual acquaintance from Ghana who is a member of the Washington, DC, chapter of the Akuapem Association, a group for those from the mountains in Ghana (including the town of Larteh) who are living in the United States. I asked our mutual acquaintance if Okomfohema might be open to speaking with me, as I was interested in learning more about priestesses and priests from the Akan spiritual path who were part of the diaspora in the United States, regardless of whether they were born or raised in Ghana or the United States.

I had learned about Akan spirituality for some years beforehand, while I was living in a gold mining town called Obuasi in Kumasi, another region of Ghana, during parts of the years 2010 to 2012. I was conducting research for my first book called *Fires of Gold* (published in 2020), which explores the myriad legal, political, and spiritual dimensions of current transformations in labor, land rights, sovereign power, and gold mining contests and collaborations.[8] Having finished my first book, I had hoped to meet an Akan path priestess or priest, possibly in the United States, whose life journey and healing practices I might explore and chronicle for my next book.

Okomfohema did grant me permission to call her by phone. When I called her, she invited me to visit her home to discuss my purpose and possible inquiries. When I arrived, I was delighted and surprised to be greeted by a circle at her house. In accordance with Akan protocol, I presented Okomfohema with customary gifts I had brought, and members of the circle briefly introduced themselves. The elders then asked me to state my purpose and intent. I shared with them my hopes for writing a book in collaboration with them that could document their practices of working with spirit for healing and guidance from the standpoint of the light, as well as what it meant for them in their lives and journeys to be a part of the diasporic Akan spiritual community. The circle consisted of professionals, family elders, truth-seekers, and protectors. Each of them, from their perspectives, intently listened and considered what I shared. They also inquired deeply into my intentions and my hopes for collaboration. They shared with me that they would have a family meeting and consult the spirits, and Okomfohema Botwe I and I could speak again after the meeting. She later shared with me that the inquiries could be continued.

For approval, the elders requested that I participate in the yearlong Soul Journey program in order to understand more deeply the concepts and some of the practices of the Akan spiritual tradition in relating to today's world. They also asked that I take a pilgrimage and join them during an official visit to Larteh, Ghana. Several African American priestesses-in-training (*akomfowaa*) were to undergo their final rites for graduation as Akan path priestesses at the Larteh shrines.

"When we requested that you visit Larteh, it was to allow you to try to erase any preconceived notions or examinations that come from the colonial or missionary perspective, and to see the light from the Akan perspective so that you could better communicate the beauty of our culture, as seen through our eyes. Missionaries are on a mission to convert. You were on a journey to understand," Okomfohema

Botwe I shared with me, some years after I visited Larteh with them. "This was a blessing and a permission from the Abosom to allow you to make sure that you speak the truth more from the Akan perspective."

I was honored to receive this invitation to join the visit to Larteh, and I quickly made arrangements for the trip. It was illuminating and profound beyond description, and it allowed me to have a much better, more expansive sense of the project, the lines of inquiry, and the broader resonances and implications for studying things like copresent jurisdictions or constellations of subjectivity. At the divining pot in Larteh, the eldest priestess consulted Nana Asuo Gyebi, who gave me the name of Nyamekye.

I was wondering how I could be named Nyamekye when it is obvious in seeing me that I am white. Also, I am not a priestess in the Akan order.

"When you use God, whatever the name for God, you're taking it out of the birth of the person, and where they're born, to God's essence and what was the intent with the birth. That's why it's hard for you to see the name out of its context, but in spirit, they said you were Nyamekye," Okomfohema Botwe I said.

I then also passed through the formal approvals at the shrines in Larteh. Okomfohema Botwe I shared with me that the elders and the spirits validated me based on the essence of my spirit and consciousness, as one who has demonstrated the abilities to interpret light. I return to the research visit in Larteh in chapter 3, which discusses younger priestesses of the ASUO house, several of whom graduated during that visit.

Okomfohema Botwe I followed the spirits' guidance and her desire that more documentation and awareness may be generated about the Akan spiritual path for current and future generations.

"I want to remain and grow. I want people to have that perspective in order to utilize it in a time of need," she said, referring to the continuation and expansion of the Akan path of spirituality.

DREAMS, VISIONS, AND COPRESENT
JURISDICTIONS

Okomfohema noted that Nana Oparebea and other key spirits visit her in dreams to speak clearly about the matter of expanding Akan spirituality as well as other central matters related to her path and shrine cogovernance on earth. For example, Nana Oparebea recently had come in a dream to tell her that, while the serenity in Hawai'i is beautiful, it is not yet time to rest, as there is so much work to be done.

"She wanted to put me straight like, 'No, you're not here to go to peace yet. You've still got work to do. Keep working. When it's time, you will come. Just sit down, and stay where you are, and do the best you can,'" Okomfohema Botwe I said, laughing. "I said, 'Dang, I can't just sit here and enjoy?' And she said, 'No. You can have this moment, but that's about it.' It was wonderful, because as long as you know, you're able to go forward. And I know the end to all this, eventually, and I know where I will be, so I'm good."

Okomfohema Botwe I shared with me the rapid, unrelenting pace of life as a high priestess.

"Everybody wants something. Everybody is searching for a part of you. And in the middle of it, you're trying to get this little peace, and kind of bring your whole self into balance. And then everyone around you needs a part of you," she said. "It's crazy, oh my goodness. It's hard."

Dreams and visions are some of the central modes of self-knowing and spiritual cogovernance for Okomfohema Botwe I and other Akan spiritualists. The way the spirits choose to communicate and work with, and through, the priestesses and priests depends on many variables, both known and unknown to the priestesses and priests in human form. One of the key factors is the comparative permeability of consciousness when people are in the spaces of dreams or visions. When needed, spiritual adepts can ask the spirits to assist them in dream interpretation during their waking hours.

"It's like you're working in different environments, and every environment has an energy. When you are divining, it's different depending on the way the spirits transmit the information. When you're divining or if the Abosom want to tell you something about a certain incident, they come to people with dreams, of course," Okomfohema Botwe I explained. "They're able to transfer knowledge more easily when you're asleep because your barriers are not so much up. You're able to communicate to a spirit a little more easily."

She clearly distinguished the dream space from visions that people will experience in the waking state, at times in tandem with dreams: "Then, you have visions. People have visions. When they have visions, they'll close their eyes, and then they'll start imagining and have visions, and they'll talk to the spirits through there. There are all different types of mediums of how people communicate."

Rather than pure imagination generated within a person's psyche, visions serve as portals or amplification spaces for communication between spirits and those in human form.

I asked Okomfohema Botwe I if she could control her dreams at all.

"No, I don't do that. What we *do* do is learn spiritual principles to do certain things *in* your dream. That's what we do. We're taught as priests, the tools that we use," she replied. "Like the Kung Fu master was training this guy to understand how to flow, and how to reduce his anxiety, and he did it through paint, and he used the stroke of the paint to flow on the wall, to show him the movement of spiritualism. It's the same thing that we do as well. The people are taught, there are elders who teach you. They're taught how to flow through different dreams when that happens."

She also explained how spirits will come through in dreams at times, even if the priestess or priest is able to hear the spirit during their waking hours at all times. *Why* the spirit's message comes in its exact forms and *when* are usually mysteries, understood by the spirits alone.

For the priestesses and priests, one matter of central importance is to maintain the strength of connection to the divine within oneself to keep the momentum and pace of life, to stay with the tempos of spiritual cocreation that can be beautiful but very exhausting.

Okomfohema Botwe I spoke of the inviolable sanctity of the inner divine flame, the *kra* or *okra* in Twi, which is immortal and resides within every person. It is the divine soul, and it belongs to God alone. The okra is the part of a person that reincarnates throughout lifetimes and that remains when a being returns to pure spirit form after the body expires.

"It's an unknown entity of God's creation. The okra is what we talk about to the energy and the spirits that is not able to be identified. That's God's quest. We call it okra. We identified it as a soul. Because when you're born, you're born with the soul of wherever you're born," she said. "For instance, if you're Chinese, and you transcend, you come with the soul of China, the Buddha, the almighty of the energy. And that energy is what takes you into certain turmoil as a baby and a child, and you get through it because of that okra. So, we don't identify the okra. We keep it as an unknown entity of God's domain."

She also said it was a sacred duty and covenant with God that priestesses and priests do not step into the domain of the okra.

"And we don't cross those borders because God will tell you, 'Listen.' When you do an oath in any profession, let's say when you become a doctor. You take an oath to your profession. And that's one of the oaths that we take as human beings," she continued. "The oath of allowing God to have his. And that is his alone, and nobody can really explore the soul. You can't separate it. It's not an entity where they can just look at it in a microscope and just examine the soul and know what God's input is in life."

The okra is the hidden flame that is the eternal in each human being. It is also that person's connection to God. The ego part of the self is not immortal in Akan spiritual teachings.

"When you communicate with spirit, do you have to invite your ego to step to the side or take a back seat, so that spirit can flow first?" I asked.

"Yes, you do. A lot of times, a lot of things will have to stop, or you go into an area that you have exclusively set up for the stopping of all the world. You go into this tunnel to be able to communicate on the highest level," she said. "That's a part of your spiritual training, learning how to put ego aside."

The protected sacred shrine spaces allow the adepts to enter this tunnel of higher, clearer communication with the spiritual realm in ways that are safe and free from unwanted interferences from other humans, spirits, or anything else. These are the spaces that are most primed for the generation of the tunnel for clear communication between spiritualists and spirits.

"The tunnel can't operate in its highest everywhere. You have to create that tunnel. It's almost like creating your house, for you to be able to be safe in. So, you have to create those environments to have the tunnel operate at its highest level," she said. "The shrines are that. And when people come into the shrines, they feel it. It's so nice. To keep it at that balance, there's a lot of spiritual bathing. There are a lot of sacrifices that the people have to make, in order to step in that arena."

It is sometimes the case that Abosom and other spirits who preside over the shrine spaces will simply refuse entry to some people. They do not always give an explanation, but it often will be because the person does not come with a pure heart or with honorable intentions, or because the person has some entwinement with negative spirits or destructive energies.

"If you're moving forward, there's always something you have to move to the side, as you move into the light," Okomfohema Botwe I explained, making a more general observation. "When you're going with the light, there's a responsibility, and there's also a jealousy with people who are in the dark."

Regardless of the sanctity of the space, Okomfohema Botwe I and other experienced priestesses and priests are often able to drop into connection, at various levels, with their spirit guides at any time. They live as interlaced with some of them, in a form of cohabitation, and as mediums for the spirits' expressions of their words, guidance, wisdom, and action. Okomfohema Botwe I is perpetually expanding and moving on her path of entwinement with the forcefields of these Abosom and ancestors, always refining her constellation of subjectivity in cocreation with the divine spirits that run through her life. She cogoverns always with the various copresences who have jurisdiction to enforce laws, orders, and protocols within her shrine houses in Maryland and Larteh, as well as with elders from across the broader Akan shrine culture system in the United States and Ghana.

The Akan spiritualists' theopolitical work also involves engagements that take place alongside and in collaboration with those working in state institutions, not merely outside state political and legal bodies. This is true in the United States and in Ghana. They seek to further true understanding, elevated consciousness, and inclusive justice. These things are of course often not brought about through existing state-based legal systems. The Akan system of spiritual laws comes to function as a parallel copresent jurisdiction that serves as an antidote to toxic behaviors or forces.

"Do you deal with the legal system yourself?" I asked Okomfohema Botwe I one day.

"Yes, I approach the legal system specifically with a program that I devised when I was in school for social work during the era of addressing the Black perspective in a deeper and more expansive way. A part of my training was, 'How do I express the trauma that African Americans have endured? And how do I utilize this in a positive way to turn around the Black-on-Black crime in the community here?'" Okomfohema Botwe I said. "So, a part of the idea, 'it takes a village,' is for bringing out reparations and healing for these traumas that African Americans have experienced throughout time. Churches also have expanded the Black History Month to include African rites of passage, day-naming ceremonies, and utilizing the perspective of dealing with your higher self. This is what I call the Soul Journey."

Okomfohema Botwe I designed and launched her Soul Journey program while still in school. It began in the Washington, DC, area.

"I devised Soul Journey and its component of dealing with the justice system through the judges, having an interaction directly with them, where they deal with torn families or children who have been dispersed, because of whatever has happened in the community, or whatever traumas they experienced, being directly involved with foster care," she explained. "We wrote a grant that included Soul Journey as a modality for youth who had experienced crime in the DC area. It addressed things, spiritually. We did readings for them. We did hands-on communication. Prayer. We did water therapy. And we did a sacred space, where there's a place where you have quiet time, and you commune and you just be silent, just be in the silence."

Okomfohema Botwe I and other Akan priestesses and priests also work sometimes with the police in the area to help them understand important principles of culture and diversity, and how traumas from past lives and earlier in this life can deeply influence the totality of a person's experience. They also work with police when the police are interacting with their clients or people they are helping.

"When we deal with the police, and they're dealing with our particular clients or the clients that we serve, they call us, and they let us know who they have. They know that we are there to help and to try to put a positive twist on the situation. We will encourage a holistic perspective with reciprocity and restorative justice as the goals, as opposed to a punitive approach," she said.

In 2017, Okomfohema led specific training for DC police officers to help them understand the broader dynamics of problematic situations involving alleged crimes from the standpoint of larger life circumstances of the people—for example, when mental health issues are involved. She explained that she taught them, among other things, "how to approach such people who may be struggling with mental health in a way that will not leave them feeling antagonized, hurt, or defensive."

This program was a part of the larger restorative justice movement, aiming to help broaden healing approaches to working with those who had been apprehended, helping them to best navigate what they were undergoing from a place of centeredness and empowerment.

"Rather than [being] punitive, they wanted to do a restorative justice effort. I've also had to do a training for DC police officers, to teach them how to handle youth who are experiencing a lot of trauma, to teach them sensitivity. This is not just because of what they've done, but before that incident happened, there were other reasons that caused this particular issue to be there," she said.

Okomfohema added that this totality includes experiences that the community carries from the days of enslavement. She explained that the ancestors who were enslaved sometimes come to share their experience and guidance with the priestesses and priests.

"The ancestors speak to us and tell us the stories. They're our guides. They actually let you know where to go, what to do, what happened, how to help them. What did they have to rise above? It's also that everybody has choices in this world, and we like to make sure people are at least getting the choices or the opportunities, if you will, to make choices, that are good for themselves," Okomfohema explained. "The spiritualists do a level, a leveling ground. We try to level everybody off who's discontented in any way, form, or fashion and find a safe middle where they can restart or they can start and find themselves. So, we reach to our inner spiritual quest and come up with answers for them to be able to explore their horizons and go through their soul experiences. That's why we call it Soul Journey. It's not just you, the person."

From the spiritual realm, Nana Oparebea and other spirits help to advise Okomfohema and others on all of these processes. Nana Oparebea also helped to call many of the spiritualists to train in the first place.

"Nana Oparebea directed us, of course, in many different ways. 'Come back home. Learn how the elders operate. Learn what systems they use, and the tie-in of the village and the community here in Ghana—the connectedness.' And that's what we try to portray, that connectedness. It's important. When people are connected, that's when they do either good things, or they do bad things. So, we have to demonstrate positive connectedness, and demonstrate that they are successful."

Okomfohema Botwe I also works with police in Ghana, where some officers more regularly consult the priestesses and priests.

"For instance, if we have children that we've raised, in Ghana, every area has their police station, and they have meetings, they have different times where we have to interact. So, if they have one of our children, and they have done something wrong, or the person has offended, they sometimes bring them to the shrine," she explained.

What brings most people to the shrines in general? People in Ghana and the United States often visit shrines for spiritual protection, to guard against spiritual attacks or other offenses that are unlawful under the Abosom's spiritual jurisdictions. Of course, people also come for general guidance on a wide variety of issues, whether personal, familial, professional, or otherwise.

The priestesses and priests also will receive requests for evidence, helping to locate lost property or persons, or assessing the veracity of a claim. When I asked for further elaboration and confirmation about whether informal police consultations of the priestesses and priests happen in the United States in places where the Akan shrine culture is vibrant, Okomfohema Botwe I immediately replied, "Yes, of course! It's all over. It's not a secret. It's not something that's hidden, and nobody knows. The police officers deal with that now. Now they say, 'Oh, we can't find your daughter,' and people will call upon the *nanas*. They'll call upon these spiritualists, the people who touch in on spirit."

Okomfohema Botwe I noted that one key difference is that many people in the general population in the United States do not carry the same respect for the Akan priestesses and priests as they do in Ghana. For Okomfohema Botwe I, this may be a matter of having severed or forgotten ties to the traditions and powers of the ancestors and the Abosom. Or may be a matter of those who sought to cut off Africans, or descendants of Africans, from their ancestral ties. In this instance, people's ancestors are calling them back to their spiritual roots so that they can move forward in their spiritual growth, a variation of "ancestors calling from the future," as Rosalind Morris beautifully put it in a recent essay on another topic.[9]

Okomfohema Botwe I emphasized that such reconnection empowers, heals, and liberates people—or has the potential to do so if people are open to it. It helps them connect to their inner true light, their soul or okra. It can help people reconnect to their family lines in spirit and become what they are destined to become, in their soul, as well as what they always have been but perhaps have forgotten.

She also explained that many fear these processes, as they are unknown and as there has been so much misinformation spread about their faith and practices. So much of what people say that Akan priestesses and priests do, which would involve working with negative forces, is the exact opposite. The Akan spiritualists seek to teach people, if they are interested in learning, how to turn away from evil or negativity, to clear that from their lives and establish boundaries so that negativity may not reenter.

"Well, some people fear Akan spirituality until something happens in their family. The Christians sometimes will go through the back door, and they'll come to the Nanas, or the spiritualists, or the mediums," Okomfohema Botwe I explained.

However, this is not something that the Akan priestesses and priests generally discuss with regard to any particular person's situation or life because they keep an ethical code of confidentiality, much like lawyers, medical doctors, psychologists, and therapists. This is required by the Abosom and other spirits of their system, and each Akan priestess or priest must honor their oaths. If they do not, they may face spiritual and social punishments, which could include losing the privilege of practicing as a priestess or priest in the same way, something that is analogous to losing a license to practice law or medicine. This oath of confidentiality is akin to attorney-client privilege or doctor-patient privacy rules. These examples are necessarily general, since the priestesses or priests cannot divulge people's private information.

"See, we have our version of a HIPPA law. Every priest has an ethical responsibility to a person. What you come for help or guidance with, that is your business. It's nobody else's. So, if a Christian pastor wants to come through the back door, we can't go out and say to church people, 'Oh, your minister has come to our office!'" Okomfohema Botwe I said, laughing.

While this confidentiality is necessary according to their protocols and spiritual laws, it also leaves room for much misunderstanding in the popular consciousness about the ethics of their theopolitics, their copresent jurisdictions, and their spiritual practices. Their silence and careful discretion allow space for people to pass judgment and spread misinformation about their activities—by saying, for example, that they are working with evil forces, or are only pretending to have spiritual efficacy in order to obtain monetary gain, worldly power, or other forms of symbolic capital.

"So, we don't get our justice. Our justice only comes from an understanding. That's where our justice will be," Okomfohema Botwe I said. "We don't push our beliefs or push our way or push our stories or anything like that on *anybody*. But we are there with Gandhi. We are *no less* than the Gandhis and the Buddhas, and all of the big people who pray. We're there with them."

The priestesses and priests often have access to seeing and knowing in ways that untrained humans do not. They also have ways of tuning into spirit, or accessing what, to the unattuned, appears intangible or inaccessible. Affective charges and forms of visions, dreams, divinations, and other intuitive modes of knowing are central to all of this. These affective registers—or variations on assemblages of affective justice, as Kamari Maxine Clarke has recently theorized—are valuable sources of knowledge in their own right.[10] This is so even in realms where affective dimensions purportedly do not play important roles, such as in evaluating evidence, fact-finding, adjudicating, or making other spiritual-legal determinations.

The spiritual connection to the ancestors like Nana Oparebea demonstrates the power of positive connectedness, not only to spirits but also among humans in the communities. These dynamic, fluid assemblages of copresent jurisdictions can be described as intricate webs of spiritual interrelations and interconnections. The way that they course through the interstices of the state—operating alongside, within, and outside the state institutions—illustrate the theopolitical dimensions of Akan spirituality. The priestesses, priests, and their interrelated spirits animate these copresent jurisdictions. In their constellations of subjectivity, the spiritualists practice their arts with the intentions of maintaining and generating positive and sacred spiritual connectedness in order to help heal and protect people and places.

For Okomfohema Botwe I, walking this life path has brought her to her current station as a chief priestess, queen mother, and transnational leader in Akan spirituality. Through decades of devotion to the causes of healing and enlightenment, she has expanded and refined her practices of discernment and spiritual connection in order to decipher, discover, and remember who she was always destined to be in her sacred work in this human incarnation.

As she has journeyed in her path, she has become ever more deeply alchemized and complexly intertwined with her spiritual husband, Nana Asuo Gyebi, and with other key Abosom and ancestors with whom she works and cohabitates, in spirit and through her human body. As a chief priestess, she fluidly streams many trusted sources of wisdom and guidance from the spirit realm, and she can shift from one stream to another almost as if she were simply breathing. For Okomfohema Botwe I, becoming this constellation of subjectivity and navigating the many dimensions of these assemblages of copresent jurisdictions has meant further becoming what she always has been—on some level of her soul—but had yet to fully remember, realize, or inhabit more deeply during this lifetime.

TWO

Ankobeahema Nana Amoabaa Atei Asiedu, Elder and High Priestess

With perpetual streams of spiritual governance work in the shrine houses, Okomfohema Botwe I relies heavily on the aid of her brilliant spiritual collaborator, shrine elder, and high priestess, Ankobeahema Nana Amoabaa Atei Asiedu (Nana Atei). She serves as second lieutenant of the ASUO shrine house. Her title of *Ankobeahema* means the protector of the shrines, the one who remains at the shrine and protects it when everyone else goes to war. She works closely with Okomfohema as an elder and a priestess at the ASUO house and the Asuo Gyebi shrine in Larteh, Kubease, Ghana. She is a central figure in the copresent jurisdictions of the house families and works in various dynamic interrelations with state and nonstate institutions. She is deeply involved in the myriad healing activities, the restorative theopolitics, and the spiritual vibrancy of Akan diasporic spirituality.

Nana Atei flourishes in dynamic constellations of subjectivity as a priestess. She works primarily with two Abosom: Nana Asuo Gyebi, the masculine river Obosom (originally from the north of Ghana), who is a healer and protector who delivers justice, and Nana Esi, a feminine healing Obosom who focuses on family, relationships, children, and childbirth. Nana Atei also works with many other Abosom and venerable ancestors who stream through her and express themselves, either as part of her or separately, in both ritual spaces and her everyday life.

She resides in divine union, or spiritual marriage, in an energetic interlacing with her two primary Abosom, though she can hear and communicate with a vast array of spirits, including other ancestors from her physical and spiritual lineages. Nana Asuo Gyebi and Nana Esi coreside within her. She can speak with them anytime, no matter what she is doing. She does not need to be in a specified ritual space, trance, or state of spirit possession. This is the case with many other spirits as well.

In addition to her role as a chief priestess, Nana Atei is a prolific and highly engaged neuropsychologist and professor at a state university in Maryland. She often teaches in vibrant Akan cloths and sacred beads, and she exudes an unmistakable glow, wisdom, and healing aura. People with a sensibility or inclination toward the spiritual sides of life often gravitate toward the warmth of her smile, her eyes, and the pronounced sacred energy that attends her wherever she goes.

While teaching and fulfilling her roles at the shrines, she also maintains a private practice in clinical neuropsychology. In her teaching and private practice, her spiritual prowess plays a key role, though usually in a fashion that goes unseen to the untrained eye. In private sessions with clients, though outwardly silent, she frequently draws on spiritual insights from ancestors and other spirits to get to the roots of psychological issues, which often have spiritual, as well as more mundane, earthly components. She also provides expert evaluations and testimonies in court proceedings that pertain to questions of neuropsychology, particularly with respect to child custody matters or claims of nonnormative psychological conditions. Like Okomfohema, she has worked with police from the community, recently incarcerated people, youth living in potentially precarious situations, and others. She juggles all this while also undertaking the yearlong spiritual training and healing Soul Journey program that she helps to fashion and lead in other venues.

As Nana Atei has grown on her spiritual path, she has become ever more entwined with certain of her ancestors and with her Abosom. At all times, even when simply driving down the road or walking in the grocery store, she has access to the guidance of the spirits, and she hears them perfectly clearly. She says that this is true of all practitioners of the path—once they become priestesses or priests. The spirits can provide everyday assistance or guidance, such as directions to the store or advice about which food to eat or avoid. They can also furnish insights into addressing and, at times, healing vital matters, such as illnesses or imbalances, particularly when they have spiritual aspects or causes. The spirits will also advise her about when other forms of medicine should be accessed and utilized, such as so-called Western biomedicine or other forms of healing mixtures or agents, such as herbal assemblages.

Although Nana Atei did not formally train as a priestess in the Akan order until she was in her early forties, she had long had spiritual powers, particularly with dreams, intuitive knowing, and prophecy. Ever since she was a child, people acknowledged and appreciated her advanced spiritual skills. Her mother also possessed intuitive spiritual gifts of healing and knowing.

Her husband in human form, Okomfo Kwabena Duku (Okomfo Kwabena), is also now a priest. His primary divine union is with the revered warrior spirit, the Obosom Nana Adade Kofi. He graduated under the training of Okomfohema Botwe I in 2009.

Okomfo Kwabena had been reluctant to train when the Abosom and ancestors called him to become a priest. He was thriving as a jazz drummer and had already experienced spiritual connectedness in his own way.[1] He initially felt that it was unnecessary to train, and he worried that it would be burdensome to do so. Training and living as a priest involves so many rules and regulations, as well as a panoply of spiritually enforced laws and guiding principles. The path also requires one to eat and drink certain things and abstain from others, to observe certain rituals and festivals, and even to speak and think in certain ways aligned with right consciousness, as taught and guided by the Abosom and the elders. In short, the priestly life requires a person to transform into another form of subjectivity, into a more evolved state of themselves. This new priestly being is more open to the constant flow of spiritual knowledge and information, as well as dynamic interrelating with broader assemblages of spiritual copresences, or constellations.

It took the occurrence of a tragic experience for Okomfo Kwabena to have a change of heart on the matter, to surrender to the call to train and graduate as an okomfo.

"He always said, 'If God wants me to be a priest, he will tell me himself,'" Nana Atei explained.

Then, they had the devastating experience of losing a young son when he was three years old. The son, once he transcended, came in spirit to reveal to them that he had come, along with the Abosom, to bear witness to his father's calling from God to become a priest.

"It took our son's being born, passing very young, and then coming as a spirit to tell us that he had incarnated so that my husband could go through that experience, in order to understand that God was calling him to become a priest," Nana Atei explained.

She elaborated on this principle, or spiritual law, more generally.

"In life, we often go through so many things. Difficult things will happen, and we don't know why. It may only be later in life that we realize that it was preparation for the spiritual work we were meant to do," she said. "The spiritual work can't happen until the person is ready on mental, physical, and emotional levels."

For those in Akan spiritual communities, the Abosom come to announce the optimal time and space for the conferral of a higher spiritual knowledge about life's trials and the necessary processes for elevation and transformation.

"The Abosom will come to explain the deeper meanings of happenings, after you have gone through certain experiences and learned the lessons. They may issue a call to train as a priest," she explained.

During this particular conversation, we were sitting in the café of a market called Mom's, an organic shop not far from her home in Maryland. As though to illustrate the perpetual copresence and cogovernance of the ancestors and spirits, she poured a bit of her juice into the drink's cap and set it out for them to taste. She explained that she routinely reserves some food and drink for the spirits, just in case they would like to partake. In fact, if she forgets to do so, they often will spill some of her food or drink to remind her.

For Nana Atei, the path of becoming a priestess was a journey of formally acknowledging, affirming, and training in the arts of healing and spiritual knowing that had been with her since she was a child.

Her preparatory work unfolded over her lifetime before she was consciously called to train on the Akan path. In fact, Nana Asuo Gyebi had been with her since a very young age, though she only realized that he had been part of her life after she had trained.

"Nana Asuo Gyebi is inside of me. I don't have to be possessed to speak with him. I can talk to him anytime and hear him. It's like prayer," she said. "He says he has been with me since I was child, at about seven or eight. Of course, I didn't realize he was there. I just knew I had some intuitive gifts, instantly knowing things. I also would have dreams that revealed things. People around me would remark upon it, saying there was something different about me, that I was special or an old soul."

It was not until her forties that Nana Atei would learn the name of this Obosom, Nana Asuo Gyebi, who had long been a part of her. During this time, she also opened her conscious awareness of the spiritual principles, laws, and language rubrics of the Akan spiritual system.

"Nana Asuo Gyebi was with me since I was child, guiding me through all of my lessons to prepare me, but I just didn't realize it. I could talk with him, and I could spiritually hear and know things, before I ever trained as a priest," she said.

Early in life, Nana Atei closely observed her mother, who harbored many spiritual gifts. They lived in a small community in the islands in the Caribbean, and many of her family members were the descendants of slaves. She is also of Irish descent, and her Irish ancestors have come to her in dreams and waking times, in spiritual form, to remind her that some of her gifts derive from them as well.

Her mother would often console and advise people in the community, and she had a particularly strong affinity with animals. Whenever she was ill, the neighbors would always know because the animals they kept for food (chickens, ducks, or goats), even the two dogs, would take up positions on their backsteps where they sat and waited. Nana Atei and her family never knew if the animal visitors were waiting specifically for Nana Atei's mother to feed them or if they were standing vigil or praying for her well-being. They would stay there all day, unless someone chased them away. They seem to resent when people would make them leave the steps.

She said that she did not experience her life as impoverished and that she felt she had everything she needed when she was growing up.

"We did not know or realize that we were poor. Everyone around us seemed to have the same existence. We always had food and a roof over our heads, but we never went on vacations. In those days, a vacation was going to the country to visit a grandparent or relative," she recalled.

Nana had a fraught relationship with her father, who was believed to be unfaithful to her mother.

"He was a ladies' man," she recalled. "He loved the ladies, and the ladies loved him."

In fact, one of her earliest memories is from when she was about three years old, and it involved her father. She stunned everyone with her bluntness and boldness. She looked at her father and said, "Why don't you pack up and get on out of here?"

Everyone was shocked to hear her speak her truth with such clarity and insight, especially at such a young age. She could observe and intuit that things were not right regarding the way her father was treating her mother. Later in life, she recalled prebirth trauma from when she was in the womb. She was receiving the stress and negativity that her mother was experiencing on account of the constant conflict with her father. Stress manifests itself in different ways in the physical realm, and Nana Atei was born with an umbilical hernia and the whooping cough.

Nana Atei explained that her early experience with the dishonesty of her father led her to be crystal clear, from day one, with the man she would ultimately marry. She said to Okomfo Kwabena, "If you ever decide you want to take another woman, then we will go our separate ways. I would rather be alone."

Nana jokingly says to her husband, "We said till death do us part, so if you want to leave, die."

She said that she does not truly mean that. "We do not own others and have to accept what life deals out sometimes."

Her husband agreed to adhere to her standard of authenticity and fidelity. They have now been married for decades without any problems similar to those her mother faced with her father.

At the beginning of our knowing each other, I sat down with Nana Atei before we went to Ghana for the four soon-to-be priestesses' graduations in August of 2018. She said she wanted to give me more of a preview of what would be happening with the processes—as much as she was able and permitted—so that it would all make sense to me, someone who has not trained as a priestess in the Akan spiritual system.

She told me about how she had just returned from Aruba, where she and her husband have a timeshare. They go there to get away from everyday responsibilities, release tension, and relax. The clear, translucent water calls to her. Nana Asuo Gyebi is a water spirit. Her other closest Obosom, Nana Esi, does a lot of work with water as well.

"Given its size, you can travel the entire island in two hours," she explained. "As Nana Asuo Gyebi is a water Obosom, places with water—rivers, streams, oceans, lakes—really draw me. The water in Aruba has such clarity as well. You can go deep into the ocean and still see your feet or see the fish swim by you. On the Caribbean half of the island, there are no waves. I go there when I want to relax."

Nana Asuo Gyebi inhabits or runs through all pure or energetically clear water, wherever Nana Atei may be. I asked her whether he both governs and is the water, as one with it.

"Yes, he governs water and is embodied in the water. This is part of his healing. If I work with him to make medicine, I use it from any pure source, such as rivers or the ocean. If I can't get the pure source, I have to look for the next best thing, such as bottled spring water. It has to come from a natural source, as Nana Asuo Gyebi runs through pure water," Nana Atei explained.

The concept, or spiritual law, behind these equivalences, spiritual and physical, is that the element's source must resonate with the clarity and truth frequency of Nana Asuo Gyebi's spirit. The embodiment of his spirit must occur within an element that is aligned with the verity and purity of his vibrational essence. Otherwise, the healing and sanctifying powers will not be properly transmitted through the embodiment's medium to the person or spirit on whom the medicine is to work. The water used in divination should also be sourced from a natural, pure place so that Nana Asuo Gyebi's spiritual communication frequency can most clearly come through to the eyes, ears, hearts, and other forms of sensorial capacities of the spiritualists who are receiving and interpreting the information.

Pollution or other kinds of desecration of a pure elemental source can lead to the spirits taking flight from a particular element's space. Physical pollution often leads to spiritual pollution. In other words, spirits who do not work in and of the light frequencies will come to inhabit polluted spaces. These spirits themselves are baser and more occluded or opaque.

I shared with Nana Atei how, in some of my previous research on gold mining conflicts and spiritual dimensions in Obuasi, in Ghana's Ashanti region, some akomfo shared with me that Abosom would leave polluted streams and rivers.[2] I asked whether it resonated with her experiences in working elsewhere with Nana Asuo Gyebi. She said that, while that principle made sense, she had not encountered the situation herself.

"With the knowledge that I have of Nana Asuo Gyebi, I don't think he would acknowledge polluted water as a suitable medium for him to work through. I don't think that I could go to a polluted river and make healing medicine with him through that water," she explained. "I would have to find a pure source, such as a waterfall. You can't make healing medicine from polluted things."

I asked Nana Atei how an Obosom like Nana Asuo Gyebi would interact with other water spirits of the Akan spiritual pantheons and environments, such as a prominent river Obosom, Tano.[3]

Nana Atei explained that the Abosom and many of their counterparts in other related systems coreside in the spiritual realm as kin, and they commune as such. This collective kinship, coresidence, and cocreation among the Abosom extend beyond the Akan pantheon to others, too—for example, the spirits of the Yoruba. There is an underlying connection, as well as a oneness among them, aspects of unity that perhaps are counterintuitive to many human reckonings and concepts of individual or even quasi-individuated beings or forms of consciousness. In this way, there is something close to a mirroring of the reality of constellations of subjectivity in the spiritual realm and the earthly one. As with priestesses and priests who interact or interlace with various streams of conscious spirit, so it may be with various orders of resonant spirits who collaborate and communicate within the spiritual realm.

"The Abosom and other divine spirits live in their realm as brothers and sisters. They're all connected. They say we make the distinctions among them. The Akan Abosom and the Yoruba orishas are ultimately one. They commune and converse together on the spiritual plane," she explained. "They're from different regions. They speak different languages. On the human plane, we don't have an exact understanding of how they are together in spirit, but we know they interact."

The Abosom and other exalted spirits will communicate and seek assistance or empowerment from others in the spiritual realm, as needed, but they do not communicate all the details of what is happening among the spirits with the priestesses and priests in human form.

They will share only what is needed to address a problem, an issue, or an illness.

As we learn from Nana Atei's childhood and young adulthood, when she was unaware of Nana Asuo Gyebi's presence with her, the Abosom only share details with the priests and priestesses when such information is needed and it is time for them to know.

When Nana Atei was growing up in the village on the islands, she often attended a Roman Catholic church with her family. While she enjoyed some aspects of it, the religion never fully resonated with her. She always felt the sermons were lackluster or somehow deficient in compelling meaning. She found the ceremonies tedious.

"Something was missing, and I always knew this," Nana Atei reflected. "I think that, whatever my path was to be, God had to reveal it to me in a way that I could feel from deep within as true and right for my soul."

The sensation of inner truth, of incontrovertible *knowing* beyond ordinary aspects of external evidence, is something that all the priests with whom I spoke emphasized. The experience of this deep knowing has often been far more important to hearing, accepting, and following the call and its various spiritual itineraries than were external validations, although those were of course important as well. The spirits also frequently send affirmations and signs through humans, animals, and many other aspects of the physical realm.

I asked Nana Atei, after knowing her for some time, if she could share with me more of her path, how she received the call and became more integrated with her Abosom, ancestors, and spiritual connections.

"This type of spiritual healing was always a part of the culture in the islands. We were not a part of it, but it was not a foreign concept," Nana Atei said.

When she first traveled to Ghana and got off the plane, a Ghanaian man told her that she was his cousin. She felt disbelief, as though he probably said that to everyone. Her initial skepticism about her Ghanaian kinship slowly cleared as she continued her travels. She was forty-three at the time. She had gone on a trip there for a conference with some social workers and others. They passed through a town with a healer who was conducting divinations on people's ancestry. Nana Atei likened this to the DNA testing for biological ancestry that people do in the biomedical genetics realm. It was like a spiritual ancestral reading, and it cost about forty-five dollars. Her colleague said he would cover the cost for her. The colleague had long been involved in Akan sacred culture in Ghana and in the United States.

Nana Atei received fascinating ancestral information from the healer.

"She told me the region where my ancestors lived. She also determined my first ancestor to arrive in the Caribbean on a slave ship. This ancestor came from the lands of present-day Ghana," she said. "The woman added that I came from a long line of priests that runs through the maternal side. Every generation must have a priest, and I would be a priest and so would my daughters."

Her daughters were eight and eleven at the time, and they initially rejected this idea. They maintained that they would not be training as priestesses when they were older, though they later changed their minds.

Over the years, Nana Atei had had many dreams of a foreign land in which she was speaking a language she did not know. These spiritual dreams had prepared her for receiving this sacred knowledge through the ancestral reading in Ghana.

"The Abosom had already been coming to me in dreams. I didn't know who they were or what they were, but I was always dreaming that I was in a foreign country. In a way, I knew it was Ghana. In the dream, I could understand and speak in a language I did not know in my waking hours," Nana Atei said.

After she received the ancestral reading and kept having these spiritual dreams, she started to share some of them with a student she taught at the university. This student was a part of Okomfohema Botwe I's shrine house community, and he would share much about Akan spirituality with Nana Atei. She would share places from her dreams that were actually in Ghana, but she just did not realize it. She would also share people she would meet and various things she would do in the dreams. The student quietly listened to her.

It turned out that the student had been relaying the dream information to Okomfohema Botwe I, his spiritual elder. Okomfohema Botwe I was conferring with her Abosom and establishing that this was indeed a call for Nana Atei to train as an Akan priestess. It just so happened that Okomfohema Botwe I had been asking her spirit husband, the Obosom Nana Asuo Gyebi, to send a superb psychologist to help her. Many people had been coming to Okomfohema Botwe I for healing, but they had psychological disorders in addition to their spiritual ailments, which often were related. Although she was a highly trained and experienced social worker, Okomfohema Botwe I sometimes found these cases to be too much to handle on her own.

Okomfohema Botwe I eventually asked the student to invite Nana Atei to the shrine house in Maryland. When Nana Atei arrived, she began to describe things and places that only Okomfohema Botwe I knew. Okomfohema Botwe I then performed a spiritual reading and told Nana Atei that the spirits were calling her to train as a priestess in the Akan order. Nana Atei was surprised and a bit concerned about the three years that the training would require. Okomfohema Botwe I asked her to go talk with her family about this call, to see if they would support her on this journey.

Nana Atei's dreams and further affirmations in the waking realm were laying bare her spiritual path for her continued evolution and service in this lifetime. She would find that she was on her way to becoming what she already was, on a deep spiritual level, or was destined to be, in her waking human life.

There was the question, though, about the support of her family. She had to check with them about training.

"In the Akan order, your family or others close to you have to agree to support you. We ordinarily don't train someone unless they have at least one strong person in their family line. If your family line cannot support you, then we seek confirmation from a good friend or some-body who will vouch for the person and be there for them," she explained. "My husband immediately agreed to support me. I had had dreams and other spiritual gifts throughout life. He felt that this was meant to happen. My entire family was supportive."

The family's questioning arrived more after she graduated, when the Abosom told Nana Atei that her husband was also being called to train. He eventually agreed to train, as did her daughters when they were later called. Her daughters had received spiritual messages that they would have to train when they were about twenty or twenty-one. Although they said they would not be doing so when they were younger, they did agree when the time arrived.

The second daughter, Yaa Ansah, was part of the graduating cohort of priestesses in Larteh on the official visit of the group that I had joined, as part of protocol, to gain permissions and allow for my writ-ing. Nana's older daughter had trained and graduated as a priestess the same year that she graduated from college.

Nana Atei shared that all she knew about their line of female priest-ess ancestors is that they were from the Volta Region, in the eastern part of present-day Ghana, and one was on a slave ship to the Carib-bean. She said that the ancestor's captors likely did not realize she was a priestess, as many known or thought to be priestesses or priests were being killed at the shore rather than forced onto the ships. For example, those in training would have *mpese,* similar to dreadlocks, in their hair. That would have been a sign that they were spiritualists.

Nana Atei elaborated on the symbolism of the change in hairstyle when one is training, as emblematic of a deep transformation and surrendering of old habitual ways of life. Wearing hair in the locks, mpese, along with so many elements of training, is about surrendering to the higher understanding and the spiritual path. It is about relinquishing control, stepping away from what is comfortable, and tak-ing the leap into the unknown to allow for spiritual growth and evolution.

"Training involves learning to let go of the need to try to control everything. We need to let go and let God, allowing God to lead and guide. Everyone has their own path to travel and their own challenges to undergo. The trials are like spiritual tests on the path," she said. "The situation may feel impossible to navigate, but if you follow your protocol, keep the faith, and rely on the assistance of your elders and Abosom, you will make it through and see the power of the path. It is amazing."

While the language of surrender resonates with many spiritual traditions, the Akan spiritual authorities do not necessarily use words like *ascension* for what happens with a soul's expansion of its constellation of subjectivity. It is more about a process of trials, of recognition, and of expansion along the way—of realizing the deeper soul purposes involved in the processes and the path. The more profound spiritual lessons embedded in the challenges, which may seem inscrutable to people who are in the throes of them, often become clearer in retrospect.

An important element of surrender to cocreation with the spirits is an acknowledgment and acceptance of flow without our notions of calendrical, linear time. Things are in flux and ever-changing, and it is always the now, the spirits say, so a set timetable for a plan is not truly fixed with the spirits.

"As humans, we are always trying to control things with plans and timeframes. However, the spirits don't have a concept of time like we do. We might plan to begin a ceremony at eight p.m., but the spiritual energy may begin to shift at six p.m. or ten p.m. We really don't control it," she said.

For Nana Atei, the primacy of the spiritual dimension of life is paramount. Surrender allows her to become one with the spiritual-natural flow of events and the ordering of things as they are meant to be, within a context of minimal resistance to the inevitable or higher-order spiritual plan of life. In this frame of mind and openness of heart, the signs and directions from the spirit are abundant in the external world.

"To me, the spiritual leads everything else," she said. "The universe gives us signs that something doesn't feel right. We call it intuition. If you listen to this inner sense, you can learn to go with it and more smoothly navigate life."

Contrary to so many false or distorted portrayals of Akan priestly practices and those of spiritualists who work with the light in other traditions, Akan spiritual authorities do not work with destructive forces, and they do not engage in manipulating or controlling others, or overcoming others' free will through things like spells or spiritual attacks. In fact, not only do they refrain from participating in such ritual activities, the Abosom and the ancestors with whom they work expressly forbid this kind of activity. Were they to engage in such undertakings, they would lose their healing spiritual gifts and possibly even their human life. When people approach them and ask for such things, their role and duty are to try to help the person understand why what they are asking is morally wrong, and how it is incumbent on everyone to work on healing themselves, rather than trying to hurt, manipulate, or otherwise control others. This is a fundamental spiritual law that governs their sacred work.

As Nana Atei put it very clearly and unambiguously, "Of course, there are people who do the dark side. We can't do that. We will be killed. We don't engage in rituals such as breaking up people's marriages or other things to go over others' free will. We don't do that. This is *all* of us. If we use our gifts to do bad, they will take us off the face of this earth. There is no maybe about it."

I asked her if, under their spiritual laws, things like love spells were off the table, in an absolute sense. There is such a common popular notion that the priestesses and priests are often engaged to implement such things on behalf of those consulting with them.

"We don't do anything like that. What we will do, if somebody comes and asks for something like a husband, we say, 'Okay, how can we enhance you? Tell me your challenges. Tell me the things you would like to make better.' We then work from there to help the person to address things in their own lives, which in turn can help them to possibly connect to someone who could become a husband," she explained. "I can help the person heal and open up for others, but I can't do anything to coerce another person or make someone do something."

She emphasized this as an important aspect of the spiritual laws of light in their work.

"We don't do spells. We don't do the dark side. That's why we wear white, to signify that we work in the light," she said. "If someone comes to us and has prior experiences with those who work in the dark side, we have an obligation to make them aware that this is not the way they should go. We clean them up so that they can move forward. Once we know that someone is walking in darkness, it's part of our job to show that person the light and the lesson."

Her corrective instruction of clients who seek things like spells is not always warmly embraced by those desiring spiritual services. Their displeasure is not relevant to the authorities, who are duty-bound to fulfill their charge to show people the path of the light so that they know of it and may choose to follow it, if they so wish.

"I have a responsibility to let them know that there are alternative paths that they can choose. Once I have communicated this to them, I've done my job. They may never come back. I may never see them again," she said.

I then turned to the question of the existence of dark energies. If the light is so powerful, why does it not efface or eradicate all dark, destructive, or otherwise untoward forces?

Nana Atei replied by invoking the unity of the one God, or Nyame, whichever name it goes by. In this, she echoes the point about the oneness of God that Okomfohema frequently underscores. She analogized the Abosom, exalted spirits of the light, to the Christian figures of angels. As God created us with free will, there is always a choice to turn to evil or darkness. It is through learning to discern the path of the light that one may achieve healing, may help others learn to do the same, and may move forward on one's own spiritual path of enlightenment. The Abosom are powerful, but they are not superordinate over our free will. They cannot compel or coerce humans to do things against the humans' own choices.

She also clarified that this free will naturally also applies to priest-esses and priests. It is ultimately up to the spiritualists to adhere to the sacred protocols and spiritual laws that they have been taught to follow to stay on the right path. There is always the matter of human volition, and there are always the interplays of light and dark, of good and evil, which are ever-present.

The cosmic reasons for the persistence of evil in the world remain a mystery to the spiritualists themselves, as an unknown aspect of the theopolitics of their work, perhaps known to Nyame alone. The Abosom may discuss such matters, but they do not converse about these things with the spiritualists.

She then detailed how the transmission of the Abosom's healing or guiding work through the energies of priestesses and priests—through their constellations of subjectivity—entails an intermingling and cocreation with all aspects that the spiritualists bring to the table as well.

"If a client comes, it is not as though Nana Asuo Gyebi can simply jump in and heal that person. He has to work through me, including all of my experiences and my lived difference. He works through my energy as a conduit to help that person," she said.

The process of divining, learning, discerning, and healing may move slowly and take time. Eventually, with everything unfolding cor-rectly—with the wisdom and guidance of the Abosom, as well as other relevant ancestors and spirits, including those that guide the person being healed—certain key personal patterns or events are pinpointed for healing and transformation. It may be that a trait, pattern, trauma, or other behavioral-spiritual marker has been passed down the genera-tions through family lines. Ultimately, if everyone is faithful to the process, the truth of what needs to be uprooted and healed will come into view.

"It may take a year or two. It may take some time, but along the way, you learn the lesson about the person—their background, their family, their ancestry, and their experiences," she said. "Through working with spirit, we may determine that the problem resulted from a relationship or from something someone else did. Or the problem may be a generational curse or illness that is passed down that the spirits may bring to light to be healed, not only from the person but from those down the family line so that they do not continue to be affected."

She drew close parallels to her work on neuropsychology, during which her spiritual insights of course are at play, although she often cannot directly share them with a patient.

"The spiritual healing process is very similar to how psychologists work. If someone comes for psychological therapy, you find out their background information, discern habits and behavioral patterns, and try to find certain triggers or causes of issues. It's the same thing, but it's on a spiritual level," she explained. "We can spiritually tap into their ancestry and establish whether, somewhere along the path, someone did something that is manifesting as a current issue or behavioral pattern. Once we locate a cause, we can help to heal the issue to make sure that the same energy does not keep generating the same issues or patterns in someone's life or in their children's lives, for example."

Nana Atei's earlier calling to be a neuropsychologist is linked to the modes of spiritual work that she has been tasked with in this life. She sees now how the two lines of work dovetail with each other.

"With our humanness, we are embodying spirit. I can see now why the Abosom made me a clinical neuropsychologist," she said. "My studies of neurons and the pathways of communication, along with how the brain controls the emotions and the physical state, also directly relate to the knowledge I need in conducting my spiritual work."

She also shared the similar interconnections with her husband's dual callings—to be an Akan path priest and a physical therapist. Okomfo Kwabena's spiritual knowledge and wisdom run through his therapy work. While he works with patients or clients, he will also assist relatives or others who may be present with them. Sometimes, those who have brought others to him will themselves be depressed or otherwise dispirited. He talks with them and guides them in how to help the person they brought to him. At times, he prays with them.

"He's also healing on the spiritual realm. It's not only physical," Nana Atei said. "His Obosom is working through him to heal those people. Whether he heals through a massage, or through helping them to take two steps to walk, he sees his physical work as spiritual work."

The clients often will not know about her husband's spiritual dimension to his work, though it is very much a part of his physical therapy work. It is akin to the ways in which Nana Atei's spiritual work runs through her work with clients in therapy.

"They don't know that their ancestors are talking to me, for example," she explained. "At times, they will be answering the questions I ask, and they will ask me how I knew to ask about a certain matter or issue. I can't say, 'Well, your grandmother told me.'"

She said that this interweaving of spiritual and other professional roles within their lives is true of her daughters as well, within their constellations of subjectivity, even if such spiritual convergence and entwinement must remain unspoken some of the time. It is all interrelated.

"My oldest daughter is a Tegare priest. The Obosom Tegare is also about law and order. He doesn't like evil, and he doesn't like witchcraft," she said. "My daughter is a probation officer and a case manager. She works with delinquent youths who have been incarcerated or in detention. When they come out, she helps them to get services. She talks with them and their families. She sees them once a week at an office and follows up with them at school. Her Obosom is working with her to help these kids."

Nana Atei emphasized the clear spiritual imprint and empowerment within her daughter's work in the justice system, in which she strives to heal and to help people move forward in their lives.

Her youngest daughter, Yaa Ansah, is now a graduated Nana Esi priestess, and she has a similar interplay between her spiritual service and her other earthly work.

"Nana Esi focuses on children as one of her specialties. Nana Esi actually walked as a human on this earth. The story is that she died in childbirth on the way from her village to the next. She felt that she was going to deliver her baby, but she was by herself and traveled to find help. She went into labor and died during childbirth. So, her mission is to help women, pregnant women. She helps women to get pregnant. She helps women to maintain safe pregnancies. She is also about family. She likes the family to stay together," Nana Atei elucidated. "People will consult with her priests over family problems. If it is beneficial and right that the family remains together, she will work to support this. She will also guide on the matters of children."

As it turns out, Yaa Ansah sought to work with youth as an English or history high school teacher, following her college graduation, which took place around the same time as she graduated as a priestess.

She also shared how the Abosom told her, when her children were young, that she brought them through her body to the earth, but that they actually belong to the Abosom.

"When the children were young, the Abosom told me, 'They're not your children. You gave birth to them, but they're not yours. They belong to us.'"

Nana Atei did not know which children belonged to which Abosom when they were young, but she knew that they had strong wills and personalities of their own.

"The children have always been strong. They've always done what they want to do. When I would complain that my kids weren't listening to me, the Abosom would remind me that it was because they were listening to spirit, to the Abosom."

This reality of the children belonging to the Abosom brought Nana Atei, as their mother, various trials of her own. She had to accept and surrender to the fact that she could not control the paths or lessons that her birth children would have to go through. These processes were necessary for the children to learn and grow into an awareness of their soul-selves and paths of connection, integration, and cocreation with the Abosom. In order for them to arrive at these states of awakening, they would have to learn lessons through the great course of human life itself so that they could turn inward and tap into deeper levels of their spiritual selves.

She shared an experience of when she was cooking and her youngest daughter, Yaa Ansah, then six years old, spontaneously said while playing, "Mom, you know this is my sixth time here, right?"

Nana Atei was surprised and intrigued. She recently had started going to the shrines. As Nana Atei was growing in her own conscious awareness of spirit, her daughter Yaa Ansah was giving her these messages, which appeared as if from out of nowhere.

"Yaa Ansah said, 'This is my sixth time here. The first time, I came from Uranus. I'm from Uranus. The first time I came here, my name was Urania. I didn't come to America. I went to India. The second time I came, I went to England. The third time I came, I went to America. This is my second time in America. This is my sixth time here.' She's telling me this, and I'm thinking, 'Okay, they watch TV. They watch cartoons. Or maybe she's connecting to spirit,'" Nana Atei recalled. "I then said to her, 'I hope that what you did not get those other five times, that you get this time with your daddy and me as your parents.' She said, 'Okay,' then went back to playing."

Nana Atei then wrote down the details Yaa Ansah had conveyed to her. When Nana Atei later reminded her, Yaa Ansah had no recollection of telling her those things. Nana Atei then understood it as a message from spirit, indicating that it was important that Yaa Ansah accomplish her soul mission in this lifetime.

She elaborated on Yaa Ansah's personality, including her determination, individuality, musicality, and constant forward movement. She does not dwell in the past. She also plays steel drums, like her father, Okomfo Kwabena.

One day, Nana Atei offered a moving portrait of her mother, Pearl, who was always focused on helping others. She was an intuitive healer with much inborn knowledge and spiritual power. Many in the community where they lived recognized and revered her mother for these traits.

"My mother was a healer. My mother would not think about herself. She died early, nine days before my twenty-second birthday," she said. "People would come to our home. We lived in a traditional community in the Caribbean, an East Indian village. Half of the village was Muslim. Half was Hindu. There were a few families of African descent. We all lived together. I would say that we were multicultural before that was a word."

The communities joined in celebrations across faith traditions. People from the different spiritual paths would come to consult her mother for her healing knowledge.

"My mother was very open to spirit. People would come to see her. It didn't matter what religion they were. They talked to her, and she would pray with them. She knew herbs very well. Someone would come with symptoms or an illness. She would send me to go pick the herbs, and she would prepare the herbs for them and tell them how to use the herbal mixtures for healing. Our house always had people coming and going."

Although Pearl had great healing capacities and regularly used them, she did not identify as a healer. She ran the household and raised the children. She was a seamstress, as well as a gifted cook and baker.

"If she was doing a wedding, she would do the whole wedding. She would make the dress for the bride, and she would make the cake," she said. "People were always coming in and out, and they would tell her things that were wrong. She would say, 'Oh, I have a medicine for that. This is what you do.' But she never saw herself as a healer. She just thought that she was helping her community. She was a beautiful human being."

Her mother primarily learned her healing arts directly from spirit, rather than through a teacher.

About ten years ago, Nana Atei's brother, who is twenty years her senior, taught her that their childhood home had served as a safe house during World War II.

"During the wartime, this was a place where the US military came, like a base. We were strategically between North and South America, and it was a safe place because we had no wars. It was a base for a lot of American troops," she said.

Jewish people who were fleeing persecution also would arrive in the community, and her family's home served as a safe house for the refugees.

"My brother said our house was marked. The refugees knew. They would come there. My mother would feed people and wash their clothes. It was a place where people received respite, and then she would ensure their safety. My father used to get upset because people were coming, but she just opened our house to people," she said.

Nana Atei and her two older sisters carry on this tradition today, welcoming people into their homes if people need food or a place to sleep.

"We learned that from our mom, but we never thought of it as her working with spirit. She was just a nice person, and she helped people."

Once Nana Atei came into conscious connection with her calling, the Abosom helped to show her that her mother was a healer. Her sisters also have this spiritual gift but have not had the same opportunities to spiritually train.

"In their own ways, my sisters do things," she said. "My sister feeds people, she gives them medicine. She prays with them. She does the same thing. She doesn't think of herself as a healer. It's just something we learned how to do. We watched our mother do it, and we did it."

Nana Atei's lifelong spiritual gifts have come in many forms.

"I've always been a dreamer. I've always been able to see and read things, not knowing that I could do it. I would see people, and I would read them. I would know what's going on with them," she said. "People would come and just start talking to me."

In fact, a dream had revealed Okomfohema Botwe I to Nana Atei several months before Nana Atei's student introduced them. She had not even known who Okomfohema Botwe I was, what she looked like, or what her profession was. It was all a blank slate in Nana Atei's conscious mind. Nana Atei also was not yet involved in the Akan sacred culture.

The dream happened soon after the 9/11 attacks on the World Trade Center, in 2001. She had gone to a workshop in her dream, which was very vivid, in color, and waking-lifelike, as with all of Nana Atei's dreams. A social worker was leading a workshop seminar on trauma and helping people to understand and heal from it. At the close of the workshop, the leader asked Nana Atei to follow her, because she had something more for Nana Atei. As she followed the workshop leader down a corridor, she woke up.

A few months later, when Nana Atei's student introduced the two, she immediately recognized Okomfohema Botwe I as the workshop leader from her dream. Okomfohema Botwe I, a social worker as well as chief priestess, then told Nana Atei that she had long been praying for a psychologist to help her in her shrine work with conditions that are physical as well as spiritual, such as certain mental health disorders. She had been asking Nana Asuo Gyebi to please locate and bring his best psychologist, and then Nana Atei appeared.

"Nana Asuo Gyebi made that connection," Nana Atei recalled, with a gleam of wonder still in her eyes. "Then, I participated in Soul Journey. I attended the hands-on class in order to see how they pray and do things. I was discerning whether I wanted to walk this path."

Although this calling was set on her spiritual path, Nana Atei of course still had free will about whether to follow through with training as a priestess. She did elect to do so.

After graduating from her training and becoming an okomfo in 2006, Nana Atei has become an important part of the ASUO house. She is now one of the elders, entrusted with helping to preserve much sacred knowledge and ensuring protection of the shrine family.

The spirits selected her for these roles on account of what Okomfo-hema Botwe I called her spiritual age—that is, how far Nana Atei already had advanced in previous lifetimes on her path toward integrating into her light, her higher spiritual forms of consciousness. The selection also was made because of the skills and expertise that Nana Atei already had evinced and cultivated in this lifetime, even before training, as well as the sacred knowledge passed down through her maternal ancestral lines, from West Africa and from Ireland. Her mother's grandmother was Irish, and her father had been an overseer on a slave plantation on another island. Nana Atei's great-grandmother was the only one of thirteen daughters to marry an African man, and they kicked her off the plantation for it. Her father's grandmother was also Irish.

One day, a few years before Nana Atei learned about the Akan shrine culture in Maryland, some of her Irish ancestors appeared to her in a dream or a half-waking vision. They stood at the end of her bed and shared with her that some of her spiritual gifts were from them, on the Irish side, not just from her African ancestors.

"It could've been a dream, but it was so real. I opened my eyes, and there were these two white people, a man and a woman. They were dressed in old-fashioned clothes. The man was looking at me. The lady was standing behind him. She was just smiling. She didn't say anything," she recalled. "The man said, 'I am here to tell you that we're part of you. You don't talk about us. You talk about your African ancestry. You are a part of us. We are part of you.' He added, 'The gifts that you have didn't just come from your African side. They also came from our side. But we're here to let you know that we're part of you.' Then, they disappeared."

Nana Atei's father had shared with her that her Irish great-grandmother, his grandmother, was clairvoyant. She was a seer.

Nana Atei's husband's mother also has Irish ancestry. His father's ancestry is all from present-day Angola.

"It's on both sides of my family. I know somebody's telling me that I have to go to Ireland. Even if I don't meet anybody, I have to feel the land," she said.

We then discussed the spiritual nature of the ancestors, more generally. I asked her if they inhabit a separate spiritual plane from the
Abosom.

"As I understand it, we die and we change forms, as we transition from
the physical form to the spiritual form. The ancestors are spirit now, not
on the same level as the Abosom, but they're in that realm where the
Abosom utilize them, too, to do God's light-work," she explained.

If the Abosom are aiming to reach people with a spiritual message,
they sometimes will send a close ancestor to the person who is still in
human form. This is so the person will be able to hear—or will be more
likely to pay attention to—the guidance or information from spirit.

As with the surrender to the call to train as a priestess or priest,
there is a surrender to the spirits when the Abosom decide they want to
come into the body and temporarily take over the consciousness of the
priestess or priest to do their healing work, ceremonial sacred dancing
and drumming, or other kindred activities.

With the matter of possession, or with the spirit's alighting and taking over consciousness—often to the point of the priestess' or priest's
fading out—it is most often not a transformation that the priestess or
priest can control.

Nana Atei explained some of the protocol for verbally interacting
with the Abosom when they come through the priestesses and priests
in full form, whether during an Akom or elsewhere. "We always ask
them right away, 'What is your name? Who are you?' That way, we
know immediately that we're dealing with the right Obosom. We then
ask what their mission is. Usually, they will have a message to deliver,
and they will share that with us."

At times Nana Atei can negotiate with the Abosom to stop a possession of others if the time or space is not optimal. One time, when I was
present, she stopped a possession of her husband by Nana Adade Kofi
(her husband's Obosom) during an Akom that was supposed to end
within the hour. Her husband had been dancing one of Nana Adade
Kofi's warrior dances, which often summons the Obosom's spirit, and

her husband began to look a bit lightheaded and his demeanor shifted, as is often the case when the spirits begin to come into the body in fuller force. Nana Atei, with her adept spiritual vision, could see clearly that Nana Adade Kofi was starting to descend on her husband to fully take over his body for the time being. If Nana Adade Kofi were to take over, the duration of his visit in Okomfo Kwabena's body during the ceremony would have been indeterminate. The length of the ceremony itself may have been greatly extended.

As an elder in the transnational practice of Akan spirituality, Nana Atei often travels among physical locations for various Akom ceremonies and shrine events, as well as for her other lines of work. She tends to travel to Ghana at least once every two years. She and the other shrine members frequently go to Larteh for the annual Nana Asuo Gyebi festival in early January. They are usually so heavily occupied with shrine work that it is hard to travel around the area. She hopes to travel soon to her ancestral land in Ghana, to visit the Volta Region that houses many from the Ewe ethnic group.

Whether in Ghana or back home in Maryland, the spirits remain perpetually interlaced in Nana Atei's professional work in teaching and neuropsychology. The spirits will often appear unbeckoned during her neuropsychological services and teaching, though she of course is very mindful in how she uses the information they offer. Nana Atei's interactions with the court system are often for expert evaluation resources, given her professional expertise. People seek her psychological insights and analyses. She submits to the courts her assessment of the health and capabilities of people who are going through the court systems for various things, including family disputes. The ancestral spirits of her patients and those she is evaluating for other purposes often come to give her important information about what to ask to elicit the facts and elucidate the circumstances that will help for healing and for addressing the situation in a more holistic or restorative way.

As Nana Atei receives spiritual information, she also acquires other forms of data, which she analyzes and delivers in the formal, secular scientific rubrics or legal discourse required in parallel jurisdictions or disciplinary domains of expertise. Her work with copresent jurisdictions is robust and perpetual—whether it is with state-based legal and other institutions, or with the spiritual laws of Akan shrine culture.

Through her various personal and professional realms, Nana Atei navigates her multiplex spiritual realities through all aspects of her life, streaming the co-presences who flow through her with wisdom, information, and guidance. Sometimes, the spirits are even interlaced as part of her. Her subjectivity itself is a constellation of forces, at times governed by her intention and desire, and at other times guided by those forces of connected yet disparate forms of powerful consciousness, such as a primary Obosom with whom she lives in intimate interconnection and dynamic interrelation.

THREE

Several Young Priestesses of the House

Call, Initiation, Graduation, and Pathfinders

In the summer of 2018, several younger trainees (*okomfowaa*) in the ASUO house in Maryland were preparing to make their journey to Larteh, Ghana for their graduation into the Akan order as priestesses. An okomfowaa is one who has been initiated but has not yet graduated from training. An okomfo is a graduate priest. The title *Nana* is given to those who have trained others.

The first time I spoke at length with these four women, we were seated in the basement of Okomfohema Botwe I's house. They spoke about their calls to train and their spiritual journeys to that point, as well as their interrelations with their key Abosom, ancestors, and elders in the shrine house community. Some came from families in which their parents were akomfo. Others came to the path on a direct call from the spirits but discovered that they in fact were parts of lines of priestesses or priests from previous lives, sometimes of the Akan order.

We had our first initial substantial conversations on a warm day in July of 2018 as shrine elders and trainees were meeting to discuss what was to come during their August trip to the Larteh shrines. As I had requested to document some of their spiritual and life journeys, the spirits, elders, and their Akan spiritual protocol required that I travel to the Larteh shrines to witness firsthand so that I could gain the clearest knowledge and perspective possible from their points of view. A film-maker, journalist, and photographer, Eric Hill, was present as well. He would join us on the trip to Larteh. Eric is a Babalawo—a high priest of the Ifá oracle, in the Yoruba Ifá-Orisa religion. He is also a high priest of Vodou. Eric's spiritual path and training came from present-day Benin and Nigeria via Cuba and Haiti.[1] Okomfohema Botwe I shared with me that she chose Eric to attend the group on the trip to the Larteh shrines as the videographer to film interviews and selected parts of ceremonies, as he is a person sensitive to their cultural and spiritual nuances.

I spoke with the young trainees who were about to graduate for several hours. We sat on couches in a very peaceful room with purple walls in Okomfohema Botwe I's home. It was my first time speaking to them in a one-on-one fashion; the conversations would develop in fascinating ways over the coming months and years.

Okomfohema Botwe I had just performed readings and healing services for visitors from the area. When she emerged, in regal blue with silver trim cloth around her body and head, she was accompanied by Osofo Yaw, also in brilliant blue traditional Akan regalia. Osofo Yaw would prepare to be enstooled as a chief in Ghana several years later. He sat to her left, and we rose, taking turns in the circle we had formed, to greet Okomfohema Botwe I formally before she and Osofo Yaw led a discussion about the practicalities of our collective trip to Ghana. Subjects included the timing of different groups' arrivals, preparations for contributions to a collective food fund, spiritual rituals and protocols, and lodging and sleeping arrangements. Okomfohema Botwe I also spoke about various implements and other items people should bring, and, particularly for the soon-to-be graduated akomfowaa, what they could expect to hear from the elders in Larteh that might differ somewhat from what they had learned in the United States. In general, the specific taboos and requirements during training vary among locations and circumstances, or shifting copresent jurisdictions.

After the formal circle meeting closed, Okomfohema Botwe I and the other elders cleared out of the room to attend to other matters.

Okomfohema Botwe I had instructed me to speak with graduating priestesses to get their perspectives on Akan culture in the United States. She later shared with me that the concept behind this initial timing was so that I could get to know them and learn their perspectives on their spiritual journeys and subjectivities "before, during, and after the rites, because who they are, and how they see things, all of that will change. You will have their perspectives from these slices of time in the experiences."

I was later to understand the fullness of this gift that Okomfohema Botwe I had granted me, as the priestesses themselves were about to experience dramatic transformations in their interrelations with the spirits, with themselves, and with each other. In short, their constellations of subjectivity were about to undergo a rebirth or an expansion, through the performance of their final rites in Ghana. The completion of their final graduation also would place them under more advanced and robust spiritual laws and systems of spiritual adjudication. They would become even more subject to the copresent jurisdictions of the Abosom, ancestors, and shrine elders, as graduated priestesses.

At the same time, the spirits would work evermore closely through them. In this way, they would learn to cogovern through these spiritual systems of law and authority. In the course of the process, for those who continue on the path as planned, the priestesses ultimately might assume the roles of the shrine elders in human form, becoming Nanas or even chief priestesses and queen mothers.

PRIESTESSES-IN-TRAINING (AKOMFOWAA):
SPEAKING IN MARYLAND BEFORE GRADUATION
IN LARTEH
Okomfowaa Abena Baakan

I first spoke with Okomfowaa Abena Baakan—soon to be Okomfo Abena Baakan—a vibrant, deeply insightful woman close to fifty-five years old. We spoke about what brought her to this Akan sacred path, how she first intuited her calling, and how she had been negotiating her spiritual interrelations and entwinements along the way. She also shared some of her visions and aspirations, and how she ultimately came to train as a priestess under Nana Atei. Like Nana Atei, Abena Baakan has ancestry in the Caribbean, and she grew up there.

Abena Baakan's story traces back to her childhood, when she was raised in a spiritual Baptist family and church. She grew up with Nana Atei and knows her daughter, Yaa Ansah, who would soon graduate with Abena Baakan as her priestess Godsister in Larteh. All four priestesses who were about to graduate in the cohort are called Godsisters. This term connotes their perpetual interconnections, both in their human lives and once they transcend to spirit at the end of this human incarnation. In this way, they become close parts of the spiritual assemblages that make up each of their constellations of subjectivity as graduate priestesses, subject to the same spiritual laws and Akan copresent jurisdictions.

She recalled how, in her childhood, she could sense that her mother and others would have sacred and spiritually charged ceremonies at her home, often in the backyard. The adults would ask the children to stay in the house, to not participate, but Abena Baakan and other kids sometimes watched them with wonder. Her mother even sometimes held church services in their backyard.

When Abena Baakan was young, she did not have much of an inkling that she one day would become an ordained spiritualist, though she had been drawn to the services that she observed with her mother. Many things transpired for her to recognize and accept this spiritual calling to train. Certain things started to occur in her life with some frequency, and she began to interpret them as undeniable signs from the spiritual realm that she was meant to train as a priestess.

The profound signs started with challenges at work, where some colleagues were trying to spiritually attack her. One person in particular was targeting her, reporting that she had done things physically that never happened.

Around the same time, however, she also had been attending the *akwasidae* ceremonies, the holy day observances for the ASUO shrine family that are held on Sundays. This is the Obosom Nana Asuo Gyebi's sacred day. She had been regularly celebrating with the family at Nana Atei's house.

After some time with this turmoil at work, alongside the contrast of the jubilant joy that she felt while celebrating with the shrine family, Abena Baakan decided to join the Soul Journey program that Nana Atei and Okomfohema Botwe I cocreated and run, along with the Abosom, key ancestors, and other elders.

One day, she was at Nana Atei's house on a sacred day while the family was doing rituals. Okomfohene Yirenkyi I was also at the house, and he looked to Abena Baakan. He pointed to her and told her she was born on a Tuesday. He then said that she was a child of Nana Panyin.

Abena Baakan was skeptical at first, not fully understanding the call, but Okomfohene Yirenkyi I continued to tell her that she was being called. She decided she would wait until the spirits directly let her know it was time to embark on the training path.

Over time, Abena Baakan found that the signs from the spirits then intensified, as did her levels and modes of interpreting these forms of spiritual knowledge. They grew to a level where she felt she could no longer disregard or question them. Things continued happening at her job. She had a fire in her home. Her car was totaled, and then she had another car that was burned in a fire. All of this unfolded alongside her feeling drawn to the life of Akan spirituality. As she reflected on the confluences, she felt recruited to train as a priestess.

She called Nana Atei who is now her Godmother in Akan spirituality and shared with her that all of these things were happening, and she felt like it was time to join on the path. Abena Baakan also had been seeing apparitions of spirits that she had not called or beckoned. Nana Atei told her that these are the spirits who are walking with her to support her on her journey. Although Abena Baakan did not understand at first, she came to understand these spirits to be her cherished ancestors and other spirit guides, who were calling her to become a priestess.

Around the same time, the sacred spirits also were alighting on her as a medium while she was dancing during akwasidae ceremonies with the shrine family. She would take the spiritual bath, and sometimes the spirits would alight and flow through her as a vessel.

Once, when she was possessed with spirit, she began to sing, and Nana Atei asked the spirit who it was. The response was "Miriam Makeba." Nana Atei, in great surprise, asked the spirit, "Where are you from?" The response was "Rhodesia." Those who were gathered knew that this was a special occasion because that nation came to an end in 1979. Her Godsister then realized that it was indeed the spirit of Miriam Makeba, the famous singer and prominent anti-apartheid activist. It was so striking to Abena Baakan, as she would add Miriam Makeba's name to her full given name when she was a child, even though it was not formally a part of her name. She intuitively felt she should add it, and she often listened to Miriam Makeba's music. In fact, when Abena Baakan was five years old and people asked what her name was, she would always respond with her given name and Miriam Makeba, as she so admired her and her music.

These synchronicities served as spiritual validation to Abena Baakan, and she began to train. While we were talking, she reflected on how it felt to be on the cusp of her graduation rites in Larteh.

"I look back at these things in my life, and I didn't realized what was happening back then. Now that I have trained, I see the deeper meaning, and I feel *light*, like that heaviness is not there," she said. "Everything has been just falling into place."

Abena Baakan shared further signs that had confirmed for her that she is on the right path. She recently had been injured on the job, in her work as a dialysis technician, but she found that to be a mixed blessing, as it created the space for her to devote herself to spiritual study and preparation for graduation. Even though she is a single parent and needed to pay the bills, she had a good feeling, because she knew she was on the right spiritual path.

Abena Baakan had an unshakeable feeling that everything would come into alignment with her work, finances, and ability to make it to Ghana for her graduation. She had a newfound, unwavering calm that she said reminded her of her mother and Godmother, and how she believed they must have felt as she watched them in their spiritual practice and serenity when she was growing up.

"The practical things have worked out for the trip, and I'm just totally excited about going to Ghana. This is my first trip to Africa. I always said I would go. I never knew the specific circumstance, but this is a very good circumstance," she said. "I also feel blessed that every time I dance, I get possessed."

Many people, including highly trained spiritualists, will dance and not be sure whether the spirits that are called upon will come and stream through them at any particular time. However, for Abena Baakan, they come to her every time, and they began to do so before she was even training as a priestess.

When the spirits flow through Abena Baakan as a vessel, she sometimes retains some consciousness of what her body is doing. She may remember certain things that the spirit in her says or does, or other things that are going on in the space around her vessel. At other times, she entirely fades out of consciousness. Sometimes she fades in and out of consciousness. It is always a pleasant experience for her now, and she often feels like she is floating. When the spirit first arrives, she feels as though she rises out of her body.

Time also will take on a different quality, as it does for other priestesses and priests when they are possessed or in a trance. At times, it is like missing time entirely, and the experience goes by in what feels like a blink of the eye. They might wake up, or their spirit may reenter their body, after several hours of possession. Even if the temporality feels disjointed or vastly accelerated, though, their bodies register the general experience through exhaustion and sometimes soreness, especially on the following day. The subsequent fatigue was one of Abena Baakan's early signs that the spirits were flowing through her while she was dancing, even while she retained some consciousness of her presence with her mind and spirit awake. At first, she did not understand the tiredness, but the elders quickly explained it to her.

Abena Baakan said she welcomed spirit possession with the trusted spirits, though it was somewhat alarming when it first started happening, before she understood more about it. She had always wondered about it, though, ever since she was young. As part of her training as a priestess, she has learned to negotiate with the spirits and to control more of the feeling and sequence regarding things such as when they alight to fully flow through her.

In the training, the akomfowaa also learn particular dances and songs that summon certain Abosom or other spirits. The vibrations and harmonics of certain movements and music will be like magnets or calling cards to the spirit or spirits they invoke.

Abena Baakan, along with the other young priestesses, is particularly interlaced and interrelated with the Abosom and ancestors who have their primary shrines in Larteh. She was awaiting the graduation trip with great anticipation and joy. She was the only one of the four who were soon to graduate who had not yet been to Ghana.

Abena Baakan, two other akomfowaa in the room, and Eric all then spoke with me about the spirit of this ethnographic research and this book. I spoke about one aim of illuminating how the spiritualists on the Akan path work to unlock the universal light that can be found in all true spiritual traditions, as well as how the priestesses and priests become another form of self—or constellation of subjectivity—working with a forcefield of copresences, or spirits, and existing as intertwined with them.

They agreed that the best knowledge regarding their paths would come through being there and witnessing or experiencing their journeys as much as I was able to do so firsthand. They said that the spirits themselves are always available to assist and guide and that the project is a collaborative and multidimensional conversation.

The spiritualists present explained that with stillness of mind, the clearing of mental chatter, we are all so much more receptive to understanding subtle spiritual phenomena that might otherwise go unnoticed. They also spoke about the vibrations of spirit, the multisensorial aspects of constellations of subjectivity, and how spiritual assemblages entail so much more than can be rendered in language. They reflected on the spiritual laws of Akan copresent jurisdictions, along with how the Abosom, aligned with Nyame, issue directives and instructions, regulate activities, administer justice, and help to provide healing, protection, and empowerment.

Okomfowaa Ama Baakan

I next spoke at length with Okomfowaa Ama Baakan, who has been part of the shrine culture, in one way or another, since high school. She is now in her mid-twenties with one child, and is the Goddaughter of Okomfo Akua Anima Ansa, Okomfohema Botwe I's daughter who is also a Nana Esi priestess in the ASUO house. After Ama Baakan had started training with a priestess at the Asuo Gyebi shrine in Ghana, she left for some time to teach English in China. When she returned to the United States, she began training with her Godmother, Okomfo Akua Anima Ansa.

"I guess my first sighting I'd seen of Akan was in high school. I had gone to a very small, private high school in my neighborhood in northeast DC. I had never really left the neighborhood because there was no need. My teacher told me about all these African Americans getting together and dancing and singing. She took us as a class, and she just said, 'Take what you want from the experience,'" she recalled.

It was only some years later that Ama Baakan would be placed, as a foster child, into the home of Okomfo Akua Anima Ansa. Okomfo Akua Anima Ansa, Okomfohema Botwe I, and other priestesses and priests were astonished to learn of Ama Baakan's earlier exposure to Akom ceremonies and Akan sacred culture. Ama Baakan explained to them how her high school teacher had taken her class to one of the Akom ceremonies. Her teacher was an okomfowaa at the time, and she is now an Akan path priestess.

Okomfohema Botwe I, Okomfo Akua Anima Ansa, and the rest of the family took it as a sign from the spirit that Ama Baakan had been placed in Okomfo Akua Anima Ansa's foster care home for a reason. Prior to Baakan's arrival, Okomfohema Botwe I and Okomfo Akua Anima Ansa had even asked the Abosom if they could send a foster child who would be harmonious with their way of life and who would be a good fit for their home.

During a later conversation at the Maryland house, Okomfo Akua Anima Ansa shared another synchronicity—that she and Ama Baakan had shared the same government last names before they even knew each other.

"We had prayed and asked, 'Please send us a foster child who is unique and just for us.' We already knew she was supposed to be here because of her last name! Then, she already had been to an Akom," Okomfo Akua Anima Ansa said, laughing.

After Baakan started to accompany Okomfohema Botwe I at her events, she dove deeply into Akan spirituality and became entwined with it in a very enthusiastic way. Ama Baakan was so intuitively adept at assisting Okomfohema Botwe I and other chief priestesses—on account of her spiritual wisdom, her previous lifetimes, and her extraordinary intellect—that they began enlisting her as an *okyeame,* a spokesperson and an interpreter of the Abosom and other spirits, such as ancestors, when they would speak. While it was fascinating and exhilarating for Ama Baakan, it was also physically exhausting. She also helped her Godmother, Okomfo Akua Anima Ansa, with her training and first program. She even accompanied her Godmother on her trips to Ghana to assist.

When Ama Baakan initiated to her Obosom, Nana Adade Kofi, and began to study under her Godmother, she became the first in line okomfowaa (thus, her spiritual name, Baakan) to train under Okomfo Akua Anima Ansa's tutelage.

The other three okomfowaa in this cohort, who were about to graduate in Larteh, had trained with Nana Atei or Okomfohema Botwe I.

Ama Baakan had already been to a graduation, had been to Akoms, and said she basically had been raised in the culture, as she had entered it at about the age of thirteen or fourteen. She had always felt at home in it.

I asked her if she had ever felt at all fearful about the Akan spiritual culture.

"Not at all," she replied. "My teacher at school was pretty open with us, once I started asking her questions. Then, my Godmother and her other daughter, my sister, were training when I was young. When I went to Ghana with my Godmother, I saw way more than I ever could have seen here in America. So, it was never weird to me. I was never standoffish. I was very hands-on, and I was very open to everything."

She was soon to become a spiritual wife of the Obosom Nana Adade Kofi, after her graduation as a priestess. As she would live in union with him as one of his priestess wives, he would come to her to help her and to empower her. He would also interlace with her to speak and do other work through her, as needed. All priestesses and priests of the exalted spirits Nana Asuo Gyebi and Nana Adade Kofi are called their wives, regardless of their gender identities.

Nana Adade Kofi first came to alight on Ama Baakan during a sacred Yoruba dancing, possession, and spiritual communion ceremony in the United States, even though Nana Adade Kofi is an Akan Obosom. He had never come to her when she was younger, at least to her knowledge. She feels that, during Yoruba ceremonies, people are much more open to the spirits unless they intentionally close themselves to them. Even though she had been around a lot of Akom ceremonies, she had not had any experiences with the spirits possessing her until she was at this Yoruba ceremony.

"When you're in the Yoruba events, people are way more freely possessed and do things very differently," she said. "That is how I first got possessed, and they told me it was Adade."

Nana Adade Kofi is a warrior spirit, and he protects from evil. He is very concerned with efficiency and efficacy, and he helps to serve the aims of spiritual law and order in the Akan copresent jurisdictions. He brings a strength to his priestesses and priests that makes them feel stronger than they are when he is not flowing in full force through them.

"He gives you power and strength to overcome some of the things that you may not have been able to do on your own. It's a little bit of reassurance," she said.

Ama Baakan explained how her relationship with Nana Adade Kofi would become even stronger once she graduated from her training and became a full priestess. Her constellation of subjectivity would expand with his enhanced copresence. She would also more actively participate in the assemblages of copresent jurisdictions, as a Nana Adade Kofi priestess.

However, prior to Ama Baakan's graduation, many facets of the upcoming union were still unknown to her.

"I'm still learning how to show my love, respect, and appreciation for him. Right now, I'm a student and taking it all in. After I graduate, I will be a master of the craft. I will be able to greet and feed him, and I will know how to be a proper wife to him."

Upon graduation, Nana Adade Kofi would more deeply and thoroughly interlace his spiritual energy with Ama Baakan's embodied spiritual consciousness, though the meanings and features of this transformation had yet to be experienced by Ama Baakan.

Some people are born with parts of an Obosom's spiritual essence interlaced in them. For others, it arrives or unfolds over the course of their lives. In all cases, the connection, once made or activated, develops over the path of life. The patterns of spiritual infusion and modes of interrelation also vary by Obosom. Nana Esi Ketewa, the key Obosom of Okomfo Akua Anima Ansa, had walked a human life and passed during childbirth. Nana Esi does not relate to her priestesses and priests as wives.

The growing entwinement and cohabitation that happens between the Abosom and their priestesses and priests as they walk the path, whether in spiritual marriage or in other forms of bonds, is a demonstration of their dynamic existence as constellations of subjectivity. These constellations of spiritual forces also course through copresent jurisdictions, participating in collaborative forms of spiritual adjudication, truth discernment, and other forms of governance and knowledge production.

I then thanked them and wrapped up our discussion, as evening was falling, and everyone was tired. The conversations would be resumed in Larteh and then once we returned to the US.

Graduation at the Asuo Gyebi Shrine in Larteh, Kubease, Ghana

During my time in Larteh in August 2018, the graduating priestesses were engaged in intensive rites and immersive experiences, and they were completely exhausted. I first arrived after the priestesses, who had already begun their final graduation rites. Okomfohema Botwe I formally introduced me to the Ghanaian priestess and highest elder at the Asuo Gyebi shrine in Larteh, Okomfopanyin Nana Afoah Baakang (Nana Afoah). She is the oldest and highest-ranking living priestess to have trained at the Larteh shrine. Her title is Panyin, which means elder in the Akan system. She, along with a group of other priestesses and priests, has a home in the Asuo Gyebi compound in Larteh. She graciously received me. They brought me inside Nana Asuo Gyebi's sacred shrine area, a small room. The Obosom arrived and alighted on Okomfopanyin Nana Afoah as the priestess vessel. Nana Asuo Gyebi and the elders led powerful chants and songs, which the priestesses-in-training also recited and sang. The air was electrified. We all bent with our right knee down and with two fingers (index and middle fingers) of the right hand to the ground, in respect and reverence. I was in white linens, which I was instructed to wear, and everyone else was in a variety of beautiful traditional cloths, all with their own spiritual significance.

The Obosom Nana Asuo Gyebi formally received me through Okomfopanyin Afoah's serving as a medium. She communicated with Nana Asuo Gyebi via a sacred pot. Through her, he gave me the Akan name, Nyamekye. I was very humbled and honored to learn of this name, though I was also very surprised by the gift. I would later come to understand, through conversations with Okomfohema Botwe I, that this name connoted the purity of the essence of my intentions and my spirit, my readiness and fitness for this work of documentation and interpretation.

The okomfowaa were also presented for final graduation approvals at the Nana Panyin shrine (also called the Akonnedi shrine), where they presented the customary gifts that protocol instructs them to give. Akan rules of conduct also required that I perform protocols and procedures at the Nana Panyin and Asuo Gyebi shrines.

While in Larteh for the rites, the graduating priestesses had many long days and little sleep. I spoke at greater length with the elders, but I tried to fully respect the space of the akomfowaa who were about to graduate, as they were so exhausted. We spoke at greater length after their graduation was complete, once we were back in Maryland.

They had to fast for long periods and then walk to the market to gather food for sacred ceremonial meals and to feed the Abosom. They explained that they would get possessed and perform feats that would be far too difficult, physically, to complete if they were not possessed.[2]

While the spirits were in the priestesses, they would be adorned in specific sacred clothes and beads, and they would have white talcum powder placed on their skin to signify that an Obosom was working through them. This marking was significant, they said, so people knew to regard the priestess's body as the Obosom, or the vessel for the Obosom, so as not to offend or disrespect that Obosom. Often, the tones and demeanors of the priestesses would change when they were serving as a medium for an Obosom, and there would be a palpable force or electricity in the room. Their eyes would glimmer with an almost imperceptibly different light that was hard to see at first glance, but it was there.

I once walked into Okomfohema Botwe I's home in Larteh during the morning, and Nana Esi had just possessed one of the graduating priestesses. Her fellow akomfowaa caught her from falling as she swayed when the spirit descended, and then the akomfowaa seated her body on the couch to speak with Nana Esi and hear what she had to say. I left the room out of respect for what was happening, not sure if I was meant to be there. As I crossed the room to the hallway, it was as though I were wading through a form of liquid electricity, like a healing ocean balm. There is a kind of high that comes from the heightened presence of the Abosom. It was a beautiful feeling that has become a part of my affective archive today.[3]

BACK IN MARYLAND, AFTER THE GRADUATIONS: SPEAKING WITH THE YOUNGER PRIESTESSES

After the graduations, and once I was back at the ASUO house in Maryland, I spoke with some of the recently graduated priestesses at greater length about their earlier calls, signs from their spirit guides, and how things had transformed for them following graduation.

Okomfo Ama Baakan—no longer Okomfowaa, since she had graduated—explained to me that she was so consumed by the rituals while she was being initiated that she was perpetually in the zone.

"I think I was semi-possessed the whole time I was in Larteh for the graduation," she said.

Okomfo Ama Baakan told me more about how she was recruited to the role from a young age because of her intuitive abilities in knowing how to act as an okyeame, or interpreter of the spirits and a spokesperson for high-ranking Nanas (elders) in New York City as well as Maryland. Okomfohema Botwe I and Okomfo Akua Anima Ansa started taking her around to big regional Akom ceremonies and festivals.

Elder priestesses, priests, and other Akan spiritualists found that Okomfo Ama Baakan, even prior to being initiated on the Akan path, could understand some of the Akan language, Twi, without formal study. When the Abosom would speak in this language, she could often understand and communicate what they were saying through her intuitive spiritual abilities. Sometimes, the Abosom speak through American priests in English; at other times, they speak in Twi. I have asked priestesses why the spirits chose certain languages at different times, and there is no clear explanation, apart from its having to do with the language abilities of the vessel—the priestess or priest—and also with the ways in which the information is to be best communicated to those who are tasked with receiving it.

One day, when we were sitting in the basement at Okomfohema Botwe I's home, Okomfo Ama Baakan said the use of both languages, and the variations in accents and dialects, added to the work she was given to do even prior to training.

Okomfo Akua Anima Ansa elaborated: "She kind of got thrown into it, because she did not really know a lot about the culture at that point, though she had seen it."

Okomfo Ama Baakan said she felt like she was more patient when she was younger. Her Godmother laughed and disagreed, saying Okomfo Ama Baakan had become more patient now.

Okomfo Ama Baakan again recalled when Nana Adade Kofi had come to flow through her in full force, and how moving and overwhelming it felt at the time.

"The first couple of times it happens, it is really overwhelming," Okomfo Akua Anima Ansa added. "With most people, all they do is cry. I know that the first time it happened to me, all I did was cry."

I asked Okomfo Ama Baakan how her relationship with Nana Adade Kofi had shifted once she had graduated as a priestess for him, residing in spiritual marriage.

"I feel like I have to call him in, and in order to do so, I have to get in the right headspace. I have to know why I am calling him. I don't ever want to be in a compromising position where I call him, and I don't know what to do after that," Okomfo Ama Baakan said.

We all laughed. Nana Adade Kofi is very swift and efficient in his personality and judgment, manner, and execution of tasks. People tend not to call him if they do not have something very specific in mind. At that point at least, Nana Adade Kofi would only come to Okomfo Ama Baakan if she called him. He never arrived simply unbeckoned. Some other priestesses mentioned to me that, at times, the Abosom will just arrive without being called.

Although things had changed for Okomfo Ama Baakan as a priestess, they also felt like a continuation of the spiritual culture in which she was raised.

Okomfo Akua Anima Ansa recalled how children whose parents were in the Akan spiritual culture would play Akom when they were little. While their parents were doing their sacred ceremonies, the children would dress up with sheets and towels, rather than the traditional cloths; they would get some talcum powder, and sing the songs and do the dances.

"That's what we did! All the shrine kids did it," Okomfo Akua Anima Ansa said. "We would play Akom. It would be so funny. The adults would be having the real Akom, and we would be in the back, playing and imitating them."

Okomfo Akua Anima Ansa explained that she grew up not really caring for the Akan shrine culture at all, even though she would play Akom with the other kids for fun. She felt that it took so much of her mother Okomfohema Botwe I's bandwidth and time. As a child, she wanted people to be visiting the house less often, asking for things less frequently. She simply wanted her mother to focus on her. Okomfohema Botwe I was perpetually busy with her sacred duties, especially as part of the first generation of Akan path priestesses and priests in the United States to have trained directly under Nana Yao Opare Dinizulu I.

"It's such a selfless path," Okomfo Akua Anima Ansa said. "With your parent, as a child, you don't understand what it is that your parents are doing. It takes a lot of their time. I would come home and want my mother to be making breakfast or dinner, and that's just not always the case when she is doing shrine baths and Akoms, or traveling. People would often visit the home for help with things and wanting attention. There were always people coming through."

As a child, Okomfo Akua Anima said that she would never become a priestess herself. However, when she was about fourteen, the spirits and the spiritualists gave her clear messages that she had been chosen and was destined to become an Akan path priestess. At first, she told them that they were mistaken, though she did ultimately accept the call to train and graduate.

Okomfo Akua Anima Ansa explained how, when people are about to graduate as priestesses or priests, they have so many processes of affective reckoning, of working through and interacting with the past, present, and future in a different, more elevated way. This expanded perspective requires passing through apparent or actual hurdles, both internal and external, for the conscious evolution of the human existence and the spirit of the priestess or priest about to graduate. So much gets processed and brought to the surface of one's consciousness, including memories—sometimes stored in the body or the soul—of past life traumas, losses, or even beautiful experiences to which the soul of the person maintains an energetic connection or attachment. All of a person's energy that can no longer stay with them, once they become a priestess or priest, must be transmuted or released so that such energy no longer remains within the constellation of subjectivity that is the spiritualists. These clearing and leveling processes ensure that the spiritualist can traverse with ease the spiritual realms and their copresent jurisdictions.

"It's intense. You go through so many emotions, but you will think, 'I didn't come this far not to make it,'" Okomfo Akua Anima Ansa said.

"You can't be your same self," Okomfo Ama Baakan added. "I feel like I was a different person in Ghana during the graduation rites. You can't be who you usually are in life because you'll be working sunup to sundown. It was exhausting."

The akomfowaa had one particularly draining ritual that involved going to the market to get special food items for a ceremony. They were supposed to walk a long distance on foot early in the morning, in their traditional priestess cloths and beads, and then carry the items back to the shrine house in bowls on their heads. This was meant to happen early during the day, and they had been fasting for the market ritual. However, several things delayed the process, and the priestesses were not able to do this until late in the afternoon when sundown was soon to approach. They were drained, hungry, and lightheaded. They explained that it was by the grace of the spirits who were running through the akomfowaa, and assisting them, that they had the strength to complete this rite. They also got ritual marks and medicine for their seeing, hearing, and smelling, which would have not been possible without the support of the spirits.

Okomfo Ama Baakan explained that it was all complicated by the fact that she had her newborn baby with her as well. She then told me how she was about to be married. Her fiancé was the man who had been sitting quietly in the corner while we talked, tending to her baby. She introduced her husband-to-be, Five, who is Muslim but whose family is very open to traditional African spirituality.[4]

A solemn yet joyful mood then engulfed the group. We all turned to Okomfo Ama Baakan and Five, as Five was preparing to formally ask his fiancée's Godmother, Okomfo Akua Anima Ansa, for her permission to marry Okomfo Ama Baakan. He was preparing to present the dowry gifts. A sister of Okomfo Akua Anima Ansa, also an Akan path priestess and a daughter of Okomfohema Botwe I, was coming to sit with her own new husband, so they could both share their wisdom about married life.

After Five formally presented the gifts, in accordance with Akan spiritual protocol, Okomfo Akua Anima Ansa asked, "Being married, this is something you both want?"

Five replied affirmatively.

"Five, you are charged with taking care of my Goddaughter and supporting her, and the child, on a full-time basis as husband.

First, I have to ask Okomfo Baakan, are you accepting of Five's engagement?".

"Yes," Okomfo Ama Baakan replied.

"Based on that information, I will give you my blessings. We will go before Adade and Nana Asuo Gyebi in the shrines to also ask their blessings," Okomfo Akua Anima Ansa said. She then turned to asking about timing and the details of marrying within both their families' faith traditions.

Okomfo Akua Anima Ansa and the family members then turned to the shrines to present the customary gifts and to ask the Abosom for their blessings for this marriage. The spirits gave their blessings and imparted some wisdom for the journey of married life. As Okomfo Ama Baakan was now a Nana Adade Kofi priestess and spiritual wife, the Abosom's blessings were especially essential. Okomfo Ama Baakan's constellation of subjectivity was soon to become even more intertwined with a human husband, who would join her journey at her side as she navigated the copresent jurisdictions of an ordained priestess of the Akan spiritual order.

Okomfo Akua Anima Ansa started ringing the bell and chanting "ago, ago, ago" to begin the formal calling of the spirits. She then began to invoke the spiritual lineage that this house calls each time, starting with Nyame, the supreme creator, and Asase Yaa, the supreme earth goddess, and then the Abosom and revered ancestors, including powerful and cherished African American leaders, such as Malcolm X and Martin Luther King Jr.

Okomfo Akua Anima Ansa and her sister, also a priestess, poured the libations and presented the gifts to the spirits.

"We have a scotch, presented for Nana Asuo Gyebi, to ask for his permission for Five to take the hand in marriage of Okomfo Baakan. We also have one gin to present to Nana Adade Kofi, as Nana Adade Kofi is her spiritual father and her protector. We also have another gin to present for Nana Esi and Nana Adu Richardson's father, the late Nana Agyiri, to bring the family blessing. We also have one more gin for blessings. Then, we have one bottle of Mezcal, presented to turn up and celebrate," Okomfo Akua Anima Ansa said. "They have brought white cloth, to symbolize their healing. Five presents six yards to show to the mother that he can take care of and clothe her, and he also has one hundred dollars to show that he can go and buy things that are needed. We present these things to the shrine. We ask for your continued blessings for the family, for Baakan, for Five, and for the baby."

After Nana Asuo Gyebi gave the blessings and his advice through a priestess in the family, Okomfo Akua Anima Ansa asked for anyone else's requests.

People presented a few more requests and gave specific thanks. The priestesses then closed with gratitude to the Abosom and the ancestors, along with general requests for forms of protection, continued blessings, and prosperity and abundance.

One request, with which Okomfo Akua Anima Ansa ended, spoke to the light that all of the priestesses and priests carry from Nyame and the Abosom to those on Earth.

"We ask that when we go out into the world, when people see us, that they not see us, but that they see your light in us, that they see the God in all of us, so that we provide the light and love that needs to be here on Earth. We ask that you continue to light every day and everything we do, as you order our things and order our thoughts, so that we think with a clear mind, a straight mind, and so that we pay attention to everything that is going on, and that we listen to all of the messages. We have so much to accomplish, and we don't just work for ourselves. We also work for spirit. Let us keep that at the forefront of everything we do. We know that you are blessing us, and we want to say *medaase*, thank you. We ask that you help us to continue to love a lot, to keep us strong, to let us continue to grow, and to let us continue to be prosperous in everything that we are doing."

In closing, Okomfo Ama Baakan thanked the Abosom and the ancestors for her fiancé, her baby, and the family that they would enjoy together in marriage.

Okomfo Akua Anima Ansa then thanked Nana Asuo Gyebi three times, as is customary, and the priestesses closed the ceremony with bells ringing and jubilant cheering. The familial marriage matters at hand for determination in the copresent jurisdictions of the Abosom and the cherished ancestors had been settled.

I looked to my right and saw a ceremonial photo of the great ancestor, Nana Oparebea, on a table near the doorway, as if she were keeping watch and blessing all who passed into the space in truth, purity, and right consciousness.

FOUR

Nana Osofo Yaw Nkrumah

Law, Order, Vitality, and Health in Shrine
Governance

Nana Osofo Yaw Nkrumah is an energetic, determined, and erudite ritual authority charged with helping ensure law and order and smooth
business operations at chief priestess Okomfohema Botwe I's ASUO
house in Maryland. He holds a doctorate in experimental nutrition from
Howard University and practices alternative medicine while running a
flourishing independent citizen-sector nonprofit business at Budd Boyz,
Inc. a.k.a. BBiBrotherhood Stool (ƆƆICƆ), in which he guides people
through Manhood/Chiefship rites-of-passage mentorship and Akan
cultural arts exchange programs for youth of all ages and for young
adults in America. His work as a nutritionist, health consultant, and
herbalist has included serving as an analyst and expert with the US
Department of Health and Human Services (HHS). He has developed a
global system of workshops that address the detection of emerging
threats to food safety and security for government bodies and businesses
in the private sector. Osofo Yaw is also a community builder and an
advocate for social justice, especially among youth. As he has explained,
his name "embodies Nana (senior), Obosumfo (trainee), Osofo (teacher),
Osofo (dancer), Yaw (Thursday), and Nkrumah (surname)."

Now in his early fifties, he was called to train on the Akan sacred
path in early adulthood and studied under Okomfohema Botwe I in her

shrine house in Maryland. He also spent some years training at the upper Akonnedi shrine in the mountain in Larteh, Ghana, where he studied to become an expert herbalist, or Densuʒ. Recently, the Abosom, ancestors, and shrine family elders called him to prepare to be enstooled as a chief for the community in Larteh, Ghana, in order to assist in customary law, protocol, and other matters of authority. Osofo Yaw may assume the stool, or throne, of his chiefship.

In Ghana, chiefship is inherently spiritual, as chiefs are selected by the spirits and installed in formal spiritual-legal ceremonies that involve sacred rites. As chiefs assume office, they often take on many of the personality traits or other characteristics of the stool spirits, or the ancestors, that govern through the stool and the person occupying it. They become evermore interlaced and one, in spiritual and in pragmatic earthly ways.

Helping to enforce law and order, Osofo Yaw has a very close relationship with Nana Adade Kofi, the Obosom who exemplifies and, through his adherents, embodies these principles. As an *Osofo*, Yaw does not get possessed by Nana Adade Kofi or other spirits, where he goes out of consciousness and serves as a vessel through which the spirits can speak and work. This is what distinguishes him from priestesses and priests like Okomfohema Botwe I, Nana Atei, or most of the other spiritual adepts featured in this book. Rather, he possesses a spiritual-physical shrine to Nana Adade Kofi and serves as a human vessel and ambassador for the Obosom and for the wider shrine house community cultures in the United States and Ghana, to which he routinely returns when his work schedule and family life in Maryland allow. He presides over festivals, historical commemorations, conferences, and other events on both sides of the Atlantic.

Osofo Yaw was born in the Bronx in New York City and grew up in Miami, Florida. While growing up in Miami, his Jamaican-born father introduced him early in life to many sacred elements of healing herbs and mindful farming through careful reciprocity with the spirits of the earth. His father, now in spirit, is one ancestor to whom he remains in close relation. His father was descended from those who had been enslaved in Jamaica, and his family members retain ties to the Maroon communities of the island's mountains, the groups that endured and grew in the wake of the legendary revolt of enslaved persons in the eighteenth century.[1]

In one of our first meetings, Osofo Yaw shared a cherished old Polaroid photograph of his father planting in the earth. He carries it with him to remind him of what his father told him about the important reciprocities of life in farming and in returning to the earth—in kind and with respect—what one has taken from her. His father walks with him all the time, actively participating in his daily life in both waking hours and through dreams, and he helps to watch over the children Osofo Yaw raises with his wife. Eventually, I learned that Osofo Yaw's father had died young—tragically shot in Miami—when Osofo was a teenager. He mentioned it one day in the midst of a talk he was giving at a conference on global Akan spirituality at Princeton, adding afterward to me, "Now we can include that in your book."[2]

Every time I am in Osofo Yaw's presence, he is keen to state the mission for a conversation or activity at its outset and to set the vision for the path's unfoldment that clearly and concisely will lead to the endpoint. He is also very careful about keeping the time, as this is a key element of his temperament as well as the disposition of his principal Obosom Nana Adade Kofi's no-nonsense, straightforward, and action-based approach to working with humans to accomplish his goals from spirit.

In the middle of one of my earliest conversations with Osofo Yaw, the chief priestess Nana Atei arrived to speak with us in the café area of Mom's Organic grocery store in College Park, Maryland. It was the summer of 2018. They both wanted to elaborate on what I would be witnessing when I traveled to the shrine compound in Larteh at the end of the summer, when I would accompany Okomfohema Botwe I, Nana Atei, and others (including a group of four of their soon-to-be-graduated young priestesses from the United States). The four trainees were about to make their final rites of passage at the two shrine houses in Larteh. Osofo Yaw was not able to join this trip, though he knew well the pertinent flow of events, rituals, places, and people. Okomfohema Botwe I had asked both of them to brief me on what was to come.

When Nana Atei first arrived, Osofo Yaw explained to her that we had just been discussing the opening of his path, how early in his life he had felt that he had received a call to serve the spirit.

"It started with things like simple prayers at night. Before I would go to sleep at night, I would get down on my knees and pray, something simple that reassured me that I'll still wake up tomorrow. But this is what started me on my path: this is my father right here," Osofo Yaw said, pointing to a picture of his father gardening, hands in the fertile soil while holding an intent and contemplative pose.

"That's my father, and we're on the farm, right? And he's digging up manure. And the only thing he wanted me to do was just watch what he does. Stay close, and don't wander off. See this guy? That's my younger brother. My father is what helped me become Osofo."

I asked whether his father was in conscious relationship to spirit and whether he followed a spiritual path.

"He was in conscious awareness of a lot. He's Jamaican, so he was naturalistic. He was always aware of health, wellness, agriculture, and food. That's where I learned it, from that age," he said, pointing again to the photograph, in which Osofo was about ten.

His father's plants were all organic. They would regularly take Osofo with him to a nearby farm to get manure to use as a fertilizer. This continued the cycle of spiritual-natural reciprocity with the consciousness of the earth and her inhabitants.

Osofo Yaw planned a summer program in which he hoped to bring kids, around the ages of eleven to sixteen, from Ghana to the United States to learn about agriculture and food production, as practiced in the States. In turn, he also wanted to bring kids from the United States to Ghana to learn from agricultural and food practices and wisdom there. He envisioned a dynamic of reciprocity across the cultures.

"The idea is for the youth to see the cultures in Ghana for two weeks, and perhaps get beads, stools, or drums. They also could take back insights from the culture and wisdom they learn from what they see in agricultural production and in water-related issues," he explained.

Osofo Yaw's mother is a retired paralegal. She worked for over thirty years for an immigration lawyer in Atlanta. Her ancestral background is from various places in Sub-Saharan Africa and Europe. His mother has encouraged him to partner with universities to build exchange programs across continents.

Osofo Yaw has found that his training in biochemistry and nutritional sciences correlates well with the information that he receives from spirit about what is healthy to ingest, or what is proper in certain ritual spaces or practices. Everything is interrelated and interconnected, so the registers of knowledge often nicely dovetail with each other. However, the totality of the correlations and connections eludes him, as it does anyone else.

"We were just talking about the universe. There are so many endpoints. I don't claim to know how to connect them all. It's impossible. It's too much, and it will lead to sadness."

I asked him why. This peace with the unknown struck me as so profound, a serene and sacred surrender.

"Trying to connect all of these billions of dots myself—I can't. It would be overwhelming," he replied.

He added that that kind of knowledge is only for the supreme Nyame, or God, or Source, or whatever name one uses to refer to the ultimate creator of everything that is.

"Do you have the understanding that we are all tapping into, at various levels and voltages, the same network of the universe, of God?" I asked.

"Yes. They call it different things. They call it different energies. I cannot claim to know that all groups are tapping into this thing that I'm tapping into. I don't know enough about that. I know that what we do is tapping into Source," Osofo Yaw replied.

Source, or Nyame, is unfathomable in its absolute essence. Thus, it requires a surrendering to the inexplicable and ineffable, that which cannot be captured or rendered in language.

I shared that I felt I had so much yet to learn about their spiritual tradition and the powers of language, including its (at times) inability to capture or represent certain phenomena. There are also so many things that are not to be uttered, things that must be discussed in a symbolic or a roundabout way—say, in parables, proverbs, or aphorisms—because there is a strict sacred prohibition on their utterance.[3]

In the café, a man then walked by with a print drawing of a camera on his T-shirt. It was a moment of a living parable of Akan spiritual teachings. Osofo Yaw took it as a sign and stopped him, kindly asking if he could take our picture. The guy returned in a moment. It was only when looking at the picture that we realized we had been sitting at a coffee table that was positioned in front of a wall painting of a rocket launch. Osofo Yaw said that this was affirmation, for him, of an inspired sense of collective mission from the spirit.

When the man with the camera shirt reappeared, Osofo Yaw asked him where he got his T-shirt, saying that he loved it.

"It's from a band named Spoon," the guy answered. "And they have a song called 'I Turned My Camera On.'"

I noted the synchronicity and the jovial flow. Osofo Yaw then turned to me and replied, "But if it doesn't connect that way, then we have to stop, and guess what? Make it right."

In order to discern the path of right action for making things right, they often consult with their Abosom and cherished ancestors in the morning, asking them for their guidance. This was one of the key features of the spiritualists' constellations of subjectivity, with the copresent jurisdictions of spiritual governance. Once a person has gone through training as an Akan path spiritualist, they have learned that they, as humans, are not truly in charge of things.

"We defer our own judgment and ask the spirits. We say, 'Here's a situation. What are the choices? What are the decisions that have to be made in order for the outcome to be positive?'" Osofo Yaw said.

The necessary information and guidance will then flow from the spirits. The spiritualists always have free will and choices on how to proceed in life. However, part of the Akan spiritual path is coming to learn the wisdom of the spirits' guidance. When the spirits give guidance or a directive, and an Akan path spiritualist chooses to proceed on a different course of action, then the less favorable outcomes almost always become apparent and felt. There will often be suffering or friction that will result. Sometimes, the guidance may seem too onerous in the immediate moment. However, not following the guidance can generate much heavier burdens and consequences down the line, whether in terms of time, energy, money, or other inconvenience.

The spiritual lessons tend to intensify over time if they are not learned. This gradual intensification—and the reappearance in various forms of the same underlying lesson—is an almost automatic feature of the spiritual laws and principles of reciprocity built into the Akan spiritual system. Lessons regularly happen in this fashion of replication. It is just that the sequences and variations of the lessons and their significances are not known in advance. The lessons may arrive in different configurations and scenarios, but they will be presented to the person until the person learns.

Nana Atei then furnished a teachable lesson in her navigation to Mom's Organic. She had lost her way en route to the place. Osofo Yaw had told her to use her GPS, and she did not. She explained that it likely was an Obosom speaking through Osofo Yaw. At times, they give her guidance through other spiritualists who may know a particular thing better than she does.

Osofo Yaw then chimed in. "You have to put something back in order, and you have to make it right. That's what she just did."

He added that his sense of needing to help guide and protect Nana Atei on her path came from the training that they both shared. Since she is a priestess in the Akan spiritual culture, he is responsible for helping to watch over her safety and well-being. This is part of his suite of rules, protocols, and responsibilities in the Akan spiritual order. It was also part of his responsibility to speak respectfully to her as he was guiding her to the café.

"I had an accountability to be ethical and human to her. That is part of the protocol. When they say something is a way of life, this is what it is. This is an example," Osofo Yaw said.

This is one clear demonstration of the copresent jurisdictions in their lives, how the ancestors or Abosom might be working through them and enforcing various expectations of ethics, truth, justice, and order. The Abosom or ancestors may also be speaking through them, without their fully realizing it. This is another variation on the constellation of subjectivity that characterizes life as an Akan path priestess, priest, or spiritualist. When the spiritualists act in accordance with their principles and protocols, their portals of interconnectedness stay clear. Their Abosom may even be conversing with or interacting with each other through their interconnectedness. They may not hear the conversation, but the spiritual interchange can interweave more fluidly through their human selves and lives if they remain in harmonious interconnection, observing protocols and principles. When there is disconnection or disharmony among some in the Akan spiritual family, it can affect everyone else who is connected. In this way, the Akan spiritualists have responsibilities to each other in relationships, as well as to the Akan spiritual house family, writ large.

In the event of a clash between Akan spiritual family members that is not promptly resolved and placed in alignment with divine order and protocols, a formal spiritual adjudication process through shrine family elders takes place. This is for times when the spiritualists do not directly work out the matter between themselves. At these times, they bring in an elder from the Akan shrine house family or from another

Akan house family in the broader culture to hear the facts, arguments, and issues at hand. The elder—or, at times, a council of elders—hears both sides of a case and issues a judgment and resolution, in consultation with the Abosom. The ruling must be observed in order for the shrine house family to continue to prosper. Which elders are called upon depends on the issue or subject matter in dispute.

"We go to specialists in that particular area who would be the right mediator for the situation," Osofo Yaw said.

The principle of often having elders from other shrine houses perform the spiritual adjudication procedures is that they are considered to be neutral third parties, well positioned to determine the disposition of a case. For example, the house may invite an elder from New York who specializes in the subject matter at hand. The spiritual court proceeding may last a whole day or even a weekend. It may continue all night long. The deliberations continue until the matters at hand are resolved. Once the Abosom indicate that they are pleased with the work the spiritualists have done, then the case is considered settled. The spiritualists will then pour libations, pray, and eat together. After the matter is settled, it is improper and a violation of Akan spiritual protocol to revisit it.

"When you make something right, you can't go back," Osofo Yaw explained. "But you have to wake up, and you have to stay up. You can't go back to sleep. You have to really work at it. Be in the here and now."

Remembering the lessons but moving forward on the path and remaining in the present are crucial components of flourishing on the Akan spiritual path as a way of life. Surrendering to the spiritual guidance is also important and can be very difficult, on account of the formative experiences that people have earlier in life that can tend to shape current reactions, as well as unconscious or conscious fears of or attachments to things, or our relationship patterns with others.

Osofo Yaw then turned to another teaching parable in the present moment, in the café. The employee with the camera T-shirt had let a loaf of bread fall to the ground and then placed it back on the shelf, alongside other loaves of bread, where it could contaminate the other food and still be sold to an unaware customer. Osofo Yaw respectfully shared with the guy that he was uncomfortable with this placement of the bread, and the man apologized and corrected the placement.

"If something is not right, you don't keep feeding the negativity. Don't keep feeding the bad behavior. Don't keep feeding the wrong process," Osofo Yaw said.

This same principle also informs the prohibition against invoking matters from the past that have been resolved. The lesson can be discussed and should be retained, but the particular matters that have been laid to rest should not be resurrected. Otherwise, speaking about it can reactivate or feed negativity that flowed from the prior existence of the dispute that was subsequently settled.

This principle is related to the prohibitions within the system against gossip, or speaking ill of others without constructive purpose or speaking invasively or disrespectfully of them. The spiritual law about a closed matter being closed, once adjudication is finished, is similar to the principle of *res judicata* in, for example, the American legal system, where matters already settled between parties in a court cannot be reopened by those same parties in another court proceeding.

Osofo Yaw works closely with Nana Adade Kofi on matters of law, order, health, and governance of the ASUO shrine house. Each Obosom has their specialties, and those who work closely with them resonate with aspects of the spirit's specialties. The spirit works through and with Osofo Yaw to help ensure health in food and other matters of safety and security for the shrine family. This also directly connects to Osofo Yaw's work in agriculture and food safety outside the shrine house, in both the state-based and in other nongovernmental organizational realms.

As Osofo Yaw had to run to join his family at an event, we decided to close the group meeting, though he still wanted to walk through the farmer's market outside before leaving. Osofo Yaw sent me the pictures he had taken, as well as one of his Jamaican father from when Osofo was young.

"We lived in the city limits of Miami, but we had to go out to the rural area to find the farms to get the manure to grow in the city," he said. "We all live in cities now. We have to go to the farm. We have to get that knowledge, bring it to the city, and start to grow. That's what that picture is about."

Osofo Yaw then poured libations, a bit of his juice, to the floor of Mom's Organic, to say thank you to the Abosom and ancestors for allowing us to meet and to connect, for bringing us together, for keeping us safe, for guiding the way, and for providing continued blessings.

We then ventured outside to the farmer's market. We found locally harvested honey, which Osofo Yaw said harbored healing properties from the local lands. He asked the beekeeper many questions about these matters. Afterward, Osofo Yaw emphasized the importance of gathering natural local knowledge about the resources within the surrounding environment. So much knowledge goes unnoticed, or it has been lost or neglected.

"We must learn and honor that knowledge and wisdom," he said, as he turned and took his leave.

FIVE

Okomfohene Nana Yaw Yirenkyi Opare Gyebi I, Chief Priest at the Asuo Gyebi Shrine in Larteh, Kubease

While I was in Larteh in 2018 with the elders and graduating priestesses from Maryland, I had the honor of visiting the home and shrine of Okomfohene Nana Yaw Yirenkyi Opare Gyebi I (or Okomfohene Yirenkyi I, for short). He also serves as chief priest (*okomfohene*) of the nearby Asuo Gyebi shrine in Larteh. He was raised in Ghana and trained directly with Nana Oparebea in Larteh, living and serving for eleven years at the Asuo Gyebi shrine. He now also lives in Washington, DC, where he has a shrine and a healing practice with his wife, an African American Nana Esi priestess who trained directly with Nana Oparebea in Larteh. He is now a key figure in helping to further fortify the ties and the mutual understanding of the Akan sacred shrine communities in the United States and Ghana. He helps to teach priestesses and priests in the United States the aspects of the spirits' copresent jurisdictions—the spiritual governance and also the interactions with state legal actors, as well as other religious figures—on both sides of the Atlantic. He is a Nana Asuo Gyebi priest, so his constellation of subjectivity is to live in dynamic interrelation with this Obosom, as well as other close Abosom and cherished ancestors of Nana Panyin shrine family.

During this visit and in our subsequent conversations, he shared a great deal of integral wisdom about the Asuo Gyebi shrine history in Larteh. He also spoke about the histories of some of the Abosom. In addition, he illuminated important facets of his current work in the realms of Akan spiritual leadership in the United States and in Ghana, with both Ghanaian and African American priests and priestesses.

His home and shrine in Ghana are located close to Larteh, in a nearby community called Nyambekyere, where his brother, Nana Abboa-Offei, is the chief. Okomfohene Yirenkyi I trained as a priest (okomfo) while he was a young adult at the Asuo Gyebi shrine in Larteh, under the legendary then-chief priestess, Nana Oparebea. He was the Larteh lineage's first male priest.

As Okomfohene Yirenkyi I has his own shrine in Washington, DC, he is an important elder in Akan shrine culture communities in the area and in the United States, more broadly. While he does not formally cogovern the ASUO shrine house in Maryland, he plays prominent roles in broader Akan spiritual culture in the DC area. He also has close relations with the interfaith African Traditional Spiritual Coalition, which is headquartered in DC.

Okomfohene Yirenkyi I serves a vital role of teaching and guiding African Americans and diasporic Ghanaians in the area. He has been a central elder in helping to launch recent virtual openings of parts of key sacred festivals and commemorations for transnational Akan spirituality, bringing together online communities of priestesses, priests, and other supporters. A group of elders innovated these virtual ceremonies as one way to congregate during the pandemic lockdown, and they continue to flourish, even after the lifting of travel restrictions.[1]

As an elder and a Nana Asuo Gyebi priest, Okomfohene Yirenkyi I flows with dynamic spiritual interrelations. When I arrived at his home in Larteh with my husband, Jeff, he said that ancestors and Abosom were present even during our interactions. His closest intimates in spirit are a part of him, in many ways, or stream through him. At the same time, these spirits are their own beings. They are distinct from him yet interlaced with him and with others. Here, as with the other ordained spiritualists, his spiritual subjectivity is an embodied and fluid field of complex spiritual forces, a constellation of enlightened consciousnesses.

When we got to the house, Okomfohema Botwe I, Nana Atei, and others had yet to arrive. My husband had just arrived in Ghana, after me, and Okomfohene Yirenkyi I took the occasion to introduce Jeff to his elder brother, Nana Abboa-Offei, who was also there to meet with all of us. Nana Abboa-Offei is a chief in Akropong serving as Okoman elder to Okuapehene. He lives with his brother at Nyambekyere, where he supervises the cocoa farm work on his ancestral land and also assists his brother in giving out the history of the Guans and Akans in the Akwapim area.

In addition to the sacred Akan ancestral rites that Nana Abboa-Offei performs in Akropong, he is a practicing Christian. Although many of the inhabitants of the Larteh area are ethnically Guan (an ethnic group that traditionally governed much of the present-day Larteh land), many of the local chiefs who preside over the lands and people are Akan. The Akuapem people, who are the most populous group in the mountainous area that includes Larteh, emerged from the coming together of the Guans and the Akans.

"The Akans are matrilineal, and the Guans are patrilineal, in their inheritance. This means that positions in Akan societies are given to the female's lineage—that is, female-born children who specifically are uncles. Thus, in Akanland, inheritance is termed *Wofa Adidi*, meaning uncle inheritance," Nana Abboa-Offei explained. "This type of inheritance has roots in the beliefs and practices concerning the fact that the Akan believes in the reality of what they see. They see a woman in her menstrual period. They see the protruding stomach of a pregnant woman, and thus, there is no way that a woman's child cannot be hers. Hence, the need to pass on the inheritance to a woman's child."

Nana Abboa-Offei also elucidated, in a fascinating way, the contrasting understanding and practices of the Guan people.

"On the other hand, inheritance in patrilineal Guan society is governed by spirituality. In the past, the paternity of a child in patrilineal society is this: after the female announces her pregnancy, the husband invites his family and that of his wife and provides a fowl for cooking a meal for the two families. If both families enjoy the meal, and the pregnant wife does not experience the mishap of sickness or death, then the child is seen as the true progeny of the husband and therefore can inherit the family paternal property. Rattray in his book published in the 1920s about Ashanti customs, tradition, and culture reveals this," Nana Abboa-Offei shared.[2]

As a custodian of the histories, Nana Abbao-Offei is very well versed in the histories of the people and the group in the area.

"The Guans were the first to migrate from the old Ghana Empire, which existed in the current locations of Mauritania and Mali. They migrated because of religious wars that threatened the growing economic prosperity of the old Ghana Empire. The Guans were peaceful and spiritual, so in their location on the Akwapim Ridge, they established farms and protective shrines. The leaders of their shrines were traditional priests and priestesses who also doubled as community leaders," Nana Abboa-Offei explained. "As they lived peacefully on the Akwapim Ridge, the Akwamus, a warlike clan, came and subdued the Guans and visited untold wickedness on them. The Guans, therefore, looked for liberating warriors to help them fight the Akwamus. They found Offei Kwasi Agyeman from Gyakiti. Offei Kwasi Agyeman, who was a merchant in arms and an expert hunter, invited his clients from Akyem Akropong to help in a liberating war of the Guans against the terrorizing Akwamus. The war was fought, and the Akwamus were defeated and chased out of the Guan settlement. For fear that the Akwamus might return with their harassment, the Akwapim state was formed through the Abotakyi Accord. In that accord, the Guans pledged their lands to the Akyem Akropong warriors, and they also made the junior brother of Akyem Abuakwa Omanhene, Ofori Kuma, the Omanhene [chief ruler] of the Akwapim State in 1733."

Nana Abboa-Offei then imparted the history of the current relationship between the Akan and Guan structures.

"The Akyem warriors, who were well known in Akan chieftaincy, established chieftaincy structures and systems that replaced the traditional spiritual leadership of the Guan priests and priestesses. The relationship between Akans and Guans had been of mutual benefit since the establishment of the Akwapim state in 1733," Nana Abboa-Offei said. "Some Akans originally helped the Akuapem to fight off the Guans, who were seeking to rule over them. Now, they all live in the area, with Akan chiefs serving in many of the customary leadership roles."

Nana Abboa-Offei, like many local chiefs, is not only a custodian of histories but also a vocal supporter and active participant in many of the Larteh shrine events. He holds deep respect for Akan spiritual culture, which he—like Akan priestesses and priests—routinely refers to as traditional to distinguish it from Christianity and Islam and to denote its long-running roots and presence in Akan and other indigenous faiths among people in Ghana.

Once we had settled at the table, Okomfohene Yirenkyi I started to tell us about how he had first come into contact with Okomfohema Botwe I and some of the other African American priestesses and priests. He first met Okomfohema Botwe I around 1993 at the Asuo Gyebi shrine in Larteh, while Nana Oparebea was still alive in human form. She had traveled to Larteh with a group of African Americans, and Okomfohene Yirenkyi I spoke with them.

"Back then, I was the only man in the shrine, so I explained to her that I would like to work with her. So, she gave me an assignment, to make some things. It was about the shrine stuff," he recalled. "So, they gave me some money. I took it around to the village. I prepared all of the herbs, and then she was happy to have all of these herbs I brought to her."

Once Okomfohema Botwe I and the others returned to the United States, they remained in touch with Okomfohene Yirenkyi I, further fortifying their bonds and collaborations across the Atlantic. They became spiritual colleagues who would provide mutual assistance from afar.

He then explained how the spirits chose Okomfohema Botwe I to be the queen mother of the Asuo Gyebi shrine in Larteh, some years after Nana Oparebea passed, before he was asked to be okomfohene. Okomfohema, some elders, and the shrine spirits then realized they also wanted a male priest to help lead and govern the shrine.

By this time, in the 2000s, Okomfohene Yirenkyi I was already living part of the year in the United States with his wife. The elders sent him a letter about the call to take the stool at Asuo Gyebi in Larteh. He was at first reluctant to assume this position. He did not respond initially, as he was wary of the politics at the shrine. However, someone in Ghana suggested to him that he would be well advised to accept the stool, as the spirits were clearly calling him.

"A stool elder and a kingmaker of the Asuo Gyebi shrine, the late Brother Agyiri, told me, 'Nana, if they want you to be Okomfohene, and you don't accept it, it will be a mess for you.' We believe that when people say something about you, the voice of the people is the voice of God. Plenty of people have said it. 'Okomfohene Yirenkyi I, you are needed. Why are you not responding to this call?' So, I switched my mind and responded to the letter, and they told me in two years, I would be okomfohene."

He was enstooled at the Asuo Gyebi shrine two years later in a large ceremony.

Since he spent eleven years at the Asuo Gyebi shrine while Nana Oparebea was alive, Okomfohene Yirenkyi holds a great wealth of knowledge about shrine history, healing practices, protection, and governance.

He first began his training as an okomfo in 1983, and he graduated in 1986.

"My family didn't want this thing, where I would train for three years as an okomfo. They wanted me to be Christian. But the spirit came on me, and I had no alternative. It was so much for me not to accept it. It was bringing my mind to this feeling, like I was crazy," Okomfohene Yirenkyi I explained.

He began to tell us how the Obosom Nana Asuo Gyebi spontaneously appeared to him in flesh as an enigmatic person, visiting the small
drinks shop that Okomfohene Yirenkyi I was running at that time, as
part of the beginning of his call to train as an okomfo.

As he began to share the story of receiving the initial call from Nana
Asuo Gyebi, there was a knock on the door. The others had arrived. He
would resume the story after we greeted the others, who joined the
meeting.

Okomfohema Botwe I and Nana Atei entered the room in royal
regalia, along with Okomfo Baakan (one of the new graduates), the
filmmaker Eric, and Okres (Okomfohema Botwe I's driver and her lead
okyeame, or spokesperson). They all sat at the table to join our conversation and meal. Eric was also there that day to shoot a short film of
Okomfohene Yirenkyi I, meant to explain his story and wisdom, along
with the other priestesses and authorities. Those who arrived formally
greeted us, each in turn. It was my first time introducing my husband
Jeff to Okomfohema Botwe I, Nana Atei, Okres, Okomfo Baakan, and
Eric. Jeff had arrived in Larteh after I did. Dr. Walker, an African
American spiritualist, professor, and elder at a related shine house
based in Washington, DC—as well as at the Asuo Gyebi shrine in
Ghana—also joined us.

The rain was pouring outside when they entered, making music on
the metal rooftops nearby. As it was Jeff's and my first visit to the home,
we presented Okomfohene Yirenkyi I with some money in exchange
for Schnapps he had on hand so that the elders could pour libations to
call in the named spirits, to ask for their guidance and blessings, and to
formally open our discussion. We then went around the table with formal introductions.

Nana Abboa-Offei shared some of the historical backdrop in the
area, in describing his position as chief.

"Akropong-Akuapem is a traditional area. And I'm the chief within
the traditional area. Of the Akuapem's palace, I am a warrior chief,"
Nana Abboa-Offei added. "We called it *akuma*. The akuma fought

to liberate the Akuapem from the Guans who came and suppressed them."

Nana Abboa-Offei also described more of the relations among the Abosom of the Nana Panyin, or Akonnedi, pantheon. Akonnedi is the leader among the Abosom of the shrine. The Abosom of Nana Asuo Gyebi and Nana Adade Kofi, for example, execute directives or implement ideas after the spirits of the shrine have been consulted.

Over time, there were two shrines in Larteh that had come to exist as geographically distinct from each other and yet were connected in the same pantheon. The upper shrine, often called Akonnedi or Nana Panyin (alternate names for the same principal Obosom) for short, includes the Abosom Nana Panyin, Nana Adade Kofi, and Nana Esi. The lower shrine is named for the Obosom Nana Asuo Gyebi.

"All of the Abosom are together. They move together, and they are close. The reason the two shrines are in separate places is that Nana Asuo Gyebi has only been with them since 1957. Nana Asuo Gyebi was Okomfohene Nana Oparebea's father's spirit, originally from the North of Ghana. The big spirits at the shrine—Akonnedi, Nana Essi, and Nana Adade Kofi—chose Nana Asuo Gyebebi to be an *abrafo* [warrior] for them, because of his character and personality. They liked him so much," Okomfohene Yirenkyi I explained. "The reason they live separately is because the spirits like different food for their offerings. At the top, they like the ram and chicken, but they don't like goat meat. At the bottom, for Nana Asuo Gyebi, black goat and cow are his favorite. He also like rams, chickens, and fowls. There are different rules regarding how to handle the cows at the shrines. So, they gave Nana Asuo Gyebi his own place to stay when he joined them. But they all are close. They have the Nana Panyin festival in October, and the Nana Asuo Gyebi festival in January."

Nana Abboa-Offei explained that Nana Oparebea had a vision from the Abosom that some African Americans should be initiated and graduated to the divine spirits. The spiritual vision also indicated that she should authorize sacred shrines to be set up in the United States. Nana Oparebea was then chief priestess of the Akonnedi shrine.

"The spirits and shrine elders determined that the head Obosom, Akonnedi, was not able to travel to the US, but Nana Asuo Gyebi and, later, Nana Adade Kofi and Nana Esi could go," Nana Abboa-Offei explained.

Okomfohene Yirenkyi shared how the first president of Ghana, Dr. Kwame Nkrumah, had built the Aburi home and other infrastructure for Nana Oparebea in the late 1950s, when she was a close friend and religious adviser to him. At that time, Nkrumah was also enjoying the strong protection of Nana Asuo Gyebi.

At this Asuo Gyebi shrine, there is now the magisterial memorial statue of Nana Oparebea, engraved with the names of many Ghanaian and African American shrine elders. Dr. Walker was one of the people who was involved in this monument, as with so much else at Asuo Gyebi. He has been involved in Akan sacred culture for more than forty years and has been an elder in the Temple of Nyame in Washington, DC. He is a literature professor in Maryland. He travels to Ghana frequently, sometimes also bringing tours of college students, and is nearing his retirement.

Okres—the first okyeame for Okomfohema Botwe I—was then formally introduced. He translates and assists in any way that is needed. He had been driving us around and doing so many things for the group. He had been involved with the Asuo Gyebi shrine family since 1993, when Okomfohema Botwe I met him through her former husband, a Ghanaian statistician based in Accra. Okres is based in Achimota, in Accra, but he travels to Larteh or elsewhere with Okomfohema Botwe I to assist her while she is in the country.

Before beginning our dinner, Nana Abboa-Offei formally welcomed us to his brother Okomfohene Yirenkyi I's home and shrine at Nyambekyere. He had opened the shrine in 1994 as the first structure in the area. There is now a large assemblage of homes around him in town.

"It's close to twenty-five years in this work at Nyambekyere," Okomfohene Yirenkyi I added.

He then shared more about their transnational modes of communication, how it works when they are physically far away, helping lead
shrine houses in Larteh and the United States. They communicate during waking hours through ordinary technological means, of course, but
they also communicate through spiritual means of possession and in
dream states.

"In the possession state, the Obosom enters the priests' and priestesses' body and, in a trance, speaks to reveal what is there for now and
the future," Okomfohene Yirenkyi I said. "It must be noted that the
training of the priestesses and priests for the three years before graduation is to prepare their body for the spiritual entry for communication.
You are in training, taking care through asceticism to keep your body
clean from lewd lifestyles. You are taught the principle that cleanliness
is next to godliness. Unless you keep yourself clean, spiritual possessions will be absent, because the Abosom will not communicate in a
dirty body. The Abosom also communicate their wishes and aspirations through the dreams of priestesses and priests."

When the spirits communicate through the dream state, an Obosom
tends to appear in the dream in the form of one of the spirit's priests or
priestesses.

"There's no confusion at all. They will bring the wives to you,"
Okomfohene Yirenkyi I said, referring to the spiritual marriages of the
priestesses and priests with the Abosom. The word *wives*, in this context, refers to both priestesses and priests who are in spiritual marriage
with an Obosom.

When a priestess or a priest appears to another ordained spiritualist
in the dream space, the default interpretation is that the priestess or
priest who was communicating to the dreamer was actually the primary Obosom to whom the priestess or priest is graduated. The priestess or priest in the dream is not understood to be merely *vocalizing* the
Obosom. Rather, the priestess or the priest in the dream is a represen-
tational *manifestation* of the Obosom.

This equation dovetails nicely with the waking-hours understanding of the priestesses and priests as interwoven with the copresences of their key Obosom or Abosom whom they serve in the first instance, as spouses or in other forms of divine union. In other words, this is another facet of their dynamic constellations of subjectivity, with various forces and consciousnesses running through their energy fields. Many truths and revelations concerning spiritual adjudication and other matters of guidance will come through the dreams as well, making dreams an important domain for the spiritual governance of copresent jurisdictions.

Okomfohene Yirenkyi I shared that there is an immediate intuitive knowing that it is the Obosom presenting himself or herself in the dream through the representation of a spiritualist. If there is someone else accompanying the spiritualist in the dream, this might indicate a connection to the spiritual message being delivered in the dream. Perhaps there is work that is needed for that other person who has appeared.

Okomfohene Yirenkyi I shared how, before he was enstooled as okomfohene at Asuo Gyebi shrine in Larteh, he had relocated to live with this wife for part of the time in Washington, DC, her hometown. They originally had met at the Asuo Gyebi shrine in Larteh, where she trained.

He reflected on how Nana Oparebea trained many priestesses and priests across the United States and Ghana. Many of those she trained in Larteh then traveled and set up shrines elsewhere, under her guidance and approval.

"We have some people Nana Oparebea trained and took to Abidjan [the capital of Côte d'Ivoire], Nigeria, Togo, a lot of places. I know some people there, too, who do the *very work* we do here," Okomfohene Yirenkyi I said.

Annual festivals in honor of the Abosom are key ceremonies for sustaining the connections among the Akan priestesses and priests who live all across Ghana, the United States, and elsewhere.

Each October, there is a large festival held in honor of Nana Panyin. Each January, a large festival is held for Nana Asuo Gyebi. Yam is central to both festivals.

"At a specific time, we eat the yam," he explained. "By August, we stop eating the older yam because there is fresh yam. So, when we do the festival for Nana Panyin, the yam is introduced for us to eat."

Yam is also eaten at the annual Nana Asuo Gyebi festival as well. There is rich symbolism embedded within the rituals, which includes a spiritual transformation and renewal of the akomfo, the Nanas, and their broader families. It is especially an occasion for strengthening and revitalizing the ties with the honored ancestors, the Abosom, and ultimately Nyame, the omnipotent Creator.

The spiritualists' relationship with the yam cycle in this festival season is connected to the interconnectedness of everything in nature, with its cycles of death and regeneration. All (or most) faiths appear to have a version of this sequence. It is similar to Christian Lent, Jewish Passover, Muslim Ramadan, or many traditions involving New Year's prayers and intention-setting. In some churches, for example, there will be all-night ceremonies in which groups of people gather to collectively pray and to usher in a blessed new year.

The yam itself has a season of regeneration, like everything in nature. The yam is universal, and everyone can eat it. It is therefore honored as such—that is, as a key symbol of universal connectivity. The spiritualists give the yam this respect of a space of recharging during the harvest season, while they also take a pause and recharge their bodies, their minds, and their spirit. All these cycles of nature, spirit, and people are interrelated, and the yam festivals are examples of honoring the new year with new hope, new faith, and new understanding.

Okomfohene Yirenkyi I explained that Nana Panyin announces when the proper time has come and then the shrine family members put on a festival. If people eat the yam before it is the proper time, they can get all sorts of digestive ailments or illnesses. Accordingly, they wait until the time of year that Nana Panyin designates as fit for yam consumption and mark it with celebratory feasts, offerings, music, dance, and other festivities.

"We the chiefs, we also do it," Nana Abboa-Offei added. "There is time we put a ban on eating of yams, especially when it comes fresh, for about six weeks. You must first give it to the shrine of the spirits to give you the blessing to go ahead and eat it."

Nana Abboa-Offei then stressed the importance of the oneness of the supreme God.

"Akans and Guans believe in the almighty God as the creator and thus revere him," Nana Abboa-Offei emphasized. "They believe that service to man is service to God. Again, the Akans and Guans believe that mountains, trees, and rivers have spirits that are the children of God. These spirits at times possess the priests and priestesses and communicate on existing things and the future."

When Nana Abboa-Offei shared this, I thought of the widespread nature of the phenomenon of children of God as the messengers and helpers for humans. This can be found across many faith traditions around the world, not only through spirits but also in the human forms of great prophets, healers, and visionaries.

In the Akan spiritual order, Asase Yaa, the Great Earth, the Great Mother, is mentioned second after Nyame in libations. This coincides with the pairings of the moon and the sun, or the earth and the sky— the divine feminine and the divine masculine, respectively.

The elders then decided to move the conversation outside, to a sitting space that had beautiful stone tiles and a canopy. Eric would film this part.

In Akan protocol, chiefs and elders do not normally introduce themselves. They asked me to introduce them for the conversation on camera.

We began with libations and asking the spirit for guidance and blessings. Those from the United States who were present stated their purposes for the visit to Ghana.

We then delved into more of the details of Okomfohene Yirenkyi's receiving the call to train as an okomfo and his surrendering to it, and his subsequent work in Larteh, Nyambekyere, and Washington, DC.

Okomfohene Yirenkyi I returned to the question of how Nana Asuo Gyebi had first come to him in the guise of a stranger visiting his drinks shop for some Schnapps. He had asked for Okomfohene Yirenkyi I, as the owner, who then realized that he didn't have any Schnapps right on hand.

"The man at the bar heard that there was no Schnapps so he called me, 'Come, I don't really need the Schnapps.' So, I sat down with him. Something pushed me back to the store to see if I can get whiskey. That one, I took. I said, 'Let's make it three tots.' And then I came to present it to the man. He just poured all of the drink down and gave the glass to me," he recalled.

The man then told Okomfohene Yirenkyi I that the two already knew each other, even though he appeared to be a stranger. The man then started talking to him about the shrine in Larteh, asking if he had ever visited.

When the man turned to leave, he invited Okomfohene Yirenkyi I to the Asuo Gyebi shrine in Larteh. As he left, he held Okomfohene Yirenkyi I's hand.

"He held my hand. Then, all the sudden, when we were going, he pressed my hand very hard! Then, I lifted my hand from his hand. When I turned, I couldn't see him."

Okomfohene Yirenkyi I then told his brother, Nana Abboa-Offei, what had happened. He also shared it with his mother. She said that perhaps he had done something to offend the spirits, and he needed to atone for that. Nana Abboa-Offei then brought someone who knew Nana Oparebea to see Okomfohene Yirenkyi I in his shop. The man told him that he should go to the shrine to see Nana Oparebea. He followed the advice.

When he got to the shrine, Nana Oparebea was flowing with the spirit, and she shared details about the encounter that he had had with the man in the shop. He was surprised and delighted to realize that it was the same spirit speaking to him through Nana Oparebea who also had been speaking through the man who had mysteriously appeared in his shop. The spirit speaking was Nana Asuo Gyebi.

This experience, to my mind, was reminiscent of the stranger in the Christian Bible who stands at the door of a church, appearing to be a beggar. In fact, it is the Holy Spirit. The parable's lesson, of course, is not to dismiss anyone who appears who may be bearing gifts from the spirit. At times, these gifts can be vital and life-changing.

After the energy had changed and Nana Asuo Gyebi was no longer speaking directly to him through the chief priestess, the others formally introduced him to Nana Oparebea. She told him that Nana Asuo Gyebi had been promising that he would be bringing a new wife to the shrine. Okomfohene Yirenkyi I then realized that he was being called to train as Nana Asuo Gyebi's wife or priest. He would become the first man to train at this shrine.

Although Okomfohene Yirenkyi I heard the call, he had yet to fully accept it. That came over time. The spirit sent him many signs along his journey to seeing the way in its totality. For example, he would feel a spiritual presence as he was eating, or sometimes, it would be raining all around him, but it would not rain on him.

"One day," he said, "I was sitting in the bush, and I heard a voice, and he said, 'Hey, who created everything on earth?' I didn't answer. 'Was he wrong to create all this?' I didn't answer. 'Then, stand up and walk through the wooded shrove.' Then, I came on myself. I said, 'Eh! This, I hear it. Then, I will do whatever.'"

At that point, after this sequence of spiritual signs and calls, Okomfohene Yirenkyi I was ready to begin the process of initiation and training at the shrine to become a priest. Nana Oparebea informed him that he would need the support of his family in order to be initiated. There are costs involved, akin to tuition paid in other school programs. As his family was not prepared to pay the tuition at that time, Okomfohene Yirenkyi I asked Nana Oparebea to initiate him; then he would pay her back by working after he finished his training and graduation. The shrine elders spoke with his brother about the plan, and his brother accepted the arrangement.

He then trained for three years and graduated. Even then, most of his family did not accept this path for him, but he remained resolute in following his spiritual calling. Nana Oparebea helped provide him with the things he needed for graduation.

He then repaid Nana Oparebea by attending to her, cooking for her, and living with her for years. The initial idea was that she would bring Okomfohene Yirenkyi I to work for a while for a king in Abidjan, (the capital of) Côte d'Ivoire. When she realized how delicious his cooking was, she said she would be taking him back home to Larteh to be with her.

Okomfohene Yirenkyi I then served Nana Oparebea at the Asuo Gyebi shrine for another eight years. With his three years of training, this meant eleven years in total.

Nana Oparebea shared with him visions of his future in training priestesses and priests. She said he should carefully observe and note her work, as he would be teaching and training many people.

After the eleven years, he felt moved by the spirit to relocate to the family land in Nyambekyere, to build a home and set up his shrine there. When he shared his plans with Nana Oparebea, she told him that he needed at least three rooms—a room for himself, a shrine room, and a room for clients. He had only built two rooms by that point. He then found help from someone who divided one of his rooms into two so that he was able to meet this requirement.

On March 23, 1994, he moved to his new home. For forty days, he went to give gratitude to Nana Oparebea and the other shrine elders in Larteh.

After some years, he met an African American okomfo, a Nana Esi priestess, who trained at Larteh with Nana Oparebea. When he first met her, he asked if she was married. She was not. He then declared that he would marry her, and she laughed. They became friends, and after many years, she asked him to join her in the United States. They got married. At this point, Nana Oparebea had passed back into spirit. Since 2007, Okomfohene Yirenkyi I and his wife have kept residences in Washington, DC, and in Nyambekyere.

After some time, Okomfohene Yirenkyi I started having dreams that he would be enstooled as okomfohene at the Asuo Gyebi shrine in Larteh. The dreams were very clear in the revelations. He shared the dreams with some family members. He explained that Okomfohema had been praying about him for years before this, but he did not know it.

One day, Okomfohema came to him and shared that the spirits had called for him to help her, an African American, to continue to culturally blend, learn, and lead in the Ghanaian ways. His dreams had shown him the importance of his accepting the stool as okomfohene at the Asuo Gyebi shrine, as a Nana Asuo Gyebi male priest as well as a Ghanaian. This would help to strengthen the Nana Oparebea lineages in the United States and Ghana. When Okomfohema shared with him that the spirits were calling him through her to the stool, he shared that he had been having dreams as well. The shrine elders then sent him the official letter, asking him to accept the stool, or throne.

In 2014, he was officially enstooled as okomfohene at the Asuo Gyebi shrine, and he has been further empowering the shrine as a leader for many years, before and since then, helping it to flourish and grow. He also continues to develop and expand his shrine in Nyambekyere. He likewise helps the surrounding communities. For example, he helped to create a road to the junction from the community, so that it is easy to reach a market in a nearby town called Koforidua. At first, he and his brother, along with his children, were the only people in the immediate area. Now, others have joined with houses around them in the community.

As sunset was approaching, we finished this discussion that was filmed at his home. We all shared our formal expressions of gratitude and bent down in reverence, as one of the elders brought out the trophy that a group of akomfo in America had given to Okomfohene Yirenkyi

I. This trophy was a gesture of deep appreciation, and the African American priestesses and priests had filled it to the brim with coins when he first received the gift. The trophy also contains a diamond, which the elders explained as of great significance to the Americans—the strength, truth, purity, and great courage that the diamond represents symbolize his qualities as a great leader and his inclusion as a key figure who is strengthening the connections between Akan spiritualists in the United States and Ghana.

GUARDIANS OF TRADITIONS AND KEEPERS OF SHRINE HISTORIES

Over the course of my knowing Okomfohene Yirenkyi I and other shrine elders, they have shared histories about the Abosom and the Akonnedi shrine in Larteh, as well as about the nature, movements, specialties, and philosophies of the Abosom, key ancestors, and other spirits. They also have shared some of the visions and vital synergies of the copresent spiritual jurisdictions in Ghana and the United States.

Okomfohene Yirenkyi I is a profound wellspring of knowledge about the shrine histories and about Nana Oparebea and her family, as he trained and worked so closely with her for so many years while she was alive in human form. He shared that Nana Oparebea's mother was Akan, and that her father was Guan. It was her father who originally had brought Nana Asuo Gyebi, as a strong warrior and healer spirit, from a town in the north of Ghana to the Larteh area. Akonnedi welcomed Nana Asuo Gyebi as an Obosom in the shrine family pantheon. Nana Oparebea was enstooled as the seventeenth chief priestess of the Akonnedi shrine, where she worked closely with Nana Asuo Gyebi and the other Abosom of the pantheon. When she led the shrine, she was practicing in the Akan spiritual traditions. Akonnedi also goes by the Akan name of Nana Panyin, which means the elder in charge. The luminous spirit of Nana Oparebea of course continues to be actively involved in guiding and protecting the Akan shrine culture in the United States, in Ghana, and elsewhere. She is said to have trained thousands of akomfo in her lifetime.

Okomfohene Yirenkyi I emphasized that in Ghana, more broadly, ancestral remembrance and veneration are central and cannot be sidelined, neglected, or removed from cultural and spiritual practices.[3] Every family has honorable ancestors, and every family has an obligation to remember, honor, and communicate with them, whether it is through asking their advice during waking hours or communicating with them through dreams. They also use various objects that were sacred to the ancestors to remember them and often offer them food and drink, inviting them to join them at meals at certain times; or they leave out offerings for the ancestors to enjoy whenever they please.

For the chiefs and queen mothers, ancestral veneration is imperative. It is central not only to their office of the stool, or throne, but also to the flourishing and vitality of their human subjects and the lands over which their customary rule presides. The ancestors help to ensure the protection of people and resources, and they help farms, businesses, and relationships to flourish optimally. Neglecting ancestral veneration and observance of their wishes and guidance can result in calamity and spiritual punishment, and not only for the customary ruler. The spiritual consequences can also befall the entire community.

Of course, this holds especially true in shrine culture, where priestesses and priests are trained and highly adept at listening to the guidance, instructions, and rules that the spirits issue. Yet it is also true for customary rulers and families in Akan cultures in general. The noble ancestors—that is, the ancestors who have an honorable character and have lived admirable, virtuous lives in human form—must be attended to and their guidance must be heeded. Elders of families are charged with making sure the younger generations heed the ancestral guidance and understand ancestral copresences. This is true in the families of Christians and Muslims as well. The vast majority of the Akan people in Ghana belong to Christian churches, but they still retain their conscious ties and relations to their ancestors.

Engaging with, relating to, and cocreating with the Abosom, is less common, and it is the jurisdiction of the spiritual adepts, the priestesses and priests.

Many Ghanaians simultaneously respect and fear the Akan priestesses and priests. Some are apprehensive of the Abosom because they see and reveal truths very clearly, which many may wish to keep hidden. Also, some fear them owing to the prohibitions of some Christian pastors.[4]

As Okomfohene Yirenkyi I explained to me one day, "We Akans have ancestral worship. That is what all the chiefs and queen mothers do in Ghana. We do ancestral worship *more* than the Abosom. The chiefs and the queens in Ghana, all of them are on their ancestral stool. They are not doing Abosom. That is the thing people have to *know*—that every okomfohene has a stool in his family, and it's passed through the ancestral spirits. For ancestral worship, no Ghanaian hates it. But when it comes to the adoration of the Abosom, then they don't like it. When they see we are doing Abosom, then they run away from it. They don't want to be part of whatever the Abosom are doing because the Abosom will come out and say something which they don't want to hear."

The truth is hard for most people to hear. And truths that people do not want revealed often are not kept hidden by Abosom, with these spirits' heightened access to information about facts, wrongdoings, misgivings, and distortions of veracity. They also can access information from different spatiotemporal realms in which they can be present at once—a key aspect of their copresent jurisdictions. As the priestesses and priests exist in dynamic constellations of subjectivity with multiple streams of spirits and receive information from the spirits, the Abosom may simply choose to utter the truth through them as mediums as soon as they observe something that the spirits determine is important to share.

During many consultations, priestesses or priests will call the spirits and either the Abosom or the ancestors will come. The spiritualists can consult the spirits through a sacred pot, which is a transmitter of spirit, a portal of sorts. Or the Abosom or ancestors can simply come through an open vessel, usually a priestess or priest, and speak. Beyond those in shrine families, people tend to believe and pay more attention to information that they directly receive from a spirit speaking through the priestess or priest, whose consciousness is often faded out or withdrawn as the spirit enters to speak and give guidance and information. The priestesses or priests say that, in general, people will much more readily follow such advice and trust in its accuracy and authenticity.

It is common that the spirits speak through multiple timelines, accessing and offering information from the past, present, and future—or what is experienced as such on the earth. They also can traverse conventional boundaries of spatiality and, say, give information about people in Ghana to those in the United States or vice versa. Not everything can be foretold, because things in the future may change, and because people have volition, or free will. But some things are predestined or fated, and thus impossible or at least unlikely to be circumvented, and these things, the spirits can share with relative certainty.

This ability to have the spirits speak through people, and for their souls to have this access to the worlds beyond the physical plane in waking life on earth, also means that it is impossible to truly imprison or control people in an absolute sense. Oppressors may have the illusion that they are doing so, but it can never be done fully, as a person's soul cannot be subjugated, imprisoned, or taken in its totality. The essence of the soul is immortal, divine, and untouchable—the flame (*okra*) of the creator god, Nyame, that burns within every human being.

This ultimate unknowability of the totality of the divine, that which is inaccessible to humans and cannot be said or fathomed, also ensures that this divine flame is always present as a portal or source for resistance and liberation from the confines of oppressive institutional systems or spiritual forces. The essence of the soul power can only be hidden from people or forgotten, but it can never actually be stolen or destroyed.

Okomfohene Yirenkyi I and other priestesses and priests said that, although there is this fear and prohibition, particularly among Christians in Ghana—and Ghana is heavily Christianized—many Christians, Muslims, and others come to seek the priestesses and priests' assistance. This is even true, sometimes particularly true, of Christian pastors, especially when they are wanting to wield healing spiritual powers that they themselves do not fully possess. It happens with pastors in Washington, DC, and Maryland as well. They just tend to do it covertly. For example, the pastors may seek assistance when they want help with a clearing a negative entity that is possessing one of their parishioners. Okomfohene Yirenkyi I is a specialist in dealing with such spirits and banishing them. Just as medical doctors in clinical settings or lawyers in legal settings have various specialties, the Akan path priestesses and priests have various specialties in their spiritual governances concerning medical maladies and legal issues. Okomfohene Yirenkyi I is a doctor of the spirit who is highly skilled in assisting when people fall down with the spirit and pastors or family members do not know how to converse with the spirit or deal with it. Although the pastors may not openly endorse the Akan shrine culture, they will draw on their wisdom in various ways. Some of the shrine elders even attend a Christian revivalist church in Maryland.

These doctors of spirit, Akan path priestesses and priests, can heal and also ascertain what is needed to bring forth justice in a community or a situation. The spiritual justice system runs parallel to other state laws and community-based justice organizations. The spiritual laws serve to guide the healing and the soul growth not only of Akan priestesses and priests but also of people within their wider orbits, including their families, communities, and other stakeholders. All this work is accomplished and enhanced in the priestesses' and priests' own dynamic lives and journeys, as they intertwine with spiritual copresences that run through them and work with them.

Okomfohene Yirenkyi I's role as a spiritual leader in both Ghana and the United States helps to ensure that all of this flows in its full flourishing and that Akan spiritual governance, strongly connected to the vital ancestral and cultural roots, continues to grow in its proper ways.

SIX

Okomfopanyin Nana Afoah Baakang, Eldest Priestess at the Asuo Gyebi Shrine in Larteh, Kubease

Okomfopanyin Nana Afoah Baakang (Nana Afoah Baakang), now in her eighties, is the eldest priestess at the Asuo Gyebi shrine in Larteh, Kubease. She trained directly under Nana Oparebea, after training for two years with her teacher who then passed, the then-queen mother of Akonnedi, Okomfohema Panyin Nana Ama Ansaah. Nana Afoah Baakang holds vast wisdom from her many years in the evolution of her consciousness in human form and from her working very closely with the Abosom and ancestors from a young age.

After Nana Oparebea passed to spirit in 1995, Nana Afoah Baakang was put in place as the leader of the Asuo Gyebi shrine. It was Nana Afoah Baakan, along with Nana Kwasi Agyiri Richardson (here Nana Kwasi Agyiri, for short)—the late head of the family that owns and manages the shrine—who recommended Okomfohema Botwe I to the stool of queen mother at the Asuo Gyebi shrine in 2005, to denote the importance of the African Americans who patronized and participated in the shrines. In 2014, Okomfohene Yirenkyi I was enstooled as chief priest at the Asuo Gyebi shrine, on the recommendation of Nana Afoah Baakang, Okomfohema Botwe I, and Nana Kwasi Agyiri.

Shrine members, including the leaders, will regularly collaborate with Nana Afoah Baakang when making decisions for the shrine family. In the Akan spiritual system, as in so many settings around the world, the wisdom of the elders who have done the genuine spiritual work throughout their lives is unsurpassed.

Nana Afoah Baakang worked very closely with the elder Nana Kwasi Agyiri while he was alive.

"Nana Kwasi Agyiri dedicated his life, time, and every other resource he had at his disposal to ensure that everything was in place for smooth running of the shrine," his son Nana Adu Richardson shared. "He worked tirelessly in tandem with Nana Afoah Baakang to ensure smooth operation of the shrine."

Nana Kwasi Agyiri would assist Nana Afoah Baakang with interpretations between her language of Twi and that of English for her work with English-speaking priestesses and priests in the United States and in Ghana. He would assist in translating her pouring of libations and her communications to English-speaking family members and other participants. Before major festivals, Nana Kwasi Agyiri would ensure that priestesses and priests in Ghana, the United States, and elsewhere were informed and that they had in place the food, travel, accommodations, and other things they may need to comfortably attend and participate. These two prominent shrine elders worked very closely with great success, and this was apparent to all whom they guided and assisted from around the world.

Nana Afoah Baakang holds the title of Okomfopanyin, as Panyin means elder in the Akan order. This title is an honorific she holds on account of her rank as the eldest living priestess at the Asuo Gyebi shrine.

She serves as a perpetual source of wisdom, spiritual adjudication, practical determination, and a protective buffer to ensure that things function smoothly at the Asuo Gyebi shrine. As Okomfohene Yirenkyi I and his brother Nana Abboa-Offei, the chief in Aburi, stated, Nana Panyin is the overall head and Nana Asuo Gyebi works as her helper.

Nana Afoah Baakang has made several official visits to the United States, during which she circulated on working tours of key Akan shrine houses to help maintain the traditions of the culture and shrines in Ghana. She also attends some sacred Akan celebrations, festivals, and memorials while in the United States.

Nana Afoah Baakang has lived for many decades within the compound of the Asuo Gyebi shrine and holds the keys to a great deal of sacred wisdom and shrine history. Prior to living at the Asuo Gyebi shrine, Nana Afoah Baakang was part of the geographically upper shrine, Nana Panyin, in Larteh while Okomfohene Nana Oparebea reigned as chief high priestess. Nana Afoah Baakang was there supporting her.

I first met Nana Afoah Baakang in person when I was in Larteh in August 2018 for the graduations of the four young African American priestesses, several of whom are featured in chapter 3. She is the priestess through whom the Obosom Nana Asuo Gyebi first addressed me while in Larteh. In accordance with Akan protocol, the shrine elders, owing to my vision of disseminating information for public knowledge, sought confirmation and permission from the Abosom. As a researcher and teacher, I sought the information on healing and spirituality from an Akan spiritual, rather than a Christian or other religious, perspective. By way of divination and through her speech, he greeted me and gave me the Akan name of Nyamekye, which the priestesses explained meant that he was acknowledging my presence.

Nana Afoah Baakang prepared my first sacred herbal bath mixture for spiritual cleansing after I arrived at the shrine. When I was leaving, she also presented me with a sacred gift of a beaded bracelet from the spirits and the family to honor my humility and to indicate their acceptance of the work that I was conducting at that time. I was very honored and humbled by this gift. They were not focused on my superficial appearance but on my conscious relationship to the divine within me. This type of bracelet is ordinarily only given to those individuals who have gone through special spiritual rites as part of their induction.

Chiefs and queen mothers are also given the distinction of this type of bracelet when they have completed their enstoolment.

I had a chance to speak with Nana Afoah Baakang at greater length when she was in the United States, during one of her stays with Okomfohema Botwe I in Maryland. During one conversation, I asked how she received her call to become a priestess. She explained that she was in third grade, and it was during the school day when she received the call. She had not seen a vision or anything like that in advance. The spirit simply visited her, and she fell to the floor and fainted. Her teachers then took her to her father.[1]

In the Akan culture around Larteh, when someone spontaneously faints, the family usually takes them to a shrine to ask the Abosom what has happened, whether is a spiritual issue at play. The fainting may indicate a spiritual message, or it may be generated by a physical issue that is considered to be within the domain of biomedical doctors. If the spiritual divination and consultation indicate a spiritual matter or message, then the Abosom at the shrine may indicate next steps.

In Nana Afoah Baakang's case, it was Abosom of the Nana Panyin shrine pantheon calling her to become a priestess. Her family took her to Okomfohema Panyin Nana Ama Ansaah, who was the queen mother of the Akonnedi shrine at the top at the time, to ask for a consultation with the spirits to see what had caused the fainting. Okomfohema informed Nana Afoah Baakang's family that it had been Nana Asuo Gyebi and one other spirit who had arrived to deliver the spiritual call while she was at school.

From that time, Nana Afoah Baakang started her training to become an okomfo—first, with Okomfohema Nana Ama Ansaah for two years and, once she passed, then with Okomfohene Nana Oparebea, her successor in the role of chief high priestess.

While Okomfohene Nana Yirenkyi I and Okomfohema Botwe I are physically away from Larteh, Nana Afoah Baakang—in collaboration always with the Abosom, ancestors, shrine elders, and family—presides over many functions of the shrine governance.

Nana Afoah Baakang shared how she helps people through spiritual consultations, cross-cultural education and incorporation, and shrine house advising while she is in the United States.

"When people come to consult, I pour libation and then ask the Abosom for the answers. While incorporating the needs of the particular person who, for some reason or another, has come to seek guidance, I will tell them what the Abosom have conveyed for their different circumstances. The Abosom will speak to me spiritually, and I can hear their voices. That's how I do my consultations," she explained.

Nana Afoah Baakang noted how her consultations with the spirit come both through divination tools and through the Abosom coming to directly speak through or to her.

When the spirit is fully flowing through her, she can speak many languages, just like many other Akan path priestesses and priests, as well as people in other spiritual systems, can.

Nana Afoah Baakang explained that when the spirits flow through her in full force, she will not usually be aware of what she is saying or be able to recall it afterward. Her okyeame, an interpreter and auditor of spirit, will inform her of what had happened and what the spirits said. The family and the shrine members will all come together and determine the next steps to take.

When the Abosom or ancestors are speaking through an okomfo in Ghana, they often use local indigenous language (for example, Twi), but if the priestess or priest is in the United States, they sometimes use English. The spirits will do this to accommodate local circumstances. The spiritualists' understanding is that a universal, omnipotent Creator can communicate in any language. It is also the case that the divine wisdom is beyond language. When it comes through language, it can take the form of proverbs, whether in Akan teachings or in the Christian Bible or elsewhere. Proverbs often give to words a higher understanding that the Creator or intercessory exalted spirits, such as the Abosom, wish to impart.

Some priests and priestesses who know multiple languages will hear the spirits speak in different languages at various times. The same spirit may come in a different language at certain moments. The reasons for the shifts in languages are not always known to the priestesses or priests. They simply observe the changes.

For Nana Afoah Baakang, as for so many other priestesses and priests, some of the most important messages from Abosom or other spirits come through the conduit of dreams.

"When the Abosom give you the message in a dream, even if you forget it afterward, they will remind you," she said.

At times, the Abosom or other spirits will even communicate with each other through the priestesses and priests while possessing them. Others who are in human form may have no idea what they are talking about, but the spirits will be talking to each other through possessed priestesses or priests.

I asked Nana Afoah Baakang if she could explain some of how it works when spirits access and reveal things from the past or the future, or from spatially distant places.

"When somebody wants to know something, I will not know much about it," she replied. "What I will tell you is, when the spirits possess, it's what you bring to the conversation. You bring something to ask from the shrine. When they possess me, they will say, 'This will happen in the future,' or 'This has happened before in your family.' Most of the time, the ancestors help them to understand what has happened before in the family."

In Nana Afoah Baakang's own ancestral lineage, there is a line of akomfo.

"My aunt was also one of the great akomfo in Ghana," she said. "She possessed about four shrines, including those for Akonnedi, Nana Adade Kofi, and Nana Esi Ketewa."

Her aunt was at the Akonnedi shrine in Larteh.

While Nana Afoah Baakang's ancestors are Guan, the shrine akomfo became identified more over time with the Akan people. The Guans are indigenous to the lands of Larteh and the surrounding areas, while Akans arrived later, a history that the previous chapter addresses. Nana

Oparebea had Akan ancestry on one side and identified more as an Akan. She made the Akonnedi shrine system in Larteh more Akan during her reign as queen mother and chief priestess in the mid- to late twentieth century. The Abosom at the shrine were happy to work with everyone, Guan or Akan.

Nana Afoah Baakang shared that this was her ninth visit to the United States. Whenever she returns to the shrine in Larteh, it presents some pressure on her, as people want her to return with many things. However, she said that she enjoys her stays and that the visits help to continually revitalize and fortify the ties between the Akan sacred cultures in the United States and Ghana. In addition to the spiritual readings and cultural teachings that Nana Afoah Baakang conducts in the United States, she brings and sells vibrant Ghanaian cloths, jewelry, and related items, which help her raise funds to bring back to the shrine family in Ghana.

Nana Oparebea, from spirit, advises Nana Afoah Baakang to help those in the United States. She is called to do so and is happy to do it. She longs to build an additional living structure at the Asuo Gyebi shrine compound in time. She has collaborated with shrine elders in both the United States and Ghana to help raise funds and execute the plan for a new borehole for fresh drinking water. They also helped to repair the road next to the shrine so that it is easier for the shrine family members and others of all ages to reach the sacred shrine in the mountain. The priestesses and priests work together, across the Atlantic, to keep the Asuo Gyebi shrine in Larteh flourishing and moving forward.

SEVEN

Okomfokese Nana Baakan Okukuranpon Yirenkyiwa, Chief Priestess

Okomfokese Nana Baakan Okukuranpon Yirenkyiwa (here, Okomfokese, for short) is a pioneering, luminous chief priestess of a prominent Akan path shrine house in New York City called Obaatanpa N'Abosum Fie. She is part of the third generation of Akan path priestesses, having trained directly under Okomfohema Nana Botwe I as her first graduated Okomfo. Her title of "Baakan" means first in a line of graduates. In addition to presiding as the head of her own shrine house family in New York City, she has served for many years as the first lieutenant for the ASUO shrine house in Maryland. In this role, she is entrusted with sacred guidance and spiritual protection for the family, and especially for Okomfohema. She is also the leader of the umbrella organization, Obaatanpa House of Hope, Inc., which includes her shrine house and the ASUO house. The group promotes religious, cultural, and community development from the perspectives of the Akan spiritual order. The name "Obaatanpa" stands for "home of the good mother," honoring the memory of Nana Oparebea and all loving mothers, recognizing everything they do to nurture their children and communities, both spiritually and physically.

Okomfokese grew up in Harlem, New York, and came to know Okomfohema Botwe I when they were teenagers in that city. They were both part of the African sacred culture community founded by Nana Opare Yao Dinizulu I. This community later expanded after his visionary trip to Ghana, where he was initiated into the Akan tradition. While there, Nana Dinizulu received official permission from Nana Oparebea to bring Abosom back to the United States to serve the African Americans who wished to connect more deeply with their ancestral roots and who sought enlightenment and spiritual empowerment through the Akan philosophies and practices. Okomfokese, now an elder, is one of the key spiritualists in the United States involved in planning, cogoverning, and convening events for the Akan Abosom, cherished ancestors, spiritualists, and broader communities in New York City and elsewhere. She helps to preside over many of the jurisdictions—or Akan spiritual governance realms—in the city and beyond.

Nana Baakan is also a pivotal figure in helping to nurture and fortify the transnational ties between the Larteh shrines in Ghana and Akan sacred shrine houses in the United States. She serves on a key advisory board of spiritual elders for the shrines and helps to advise, protect, divine, and adjudicate in many vital matters concerning the shrines' governance.

Professionally, Nana Baakan served the New York City educational system as a teacher. She brought her spiritual gifts and intuitive guidance into the classroom to impart knowledge and to positively impact the lives of young people.

Teaching is also a central component of her role as a chief priestess for the house.

"Education is an important part of the priesthood, at least in what I am doing. I want people to understand things and be able to find themselves. Even as young children, you can teach them to bring out the best in themselves," she said. "It's also about learning to relate to your peers. Even if they don't understand you, you want to make sure that you understand them. You don't want people to be able to take you down. You want to always keep yourself up. African spirituality is a blessing to the world. We have to make sure that our people here in the diaspora know this, know that it is good."

Okomfokese continues to help train the next generations of Akan path priestesses and priests in New York City. She also helps to lead them, when possible, to Larteh for official visits to the shrines there. She and her house members facilitated the more recent flourishing of virtually presenting festivals and commemorative events. The festivals are held to unify and revitalize members and supporters of the Akan tradition, wherever they may be physically located. In this way and in many others, she works to help foster consciousness of a spiritual oneness and interconnectedness among community members.

As a chief priestess, she exists in dynamic interrelation with key copresences—or spirits—who are connected to her and whose wisdom and consciousness flow through her in dynamic assemblages of spiritual energies that heal, fortify, and enlighten those around her. In this way, as with the other Akan priestesses and priests, she exists as a vibrant constellation of subjectivity, with various spirits and energies of consciousness informing her, helping to guide her and flowing through her in fluid fashions as she goes through life in sacred ritual spaces—in her professional life beyond the house, and in her everyday activities.

She is a wife of the Obosom Nana Asuo Gyebi, the healing and warrior spirit. In this way, he could be said to be the spirit that is most closely intertwined in cocreation and cohabitation with her. She twice received the direct call from him to train and graduate in order to become his wife, as an Akan priestess, before accepting the call at a later stage in her life. She was fairly young the first time she received the call.

She grew up in the 1960s and 1970s, when many political changes and movements for change were sweeping American society and the world.

"Especially with African people, whether in the diaspora or in the motherland, or in other places, there was a lot of unrest. People were looking for justice," she said.

She spoke about the broader atmosphere of the Vietnam War and the intensifying protests over racial, social, and economic injustices. Pan-Africanist political mobilizations were also prominent in local and transnational activism. The civil rights movement and organizations such as the Black Panthers were in full swing.

In the midst of all of this societal transformation, Okomfokese enjoyed a deep sense of cultural flourishing in her family and broader community. She was very involved in the local music scene, in African jazz, jazz, Motown, and rock 'n' roll.

"In our community, we had so many pioneers who gave a lot to what people call 'American culture,'" she recalled. "One song, in particular, with the lines—'Say it loud, I'm Black and I'm proud' [1968 song by James Brown and Alfred Ellis]—was amazing because it represented the awakening of the new generation of Black people. It really gave energy to us to push us forward."

Okomfokese said that one of the most impactful moments of her life and consciousness was the 1955 murder of fourteen-year-old Emmett Till by two white men who bludgeoned him to death, supposedly for looking the wrong way at a white woman in a grocery store. At the time, an all-white jury in Mississippi acquitted the two white men, the white woman's husband, and his half-brother.

Prosecutors charged the men with murder. When the all-white jury failed to convict them, it sent shockwaves through much of the nation as emblematic of systemic racism and the failures of the justice system. More recently, the white woman in the store, Carolyn Bryant Donham, had admitted that she falsified parts of her testimony in the courtroom. Of course, these things have been much too little much too late. The murder cannot be undone, and the event is seared into the consciousness of the nation as an unforgettable instance of vicious, violent racism in the United States.[1]

"It upsets me even now, talking about this murder, as just one example of what white people do to us. I think of what was taken away when we were taken from Africa. Our ancestors were taken as enslaved people under such harsh conditions, I don't even know how they survived," she said.

In school growing up, she felt that a great deal was missing from the story of her ancestors and what they had gone through in the United States. Some of the great freedom fighters were part of the curriculum, which served as a source of sustenance and empowerment. Frederick Douglass, Sojourner Truth, and Harriet Tubman were among those whose stories were taught when she was young. In the community in Harlem, they had the cultural icon of freedom fighter Malcolm X, who preached at the Nation of Islam's legendary Mosque No. 7. (It is still in operation, now as a Sunni mosque known as Masjid Malcolm Shabazz.)

Although there was economic poverty in the community, Okomfokese remembers so much flourishing and joy from her days of youth.

"We were always having block parties. It was so family-oriented, in spite of what was known as poverty. And people would come up from the South. Farmers would be bringing up food for us to eat, and it felt so good. It would nourish us."

She was the oldest of seven children and was very close to her family. Her parents had come from the South, and they were involved in Marcus Garvey's political movement.

Okomfokese did not regularly attend local churches when she was young, but she was connected to her spirit from a young age. When she was between ten and twelve years old, she guided herself to be baptized in a Christian church. She simply went on her own one day. She felt light afterward, as though it had been a good thing to do for herself, though she did not feel the need to join or attend a church.

Her sense of intuitive guidance from the divine was always present with her. She described how, even when she was very young, she would look to the sky, and she could feel her spirit rise or move upward.

At the same time that she experienced sacred connection with her own spirit and in her own community, she continually encountered racism and injustice in the broader societies around her.

She shared another deeply impactful and hurtful experience that had occurred in her presence when she was young, visiting her grandparents in the South. It has stayed with her throughout her life.

Her grandfather was delighted that she was in town with them, and he was excited to introduce her to people in their local town community. He brought her, then a young girl, into a town store, and the white owner of the store was present. The white man looked at him and told him that he should know he shouldn't be in there, meaning as a Black man. The white man said something about going to another store for Black people, using a racial slur.

"I looked at my grandfather, and he looked so dejected, because he just wanted to introduce his granddaughter," she recalled.

Another major event in her life and consciousness was when Dr. Martin Luther King Jr., was assassinated on April 4, 1968. She was in middle school. All of a sudden, her teacher told the class to stop everything. He had just received the news that Dr. King had been murdered.

"I remember thinking, why would someone kill a man of peace? I didn't understand. And I couldn't get an answer to this. He was trying to pull people together under a loving Christian mindset. That was really hurtful," she said. "Other incidents happened. Bobby Kennedy got assassinated [on June 6, 1968]. Before that, Malcolm X had been assassinated [on February 21, 1965]. All of this was very upsetting."

As all of this was happening, she grew in her commitment to pursue justice and liberation for the people in her community. She also reveled in the many treasures of African and African American music, art, and culture that were flourishing around her.

In high school, she emerged as a self-aware leader. She could feel it in her style, her dress, and her demeanor. She could clearly sense it in her mind, her spirit, and her actions. She was part of the first class that was coed at her high school. It had previously been a girls' school. She was elected as a leader in high school and continued her leadership activities into college.

It was in college that she first met Nana Yao Opare Dinizulu I. He was teaching an African history and culture class, and Okomfokese enrolled in it. As part of the class, he required that she go to the African spirituality temple that he founded, Bosum Dzemawodzi. She was given an assignment to observe the practices there and write about them.

"That was so impactful because I had never seen people do things like they did them there. They would bow and greet him, and they wore white attire. They had the *mpsese* locks [often worn by those in training] or dreaded hair. Seeing the senior priests, how they carried themselves, I said, 'Wow.' I remember saying to myself, 'This is what it's like in Africa.' I just knew, period," she said. "That's also when I met Nana Botwe. She was a trainee at the time, too. That really stuck with me. I started going to the Akoms, but I didn't train then."

Although she did not initiate right away, she became part of the Akan spiritual community and the broader African traditional spiritual culture in the city in the 1970s. She remembered going to Nana Dinizulu's wedding, where about five hundred people were gathered. People still speak of it to this day. She shared how moving and beautiful his singing was. She also became part of the African jazz scene.

"A lot of things happened around this time that reinforced my identity as an African woman and that reinforced my sense of being proud of myself, proud of all of the accomplishments of my people. All of this encouraged me to not give up," she said.

Okomfokese had visions of her future travels to Africa in the dream state, in the form of a recurring dream. Her mother, whom she described as a very conscious person, always intuitively knew that Okomfokese would go to Africa. She would tell Okomfokese not to worry, as she would one day be in Africa. The dream involved, along with some other things, a woman in Africa going to a well. She had been having the dream since she was younger, and it continued into her young adulthood.

When she first met Okomfohema Botwe I, then in training, Okomfohema relayed a message from Nana Asuo Gyebi that Okomfokese was meant to be his wife. Okomfokese at first was surprised and said she could not imagine it for herself. He accepted her hesitation at that time.

Even though she was not yet ready to train, Nana Baakan continued to be involved in the African traditional spiritual community. She also continued with her education and career, and she married and had children.

She later visited Ghana and spent time in a town called Mampong in the Akuapem area in the mountains, not too far from Larteh. She became ill and received a vision in a dream in which she was directed to find a priestess of Nana Asuo Gyebi. When she subsequently met with Okomfohema Botwe I, Okomfohema washed her head, conducted a divination, and again delivered the message that Nana Asuo Gyebi wanted to marry her.

This was astonishing to Okomfokese, since she was receiving, in 1982, the same message that she had received from the Obosom in 1975. Okomfokese replied that her children were back in the United States, and Okomfohema told her that Nana Asuo Gyebi said he would wait for her.

After this, something shifted for her. Things around her started happening differently, and she felt different.

"I knew it was something spiritual," she said.

She started learning more about the Akan spiritual culture from an elder Akan priestess who lived in Brooklyn at the time.

After Okomfohema Botwe I had graduated as a priestess in New York, she moved to Maryland to set up the ASUO house under her leadership. Around that same time, Nana Asuo Gyebi also claimed a very good friend and mentor of Okomfokese as his wife. The three of them were at a festival in Maryland, and Okomfohema Botwe I told Okomfokese that Nana Asuo Gyebi said that it was time for her to train.

After this festival, Okomfokese no longer hesitated. She was ready to be initiated, to train as a priestess and a wife of Nana Asuo Gyebi. She accepted the call, and her husband was supportive, even with all the time, energy, and resources that were necessary to commit to the process.

Nana Oparebea had told her about the process for training. Okomfokese began training in 1987. It was meant to be one year, but Nana Asuo Gyebi said he was waiting for Nana Oparebea to get back to the United States for her final graduation. However, she was not ultimately able to make it back in time for Okomfokese's graduation in 1989.

Training with Okomfohema Botwe I was a very thorough, meticulous, and exacting process for her. In the Akan tradition in general, trainees have to start at a level base line at the bottom, and they rise through the ranks in the community over time.

"First, you have to start from ground one on your knees, and you continue. That's something that's important about Akan spirituality. You can't just jump out there and say, 'I have a following, and it's good.' It doesn't go like that," Okomfokese explained. "You have to work hard. You have to be on your knees, humble. You listen. You learn. This is all something that is within us, and it carries on into the tradition."

The respect for elders in the sacred community is very important. The elders of wise consciousness have already traversed so many of the lessons that the younger are still living through and learning from. A key component of training as an okomfo is the humbling of oneself before the wisdom of the elders and the Abosom.

"Nana Botwe was very disciplined about training. She wanted you to follow guidelines to a *T*, and I did that. I was loyal in that way, following her lead," she said. "That's important. You have to humble yourself. If the Abosom say something, you have to take it seriously. As an okomfowaa, humility is very important as you prepare to graduate."

Okomfokese also had the added dimension of being the only one in training under Okomfohema Botwe I for a time. She would commute each month between Maryland and Brooklyn, where she lived with her husband and children. This helped to further fortify her spiritual bonds and her inner relationship to her personal strength.

She also helped with the growth and expansion of the ASUO shrine. After some time, she brought in Okomfohema Botwe I's second trainee and others as well.

"I've had the opportunity to sit at the feet of the elders and train, and to become an elder upon my graduation. I was the youngest among those elders present at that time," she explained. "It was a lot, because I understood then. Now, I see the new elders coming in, and I can be a role model for them, and I understand it."

Having become a priestess and now chief priestess and elder has transformed her life and her multisensorial ways of knowing truths and navigating life. As she has expanded in her own consciousness and spiritual capacities, she has also enhanced her natural leadership qualities. She helps many people learn to heal, empower, and liberate themselves and others in collaboration with the Abosom, cherished ancestors, and supportive community members.

"Being part of the culture has allowed me to open my eyes and my ears. I see things in different ways now. I hear things, and I know if I hadn't gone under, I wouldn't hear those things. I have visions that are different now. All of that," she said. "The journey has meant everything to me in my life."

Okomfokese has raised her children in the Akan spiritual culture. She has continually met remarkable, transformative people through the sacred community at every stage of her life as a priestess. She has collaborated with many people who are laying new groundwork or frameworks for spiritual change and empowerment in all aspects of life. When people do not find the justice or sustenance they are looking for in extant institutions, in the state or elsewhere, they can turn to the spiritual authorities and their copresent jurisdictions, which provide alternative or parallel avenues of caring, healing, and providing.

"I've seen miracles happen. They do. I've been part of them. They transform people's lives. I've seen it. It's that connection to home, back to Africa, which is what we want, which is what I was born from. I know that my family had it in them. I guess I was the one who had to step out there and do it," she said.

Okomfokese reflected on the powerful leadership of Nana Oparebea, who took her under her wing and taught her so many things. She continues to guide and protect from spirit, of course, as a cherished ancestor.

She also shared more about the nature of her spiritual husband, Nana Asuo Gyebi, and other Abosom.

"He is a protector and a healer. He helps people find their destiny. He's water inside a rock—gentle and solid, and he is so graceful. Each of the Abosom have their ways. The Obosom Nana Adade Kofi, if he takes you under his wing, you're going to get it done. If he tells you that it's not this, take him at his word—that iron," she said. "For spiritual evolution, you have to put in the work and follow the instructions of the Abosom, and as long as you put in the work, you'll be good."

She spoke of the foresight and vision beyond linear earth time that the exalted spirits possess. She gave an example of when Nana Asuo Gyebi manifested to deliver a prophetic message during an international arts festival that the priests and priestesses were doing. He told one man at the festival that, one day, the man would tell a great story. That same man ended up in the famous film, *Sankofa* (released in 1993 and directed by Haile Gerima).[2] Sankofa, in Akan, means "one must return to the past in order to move forward," and the sankofa is known as a "bird of passage."[3]

Okomfokese said that some of the most rewarding parts of her life have involved her being able to help her people to find their ways in navigating through society in the United States or in traveling home to Africa, or in helping through various spiritual and physical healing projects. She shared how even physical healing, for her, involves a spiritual aspect, as the Abosom are always part of it in her life. She has witnessed how these exalted spirits have helped her and others on physical and spiritual levels. Her constellation of subjectivity—as chief priestess, mother, leader, wife, teacher, and community member—is ever-expansive and helps her to cocreate avenues of justice, protection, and belonging beyond the constraints of other societal institutions.

"Our people have been devastated in such a way that I can honestly say is unique to us. All other immigrants have come for reasons, sometimes because of trials and tribulations in their homelands. We are the only ones who were forcibly brought here and detached from everything we knew—our culture, our ancestors, our lands—and the suffering and abuse still continue," she said. "Our Akan spirituality helps people to heal and find a place for themselves, even if it means that they will continue in other traditions. It is helping people to reconnect and be strong. That bridge we talked about earlier—I would say I'm a bridge."

The Abosom help people to identify their soul's purpose and their particular gifts, and then they help people to cultivate and further develop these gifts—if they wish to do so. The elder priests and priestesses also often do the same for those who are newer to the Akan spiritual path. This is part of the spiritual bridge that Okomfokese helps to provide in her myriad roles in the community.

She reflected on the beauty and the power of the call to serve as Akan priests and priestesses, and how the divine spirit has always been with the people through everything. She also related the divine spirits of the Abosom to the Holy Ghost of the Christian churches.

"I know this Akan spirituality gives us the opportunity to reconnect with our family, to know our spirit, to rejoice in our spirit, to be loved and to express our love for our people and our spirit. For these Abosom to call us to train and be with them, that itself is amazing. In the Black churches, people know about the Holy Ghost. People know that," she said. "Our people have always been spiritual—even through the trials and tribulations of slavery, that spirit has never left us. That spirituality will never leave us. It will always be with us."

She emphasized that the Akan spiritual focus is on making things right and good in this lifetime, which will influence the next life and the ones after that. There are cycles of spiritual reciprocity that continue throughout a soul's reincarnations that are similar to the cycles of reciprocity in nature. The Akan spiritualists do not wait for a faraway heaven or a place where people get their just dues solely in the afterlife. Life here in this incarnation is just as important as life when one crosses over, back into spirit.

Okomfokese and her shrine family continually help to fortify the bridges of connection to the shrines in Larteh. They recently have been helping to restore the house structures, the road, and the water infrastructure at the Asuo Gyebi shrine in Larteh. She shares with a group of elders a dream of creating a museum and a library in Nana Oparebea's house in Larteh. Okomfokese and her house helped with the commemorative statue to Nana Oparebea in Larteh. She plays key roles in helping to organize or lead festivals, Akoms, and other events in the United States and in Ghana—and now, in the virtual sphere, as well for select occasions. She also has held a public Akom for thirty-four years, honoring Nana Asuo Gyebi at the International African Arts festival, which has been occurring annually for almost fifty years in New York City.

She and her shrine family members seek to help empower those in the community on any level they wish—whether physically or spiritually, or through education or community service. They lead various rites of passage for people. They also provide a forum for mediation and conflict resolution, including spiritual courts and adjudication, for matters arising within their community. The Akan path spiritualists also conduct or preside over naming ceremonies, marriages, life celebrations, and transition ceremonies for those who have passed.

Okomfokese reflected on the significant work that goes into establishing and maintaining a shrine house community. The energy must be sustained, and the shrine family members must always raise the new generations and keep the shrine work and education relevant to what is going on in people's lives.

"You raise your shrine house by raising the people," she said. "The shrine family is like a mini-village. Everyone has their roles."

Members of the Obaatanpa House of Hope also make sure to circulate in the wider Akan diasporic community, participating in lectures, Akoms, festivals, and community events at the other shrine houses in the area so that they can all support each other and stay connected as a spiritual community. The shrine house family and the broader networks are vital assemblages of spiritual healing and liberation, always expanding in dynamic and elevating ways.

Conclusion

Revitalized Visions and Transatlantic Copresence in
Akan Spirituality

Akan spirituality in the United States is more vital than ever and is continuing to undergo further expansions and growing interrelations with the shrine families in Ghana. In 2018, Ghana's president Akufo-Addo declared that 2019 would be the year of the Great Return, as noted in the introduction. In this commemoration, he marked the four hundred-year return home, in which he opened the door so people could come back to explore their deep histories and future horizons as Africans in their vibrant independence and freedom.

The Akan spiritualists featured in this book, each in their own particular and profound ways, are part of this broader revitalization. Each spiritualist who has shared parts of the stories of receiving the call and becoming priestesses and priests, with their dynamic constellations of subjectivity and their assemblages of copresent jurisdictions, has contributed to a clarification and revelation project of helping to bring to light a broader understanding of the truth and the spiritual principles of their sacred art. So much about the Akan sacred tradition, both in the United States and in Ghana, has been misunderstood in so much of what counts as popular consciousness.

This book is not merely a rarefied academic exercise. In full collaboration with the spiritualists who are the keepers of the sacred knowledge, I have tried to document and help to illuminate the truth of the Akan sacred order, its spiritual laws, and the lives of the spiritualists who, through sacred and other professional work, variously interact with legal, political, social, and other institutions. They chart novel paths of spiritual liberation, healing, awakening, and belonging, both reconnecting to their West African ancestral roots and reformulating these deep spiritual histories to speak to their circumstances in contemporary society. Their copresent jurisdictions feature the assemblages of spirits and spiritualists who govern those under the Akan spiritual jurisdiction and who interact with state and other institutional authorities with their secular jurisdictions. Their lives as ordained spiritualists invite a new expansive concept of constellations of subjectivity, according to which people themselves become dynamic assemblages of powers, with spirits running through them and, in some cases, becoming part of them in their lives, interwoven as one, for their sacred healing work. Their spiritual work charts novel avenues for justice and belonging as a space for emergent politics, or "sovereignty from below." Their lives and spiritual work also evince a historically informed and spiritually connected cosmopolitics in which multiple ontologies are at play, both in the spiritual lives of copresent jurisdictions and in their expansive understandings of ever-emergent subjectivity.

As the Akan spiritualists have their own forms of spiritual adjudication, healing, and policing, which work alongside, as well as in the interstices of and sometimes in conflict with state-based institutions, they are also part of the recently theorized "after law" moment. The theorized era posits a "post-juristocratic transition" in which state-based legal domains are no longer featured as the privileged site of political life. Instead, people are seeking their forms of community, authority, belonging, inclusion, and securing of rights in other ways, including these interrelations among Akan spiritual families in the United States, Ghana, and elsewhere in the diaspora.

Over the course of this book, I have interlaced both dialogical exchanges and other prose that my interlocutors have collaboratively edited and reviewed for accuracy and approval, and I have strived to achieve the most accurate form possible in light of our exchanges. To my mind, this form of writing and this collaborative ethnographic engagement are very important aspects of efforts to generate decolonial knowledge production. It is through these collaborative research modalities and the subsequent writing conversations that I have sought to generate and evaluate the book's key conceptual contributions—copresent jurisdictions and constellations of subjectivity—and to build upon the broader theoretical interventions of theopolitics, cosmopolitics, and the "after law" moment.

With a newly flourishing turn to virtual ceremonies, gatherings, and conferences, the transatlantic copresences of priestesses, priests, other shrine family members, and their Abosom and cherished ancestors have taken on new dimensions and import. The shrine families in the United States and Ghana have become evermore connected since Nana Yao Opare Dinizulu I established the first approved Akan shrine house in New York City in 1969, under the authorization of the powerful chief high priestess Okomfohene Nana Oparebea.

A part of the expanded virtual domains of meetings and events came by necessity, while I was conducting this research. The COVID-19 pandemic descended on the world in the early spring of 2020, while I was in the middle of researching and writing this book. While the pandemic could have dampened the activities of Akan spiritual culture, as elsewhere, especially since in-person gatherings and international travel were so difficult, the two principal shrine houses featured in this book, along with others, actually witnessed an expansion of engagement. Elders from the ASUO house in Maryland and the Asuo Gyebi shrine in Larteh, in cocreation with the Abosom, key ancestors, and other elders, have started to open parts of major festivals and commemorative events to participation via Zoom for the first time. Access to formal shrine events through these newer virtual spaces has brought the participation of many more people in Akom gatherings and sacred festivals, at least the parts that are appropriate to open to the more general public. These expansive participatory modalities in virtual spaces, in turn, have led to increased membership, initiations, graduations, and plans for travel from the United States to the Asuo Gyebi shrine in Larteh, as awareness is spreading well beyond existing shrine families. The rise or expansion of virtual spaces for the communities are inspiring a deepening and widening of new constellations of subjectivities for priestesses and priests, as well as an expansion and revitalization of copresent jurisdictions among Abosom, ancestors, spiritualists, and others. In addition to the pandemic, there was a broader intensification in racial justice consciousness movements, including the Black Lives Matter movement. This coincided with the continued growth of transatlantic Akan spirituality. The elders also have shared—and have asked me to note here—that Akan spirituality is available to help everyone raise their consciousness and find paths for healing and liberation.

The Akan spiritualists, along with many others, are seeking newly expanded forms of belonging, empowerment, healing, and political mobilization outside or alongside other formal legal systems and political statecraft institutions in the United States and Ghana. They are reconnecting in a deeper fashion with ancestral ties and other forms of spiritual and political belonging, refashioning them to meet the needs and desires of those in contemporary society, while maintaining and continuing the teaching and the practice of the essential Akan protocols and the spiritual laws of right versus wrong acts and deeds. Far from a static spiritual consciousness inherited from the past, Akan spirituality in the United States and Ghana summons the sacred powers of the past and activates them within the contexts of ever-expansive Akan spiritual consciousness for the present times and for the future.

As many people today are disenchanted with current legal and political institutions, they are cocreating and collaborating in new forms of politics that can be more lateralized and diffuse, and that can course beyond, alongside, and in the interstices of, or in resistance to, state-based institutions or legal domains. As the Akan path copresent jurisdictions reveal throughout this book, the recent theorizations of a "theopolitics"—or "sovereignty from below"—are of even more expansive applicability and theoretical power than perhaps has yet been realized, as rich and compelling as the initial works on these orientations have been.[1] These new theopolitical forms are also flourishing within post-juristocratic orders, or the "after law" moment.[2] In other words, they are charting a path through the crossroads of the contemporary, including the many fault lines and misalignments of secular liberal democratic promises. People are finding new meaning and sustenance through theopolitical phenomena and alternative spiritual paths, such as the Akan shrine culture, which is also being amplified with broader African or African-related forms of spirituality through interfaith theopolitical programming and collaborations—for example, with the national African Traditional Spiritual Coalition, headquartered in Washington, DC.

More broadly, many people are turning to the spiritual healing paths for support during these times of stress and rapid transformational change on so many levels of American and global societies—the pandemic, a deepening economic recession, political polarization, and the intensification of multiple social justice movements. Many people from all walks of life and faith are calling for change at an even higher pitch than usual. Where they are not finding holistic solutions within formal state bodies or other societal institutions, they are turning to alternative forms of political mobilization, social belonging, healing, and spirituality. As Akan path spiritualists chart shrine communities' ways into the future, the priestesses, priests, and other members are also renovating concepts and practices they mobilize as part of their spiritual work in their broader suites of sacred activities and everyday life.

As the spiritual pathways and life experiences of those featured throughout this book demonstrate, these dynamic Akan path practices, subjectivities, and assemblages work in many experiential modes and affective registers. The Akan path offers a reformulation, an opening, an expansion, and a reorganization of the very personhood, or subjectivity, of a priestess or priest. They do not simply walk a path. They become the path, and the path becomes them. These dynamics of spiritual reconstitution or reconfiguration work through dreams, visions, spiritual visitations, mediumship, and other forms of mystical modalities that help to inaugurate more expansive and multivalent forms of spiritual subjectivity.

I have argued throughout this book that these dynamic assemblages of copresences can be productively theorized as *constellations of subjectivity*. As Akan path priestesses and priests become connected—or come to understand that they are already connected—to Abosom, ancestors, and other spirit guides of the light, they also discover aspects and powers within them that they had yet to consciously unlock and with which they had yet to cultivate relationships. In this way, their subjectivity is less bounded than they initially may have thought. Furthermore, their more expansive subjectivity involves ways of knowing, sensing, and communicating that they previously did not recognize as parts of their lived experiences. These modes of perceiving, sensing, and navigating social and spiritual worlds lie beyond most dominant, mainstream performative discourses of subjectivation—or subjects-making through regimes of truth or power-knowledge, which create "subject-effects," to use the Foucauldian language. In the Akan cosmopolitics, the Abosom and cherished ancestors are part and parcel of the spiritualists' dynamic assemblages of copresent jurisdictions and their constellations of subjectivity. These spiritual communities help generate belonging and foster justice in ways that resonate with broader shifts toward interweaving alternative faith orders into the fabric of contemporary society and everyday life. In Arturo Escobar's prescient words, as he wrote about his theory of pluriversal politics, the Akan spiritual orders are part of a broader conceptual and political shift that posits "another possible is possible"—that is, flourishing and justice can occur outside the confines of would-be secular liberal orders. There are other parallel, complementary, or even sometimes conflictual avenues of justice at play. The spiritual laws and paths of the sacred Akan order in the United States and Ghana furnish one such example, and a powerful one at that.

While the path of priestesses or priests may appear to others as a matter of preordained destiny or as the unfoldment of a personal telos, their constellations of subjectivity are fields of creative flux and contingency, as well as a great deal of freedom and volition with respect to embracing certain spiritual capacities that these Abosom and ancestral presences offer. The priestesses and priests negotiate with spirits in dreams and visions, as well as during waking hours. They do so alone and in communal settings. In this way, subjectivity is constantly negotiated and renegotiated over time in conversation with the spirits, other priestesses and priests, family members, and people from throughout their various spheres of existence. The perpetual emergence of the okomfo is an intersubjective process in the fullest sense: it involves a multiplicity of spirits as well as human consciousnesses.

These constellations of subjectivity and copresent jurisdictions generate the continuous revitalization and expansion of the Akan spiritual path in the United States and its related shrine communities in Larteh, Kubease, Ghana. These spaces of copresence help to establish, refashion, and, at the same time, continually renew cosmopolitical spiritual alliances and assemblages of theopolitical powers. These spiritual unions and communities create new spheres of healing, empowerment, and flourishing that extend far beyond the oft-secular zones of legal entitlements, social welfare, and political mobilization in contemporary public life.

The paths of these priestesses and priests reveal how, at times, becoming other can converge with becoming more. They may discover what they long had been but had yet to remember or discover. They do so through perpetual journeys of expansion into multiple worlds of illumination and knowledge, as well as into kaleidoscopic modes of navigating and evolving in spiritual consciousness.

The rise and revitalization of the Akan copresent jurisdictions involve the perpetual interchange and interaction between state legal institutions and Akan shrine house communities, including the spiritual charges and affective resonances that course with great consequence for the ongoing quests for justice, healing, belonging, and spiritual enlightenment. This is especially true in the contemporary United States, with its contested liberal democratic settlements and coursing debates about whether legal and other social systems are adequately providing full avenues for justice. At the same time, as the chapters demonstrate, the Akan path members are very present and active already in every domain of society, including medicine, law, education, public health, and social systems. As with everyone, the work they conduct in these secular domains is first and foremost about fulfilling the responsibilities of the workplace.

While they sometimes have been out of clear public view, these Akan path spiritualists, their Abosom, and their cherished ancestors have been helping to offer alternative spiritual modes of law, governance, adjudication, healing, redress, and belonging. As the resurgence of Akan spirituality courses through public life in parts of the United States, it also recharges and transforms some practices in Ghana, as the transatlantic interconnections of the spiritual assemblages remain strong. Intricate systems of copresence and cogovernance—or what I have theorized as *copresent jurisdictions*—connect all these communities, at all times. Many Abosom and some other spirits can be in multiple localities at once, bringing through forgotten or hidden information from the past or present and, at times, prophesying for and from the future. These alternative modes of knowledge production, though deeply mystical in many ways, are grounded in vital everyday pragmatics that help generate a novel theopolitics of renewal and a post-juristocratic transition within contemporary public life. As people turn evermore to alternative forms of spirituality and governance, these priestesses and priests illuminate powerful pathways into the future—for themselves, for cultural anthropology and social theory, and for revitalized realms of law, spirit, and political belonging in contemporary societies.

ACKNOWLEDGMENTS

I am grateful to so many for sharing their insights and wisdom for this book and the years of research that went into it. First and foremost, I must express deep gratitude to the Akan path priestesses, priests, and other community members—as well as to their cherished ancestors and Abosom—who allowed me to learn and write about their lives and sacred work. They are too many to name, and I also must honor their anonymity or privacy where desired, but my gratitude to them is profound.

I conducted the research and writing for this book while I was serving on the faculty in anthropology at Princeton University. I am grateful for multiple sources of funding and support that I received for this research while there from various programs and centers, including: the Humanities Council; the David A. Gardner '69 Magic Innovation Grant; the University Center for Human Values; the Program in African Studies; the Princeton Institute for International and Regional Studies; the Princeton Society of Fellows in the Liberal Arts; the Fung Global Fellows Program; the Center for Culture, Society, and Religion; the Being Human Festival; the President's Award in Distinguished Teaching; and the University Committee for Research in the Humanities and Social Sciences.

I also owe many thanks to various sources of external support that I received while at Princeton and while conducting the longer-running research that laid the foundation for this work. These sources of support include: the W. E. B. Du Bois Research Institute in the Hutchins Center at Harvard; the Athenaeum; the Institute on the Formation of Knowledge at the University of

Chicago; the US Environmental Protection Agency; the Social Science Research Council; the American Council of Learned Societies; the Andrew W. Mellon Foundation; the Some Institutes for Advanced Studies (SIAS) consortium; the Lincoln Institute; the Institute for Global Law and Policy; the Program on the Study of Capitalism at Harvard; the Nicholson Center at the University of Chicago, and various other sources at the University of Chicago; Harvard University, and beyond.

I am indebted to many friends, family members, guides in spirit, and interlocutors from various domains for generous insights and illumination. They are too many to name. I also am grateful to Kate Marshall, Chad Attenborough, Emily Park, and their colleagues at the University of California Press for their fantastic guidance and wisdom. I am grateful to Peter Letzelter-Smith and Gabriel Bartlett for wonderful copy edits, as well as to Victoria Baker for her amazing indexing work. I likewise am grateful for the enthusiastic and insightful anonymous reviews of this book for the press and for the generous final reader report. I also give thanks to the editors of *PoLAR: Political and Legal Anthropology Review* for granting me permission to publish an article that features elements that are also included in this book.

Most of all, as ever, I am grateful to my beloved husband, Jeffrey Rosen. His brilliance, kindness, prolific creations, and fierce devotion to wisdom, justice, and the light never cease to amaze me. I am perpetually fortified and inspired by his radiant presence and spirit.

NOTES

INTRODUCTION

1. I have used the terms *African Americans* and *African diasporans* rather than *Black* or other designators, as that is what my interlocutors requested I use in writing this book. I also interchangeably use the words *religion* and *spirituality*, following the usages of my interlocutors in the Akan shrine culture.

2. Okomfopanyin Afoah is the first priestess that Okomfohema Nana Akua Oparebea (Nana Oparebea) graduated at the Akonnedi Shrine (also known as the Nana Panyin Shrine) in Larteh, Ghana, in the early to mid-twentieth century. The title *Panyin* means elder. Nana Oparebea is the famed Ghanaian priestess who authorized and helped to establish formal shrine houses in the United States. After I first introduce an interlocutor in this book by their full formal title, I then include the shortened version to be used in subsequent mentions, for ease of reading. The only exceptions to the shortened subsequent usage are for when an interlocutor, on reviewing and editing the materials pertaining to them, has requested that their full title be used in particular places. All names used for living people in this book are people's actual spiritual and/or legal names (at times different), as they have requested them to be used and for which they have granted permission. The only exception to this is when people have requested that I use a pseudonym for them instead. Where this is the case, I have noted it in the endnotes. The interlocutors chose their own pseudonyms, where used.

3. All foreign italicized words are Twi, also called Akan, unless otherwise specified.

4. This ceremony differed in meaning and significance from the type of historical visits or tourism about which other scholars have written. For example, Jemima Pierre has written about her affective experiences of a castle dungeon in Ghana, reflecting on her visit to the Cape Coast Castle for a Reverential Night ceremony in 2015: "Together, we tried to make our way through the various tunnels connecting the dungeons, walking on an unstable ground that at times sloped steeply and at other times had jagged slants. In one dungeon, we saw a shrine that, judging by its lit candles and fresh flowers, seemed to have been recently visited. Within the dark walls, we could hear not only our own shrill echoes but also those of the many people walking through, as well as children screaming in what seemed like both fear and delight. At that moment, I *felt* slavery. *We* felt slavery. In her discussion of tourism to Elmina and Cape Coast Castles, Sandra Richards explains that visitors are usually forced to reenact aspects of African captives' experiences, imagining the actions that transpired when 'burdened by the oppressive presence of the confining castle-dungeons.' Indeed, it seemed that the *affect* of the dungeons was just as important as the ceremonies enacted and speeches given to recast and remember slavery." See *The Predicament of Blackness: Postcolonial Ghana and the Politics of Race* (Chicago: University of Chicago Press, 2012), 138, citing Sandra Richards, "What Is to Be Remembered? Tourism to Ghana's Slave Castle-Dungeons," *Theatre Journal* 47, no. 4 (2005): 617–37, 623. For another discussion of the Cape Coast Castle, see Andrew Apter, "History in the Dungeon: Atlantic Slavery and the Spirit of Capitalism in Cape Coast Castle, Ghana," *American Historical Review* 122, no. 1 (2017): 23–54.

5. Okomfohene Nana Yao Opare Dinizulu I received ancestral revelations in a dream, which led him to travel from Harlem to Ghana in search of the lands, kin, and sacred knowledge of his forbearers. While he was there, the mother of the high priestess and queen mother (Okomfohema) of the Akonnedi shrine in Larteh at the time, Okomfohema Nana Akua Oparebea, revealed through divination that Nana Dinizulu had related ancestry. He hailed from a line of priests, and the spirits were now calling him to initiate and graduate as an okomfo and to help bring an Akan shrine system to the United States, primarily to serve African Americans in their quests for healing, transformation, and strengthened connections with their own souls and ancestors. Akan path shrine houses in the United States have grown since Nana Dinizulu began to establish them, with subsequent visits by Nana Oparebea to assist in their establishment and in the initiation and graduation of more African American *akomfo*. For detailed discussions of the establishment of Akan shrine houses in

the United States, see Nana Kwabena Brown, "North America, African Religion in," in *Encyclopedia of African Religion,* ed. Molefi Kete Asante and Ama Mazama (London: SAGE, 2008), vol. 2, 456–60; Kwasi Konadu, *The Akan Diaspora in the Americas* (New York: Oxford University Press, 2010); Nana Yao Opare Dinizulu, *The Akan Priests in America* (Long Island City, NY: Aims of Modzawe, 1974); Nana Akua Kyerewaa Opokuwaa, *The Quest for Spiritual Transformation: Introduction to Traditional Akan Religion, Rituals, and Practices* (Lincoln, NE: iUniverse, 2005); Angela T. McMillan, "Entering the Sacred Circle: A History of the Akan Spiritual Tradition in the United States, 1965–2015" (PhD diss., Howard University, 2015); Okomfo Afoah Boakyewa, "Nana Oparebea and the Akonnedi Shrine: Cultural, Religious and Global Agents" (PhD diss., Indiana University, 2014); Doris V. Bright, "The Quest to Legitimize the Akan Religion in America (Phase One): The Akonedi Shrine, Larteh, Ghana, and the Bosum Dzemawodzi" (PhD diss., the Union Graduate School, 1977); Pauline Guedj, "Diaspora: Re-Africanization," in *New Encyclopedia of Africa,* eds. John Middleton and Joseph Calder Miller (Boston: Gale, 2008); and Pauline Guedj, "The Transnationalization of the Akan Religion: Religion and Identity among the US African American Community," *Religions* 6, no. 1 (2015): 24–39.

6. Interestingly, in Albert Raboteau's significant study on religion among those enslaved in the United States, *Slave Religion,* Akan religion appears to be mentioned only twice. In the main reference, the one that is in the body of the text, Raboteau addresses the West African influences on the religious beliefs, practices, and institutions among the enslaved, noting that they bear resemblances to each other, but all of course also have distinctions and have transformed in certain ways once they started to be practiced in the United States (as all religions, everywhere, do in their dynamism). He states, "There were, and are, too many significant differences among the religions of various West African peoples, not to mention local variations within any single people, to permit putting them all into a single category. However, similar modes of perception, shared basic principles, and common patterns of ritual were widespread among different West African religions. Beneath the diversity, enough fundamental similarity did exist to allow a general description of the religious heritage of African slaves, with supplementary information concerning particular peoples, such as the Akan, Ewe, Yoruba, Ibo and others, whose influences upon the religions of Afro-Americans have long been noted. It is important to remember also that no single African culture or religion, once transplanted in alien soil, could have remained intact: it was inevitable that the slaves would build new societies in the Americas which would be structured in part from

their diverse backgrounds in different African societies, in part from the experience of enslavement in a new environment. A common religious heritage then resulted from the blending and assimilation of the many discrete religious heritages of Africans in the New World." See Albert J. Raboteau, *Slave Religion: The "Invisible Institution" in the Antebellum South* (Oxford: Oxford University Press, 2004), 7–8. For brilliant studies of the circulations and transformations of religious ideas, beliefs, and practices throughout the diaspora in all directions, see, for example, J. Lorand Matory, *Black Atlantic Religion: Tradition, Transnationalism, and Matriarchy in the Afro-Brazilian Candomblé* (Princeton, NJ: Princeton University Press, 2005); Tracey E. Hucks, *Yoruba Traditions and African American Religious Nationalism* (Albuquerque: University of New Mexico Press, 2012); Tracey E. Hucks, *Obeah, Orisa, and Religious Identity in Trinidad,* vol. 1, *Obeah: Africans in the White Colonial Imagination* (Durham, NC: Duke University Press, 2022); Andrew Apter, *Beyond Words: Discourse and Critical Agency in Africa* (Chicago: University of Chicago Press, 2007); Stephan Palmié, "Africanisms," *African Diaspora* 11 (2018): 17–34; Stephan Palmié, *The Cooking of History: How Not to Study Afro-Cuban Religion* (Chicago: University of Chicago Press, 2013); Paul Christopher Johnson, *Diaspora Conversions: Black Carib Religion and the Recovery of Africa* (Berkeley: University of California Press, 2007); Paul Christopher Johnson, "An Atlantic Genealogy of 'Spirit Possession,'" *Comparative Studies in Society and History* 53, no. 2 (2011): 393–425; Yvonne Daniel, *Dancing Wisdom: Embodied Knowledge in Haitian Vodou, Cuban Yoruba, and Bahian Candomblé* (Champaign: University of Illinois Press, 2005). For other important historical studies of African American religions and religious practices, see, for example, Albert J. Raboteau, *A Fire in the Bones: Reflections on African-American Religious History* (Boston: Beacon, 1996); Eddie S. Glaude, Jr., *Exodus!: Religion, Race, and Nation in Early Nineteenth-Century Black America* (Chicago University of Chicago Press, 2000); Albert J. Raboteau, *Canaan Land: A Religious History of African Americans* (Oxford: Oxford University Press, 2001); Milton C. Sernett, ed., *African American Religious History: A Documentary Witness* (Durham, NC: Duke University Press, 2000).

7. In no way does this use of *tradition* imply any adherence to the imperialist fiction of "traditional" versus "modern," a distinction that has always been a missionizing, colonial, and often racializing fiction that is rampant in the history of anthropology (and elsewhere). I use *traditional religion* or *spirituality* here only because that is how the practitioners who are my interlocutors refer to it, and they have asked that I follow their usage. It is a shorthand for distinguishing from other forms of religion common in Ghana and elsewhere in Africa, such as Christianity and Islam. The very existence and flourishing of these

Akan path priestesses and priests, their transnational networks, and vital assemblages attest to the fact that this religion is far from being some sort of past reality that is unchanged in the present or some merely nostalgic reminiscence. Rather, Akan spirituality is absolutely contemporary, currently charged, and growing in its power and significance in the lives of those who choose the path.

8. Aisha Beliso-De Jesús, *Electric Santería: Racial and Sexual Assemblages of Transnational Religion* (New York: Columbia University Press, 2015), 156. In my deployment of copresences in this book, I draw on Akan philosophies of being, power, motion, knowledge, dreams, visions, and interrelations. See, for example, Opokuwaa, *The Quest for Spiritual Transformation*; Opokuwaa, *Akan Protocol: Remembering the Traditions of Our Ancestors* (Lincoln, NE: iUniverse, 2005); Kofi Bempah, *Akan Traditional Religion: The Truth and the Myths* (Charleston, SC: BookSurge, 2010); Konadu, *The Akan Diaspora in the Americas*; Kwasi Konadu, *Transatlantic Africa* (New York: Diasporic Africa, 2018); Kwasi Konadu, *Our Own Way in This Part of the World: Biography of an African Community, Culture, and Nation* (Durham, NC: Duke University Press, 2019); Kwame Gyekye, *An Essay on African Philosophical Thought: The Akan Conceptual Scheme,* rev. ed. (Philadelphia: Temple University Press, 1995); and Kwame Anthony Appiah, *In My Father's House: Africa in the Philosophy of Culture* (New York: Oxford University Press, 1993).

9. Beliso-De Jesús, *Electric Santería*, 158.

10. Carlota McAllister and Valentina Napolitano, "Political Theology/ Theopolitics: The Thresholds and Vulnerabilities of Sovereignty," *Annual Review of Anthropology* 50 (2021): 7.1–7.16, 7.1.; Mark Goodale and Olaf Zenker, eds., *Reckoning with Law in Excess: Mobilization, Confrontation, Refusal* (Cambridge: Cambridge University Press, 2024). See also Carlota McAllister, "No One Can Hold It Back: The Theopolitics of Water and Life in Chilean Patagonia Without Dams," *Social Analysis* 64, no. 4 (2020): 121–39; Valentina Napolitano, "On the Touch-Event: Theopolitical Encounters," *Social Analysis* 64, no. 4 (2020): 81–99; Maria José de Abreu, *The Charismatic Gymnasium: Breath, Media, and Religious Revivalism in Contemporary Brazil* (Durham, NC: Duke University Press, 2021); Maria José de Abreu, "Acts Is Acts: Tautology and Theopolitical Form," *Social Analysis* 64, no. 4 (2020): 42–59; Thomas Blom Hansen and Finn Stepputat, "Sovereignty Revisited," *Annual Review of Anthropology* 35 (2006): 295–315; and William T. Cavanaugh, *Theopolitical Imagination* (London: T&T Clark, 2002).

11. Diana Bocarejo, "Cultivating Justice Beyond Law," *PoLAR: Political and*

Legal Anthropology Review 43, no. 2 (2020): 304–18.

12. McAllister and Napolitano, in proposing theopolitics, ask us to "explore the forms of justice beyond its capture by rights and the law," and they push past many secularist assumptions about the state, sovereignty, politics, or even anthropological knowledge—assumptions, they note, that are entwined with the colonial history of the discipline of anthropology. They gesture to the often unnamed phenomena, the power of what is not said, the importance of the invisible or unknown, the shifting vitalities, and the uncertain features in theopolitical assemblages. As they put it, "theopolitics invites anthropologists to attend ethnographically to that which does not name itself and yet undeniably is by exploring the shades of sovereignty from below." See McAllister and Napolitano, "Political Theology/Theopolitics," 7.1–7.16, 109–24, 111. They also note a similarity to several other recent trends but maintain a distinction in theopolitics: "Theopolitics finds considerable overlap with other contemporary attempts to rethink the foundational concerns of anthropology, such as those attached to concepts of ontology, vitalism, or affect. Yet it differs from these moves by affirming that the forms of alterity in which these concepts are grounded may themselves be constituted by their extimacy to a sovereign that anthropology can only provisionally apprehend" (ibid., 119). These are fascinating theoretical debates that likely will continue to emerge for many years to come in anthropology and adjacent disciplines. For the purpose of this book and its interventions, I draw on both cosmopolitics and theopolitics in my theorizations, and I do not find them to be wholly at odds. The way I read cosmopolitics is that they are connected to histories—say, of what are often described as modern politics—yet also connected to something other. There is an ontological difference, but not an isolation or a disconnection or an ahistoricism. As Marisol de la Cadena puts it in *Earth Beings,* "Ethnographically inquiring both within the cosmos—the unknown and what it can articulate (Stengers 2005a)—and within 'politics as usual' (de la Cadena 2010), we may speculate that these cosmopolitical moments may propose an 'alter-politics' capable of being other than *only* modern politics. An alter-politics would, for example, be capable of alliances or adversarial relations with that which modern politics has evicted from its field. And this capacity would not require translating difference into sameness thus complicating the agreement that modern politics imposes on those it admits." See Marisol de la Cadena, *Earth Beings: Ecologies of Practice Across Andean Worlds* (Durham, NC: Duke University Press, 2015), 279. The author here is citing Isabelle Stengers, "A Cosmopolitical Proposal," in *Making Things Public: Atmospheres of Democracy,* ed. Bruno Latour

and Peter Weibel (Cambridge, MA: MIT Press, 2005), 994–1003. See also Marisol de la Cadena, "Indigenous Cosmopolitics in the Andes: Conceptual Reflections Beyond 'Politics,'" *Cultural Anthropology* 25, no. 2 (2010): 334–70; Ghassan Hage, *Alter-Politics: Critical Thought and the Globalization of the Colonial-Settler Condition* (Melbourne: Melbourne University Press, 2015). In a similar vein, I also draw much inspiration here from related work on the pluriverse. See Arturo Escobar, *Designs for the Pluriverse: Radical Interdependence, Autonomy, and the Making of Worlds* (Durham, NC: Duke University Press, 2018); Arturo Escobar, *Pluriversal Politics: The Real and the Possible* (Durham, NC: Duke University Press, 2020); and Marisol de la Cadena and Mario Blaser, eds., *A World of Many Worlds* (Durham, NC: Duke University Press, 2018).

13. Intricate interweaving of powers, knowledges, and states of consciousness are part of the fabric of what I am calling constellations of subjectivity. As such, the concept builds on recent anthropological work on dreams and copresence, as well as subjectivity and co-emergence, including anthropologies of cosmopolitics and pluriversal politics. See, for example, N. Fadeke Castor, *Spiritual Citizenship: Transnational Pathways from Black Power to Ifá in Trinidad* (Durham, NC: Duke University Press, 2017); Amira Mittermaier, *Dreams that Matter: Egyptian Landscapes of the Imagination* (Berkeley: University of California Press, 2010); Jeannette Mageo and Robin E. Sheriff, eds., *New Directions in the Anthropology of Dreaming* (New York: Routledge, 2021); de la Cadena, *Earth Beings*; Escobar, *Pluriversal Politics*; Escobar, *Designs for the Pluriverse*; de la Cadena, "Indigenous Cosmopolitics in the Andes," 334–70; de la Cadena, *Earth Beings*; de la Cadena and Blaser, eds. *A World of Many Worlds*.

14. For an illuminating study of Akan spiritualists' fact finding in a place in coastal Ghana, see Marcus L. Harvey, "Medial Deities and Relational Meanings: Tracing Elements of an Akan Grammar of Knowing," *Journal of Africana Religions* 3, no. 4 (2015): 397–441.

15. For explorations of some parallels in other countries, see, for example, Paul Christopher Johnson, "Translating Spirits: Medical-Ritual Healing and Law in Brazil and the Broader Afro-Atlantic World," *Osiris* 36 (2021): 27–45; Kate Ramsey, *The Spirits and the Law: Vodou and Power in Haiti* (Chicago: University of Chicago Press, 2011); Bocarejo, "Cultivating Justice Beyond Law," 304–18; J. Brent Crosson, *Experiments with Power: Obeah and the Remaking of Religion in Trinidad* (Chicago: University of Chicago Press, 2020).

16. For the work that centrally inspires my uses of pluriversal politics and cosmopolitics in this book, see Escobar, *Designs for the Pluriverse*; Escobar, *Pluriversal Politics*; Isabelle Stengers, "A Cosmopolitical Proposal," in *Making*

Things Public: Atmospheres of Democracy, eds. Bruno Latour and Peter Weibel (Cambridge, MA: MIT Press, 2005), 994–1003; de la Cadena, "Indigenous Cosmopolitics in the Andes," 334–70; de la Cadena, *Earth Beings*; de la Cadena and Blaser, eds. *A World of Many Worlds*. See also Lauren Coyle Rosen, "Mining Rituals in Vital Spaces: The Cosmopolitics of Gold and the Precarity of Mine Closure in Ghana," *Ethnos*, accessed March 5, 2024, https://www.tandfonline .com/doi/abs/10.1080/00141844.2023.2288535; Mareike Winchell, *After Servitude: Elusive Property and the Ethics of Kinship in Bolivia* (Oakland: University of California Press, 2022); Anya Bernstein, "More Alive Than All the Living: Sovereign Bodies and Cosmic Politics in Buddhist Siberia," *Cultural Anthropology* 27, no. 2 (2012): 261–85; Anya Bernstein, *Religious Bodies Politic: Rituals of Sovereignty in Buryat Buddhism* (Chicago: University of Chicago Press, 2013).

17. Justin Richland, *Cooperation Without Submission: Indigenous Jurisdictions in Native Nation-US Engagements* (Chicago: University of Chicago Press, 2021). These copresent jurisdictions also partake of multiple temporalities and the various erasures and partial recollections that are part and parcel of trauma and its various "chronotopes" in new "juridical creations" of victimhood and attempts at redress, as Mariane Ferme recently has theorized in the aftermath of the civil war in Sierra Leone. See Mariane Ferme, *Out of War: Violence, Trauma, and the Political Imagination in Sierra Leone* (Oakland: University of California Press, 2018).

18. Clarke, *Affective Justice*. For generative discussions of affect within recent anthropological and social theoretical works, see, for example, Aimee Meredith Cox, *Shapeshifters: Black Girls and the Choreography of Citizenship* (Durham, NC: Duke University Press, 2015); William Mazzarella, "Affect: What Is It Good for?" In *Enchantments of Modernity: Empire, Nation, Globalization*, ed. Saurabh Dube, (New York: Routledge, 2009), 291–309; Deborah A. Thomas, *Political Life in the Wake of the Plantation: Sovereignty, Witnessing, Repair* (Durham, NC: Duke University Press, 2019); and Kathleen Stewart, *Ordinary Affects* (Durham, NC: Duke University Press, 2007). As Kathleen Stewart rendered it in a concise essay, "In the state of emergence and precarity, points of aesthetic-material-social-political precision can appear as a flickering apparition, a flash of color, or they can come to bear, roughly, on bodies like a hard shard landed in a thigh muscle. The ethnography of such things has to be both nimble and patient, jumping with the unexpected event but also waiting for something to throw together. The ethnographic reals it approaches are not flat and incontrovertible but alchemical, traveling in circuits of impact and reaction. In this world things happen. Analysis trains itself on an effort to describe the iterations, durations, and modes of

being taking place." See Kathleen Stewart, "In the World that Affect Proposed," *Cultural Anthropology* 32, no. 2 (2017): 192–198, 197, https://journal.culanth.org /index.php/ca/article/view/ca32.2.03/148. Interestingly, Stewart, an anthropologist, tends to draw on and cite scholars mostly beyond the realm of anthropology, though her innovations have been deeply impactful within the discipline. In this short essay, she invokes and cites, for example, Karen Barad, "Posthumanist Performativity: Toward an Understanding of How Matter Comes to Matter," *Signs* 28, no. 3 (2003): 801–31, https://doi.org/10.1086/345321; Donna Haraway, "Anthropocene, Capitalocene, Plantationocene, Chthulucene: Making Kin," *Environmental Humanities* 6, no. 1: 159–65, https://doi.org/10.1215/22011919–3615934; Graham Harman, *Weird Realism: Lovecraft and Philosophy* (Alresford: Zero Books, 2012); Erin Manning, *Relationscapes: Movement, Art, Philosophy* (Cambridge, MA: MIT Press, 2009); Erin Manning and Brian Massumi, *Thought in the Act: Passages in the Ecology of Experience* (Minneapolis: University of Minnesota Press, 2014); and Eve Kosofsky Sedgwick, "Paranoid Reading and Reparative Reading: Or, You're So Paranoid, You Probably Think This Introduction Is about You," in *Novel Gazing: Queer Readings in Fiction,* ed. Eve Kosofsky Sedgwick (Durham, NC: Duke University Press), 1–40.

19. Goodale and Zenker, eds., *Reckoning with Law in Excess*. See also Charles Piot, *Nostalgia for the Future: West Africa After the Cold War* (Chicago: University of Chicago Press, 2010).

20. See, for example, Aisha Beliso-de Jesús, "Santería Copresence and the Making of African Diaspora Bodies," *Cultural Anthropology* 29, no. 3 (2014): 503–26; Beliso-de Jesús, *Electric Santería*; N. Fadeke Castor, "Shifting Multicultural Citizenship: Trinidad Orisha Opens the Road," *Cultural Anthropology* 28, no. 3 (2013): 475–89; Castor, *Spiritual Citizenship*; Kamari Maxine Clarke, *Mapping Yoruba Networks: Power and Agency in the Making of Transnational Communities* (Durham, NC: Duke University Press, 2004); Clarke, *Affective Justice*; de la Cadena, "Indigenous Cosmopolitics in the Andes," 334–70; de la Cadena, *Earth Beings*; Tracey E. Hucks, "'I Smoothed the Way, I Opened Doors': Women in the Yoruba-Orisha Tradition of Trinidad," in *Women and Religion in the African Diaspora: Knowledge, Power, and Performance,* eds. R. Marie Griffith and Barbara Dianne Savage (Baltimore: Johns Hopkins University Press, 2006), 48–71; Hucks, *Yoruba Traditions and African American Religious Nationalism*; Hucks, *Obeah, Orisa, and Religious Identity in Trinidad*.

21. In these formulations and understandings, I draw on theorizations of rhizomic, nonlinear, affective assemblages of power and worlds within anthropology and philosophy. See, for example, Gilles Deleuze and Felix

Guattari, *A Thousand Plateaus: Capitalism and Schizophrenia,* trans. Brian Massumi (1980; Minneapolis: University of Minnesota Press, 1987); Clarke, *Affective Justice*; Mark Goodale, *A Revolution in Fragments: Traversing Scales of Justice, Ideology, and Practice in Bolivia* (Durham, NC: Duke University Press, 2019); Belisode Jesús, *Electric Santería*; Piot, *Nostalgia for the Future*; Valentina Napolitano, *Migrant Hearts and the Atlantic Return: Transnationalism and the Roman Catholic Church* (New York: Fordham University Press, 2015); Thomas, *Political Life in the Wake of the Plantation*; and Elizabeth Povinelli, *Geontologies: A Requiem to Late Liberalism* (Durham, NC: Duke University Press, 2016).

22. Crosson, *Experiments with Power,* and Castor, *Spiritual Citizenship,* 168.

23. Goodale, *A Revolution in Fragments.*

24. I interchangeably use the terms *religion* and *spirituality*. However, I use *spirituality* more often, as that is what my interlocutors do.

CHAPTER 1

1. Raboteau notes the belief among many religions in Africa (and it may be all of them, in my understanding) in one supreme creator: "Common to many African societies was belief in a High God, or Supreme Creator of the world and everything in it. It was also commonly believed that this High God, often associated with the sky, was somewhat removed from and uninvolved in the activities of men, especially so when compared with the lesser gods and ancestor-spirits who were actively and constantly concerned with the daily life of the individual and the affairs of society as a whole." See Raboteau, *Slave Religion,* 8. Here he cites Geoffrey Parrinder, *West African Religions,* 2nd rev. ed. (London: Epworth Press, 1961); John S. Mbiti, *Concepts of God in Africa* (New York: Praeger, 1970); Edwin W. Smith, ed., *African Ideas of God* (London: Edinburgh House, 1950). See also, for example, John S. Mbiti, *African Religions and Philosophy* (Oxford: Heinemann, 1999). For powerful discussions of Martin Luther King, Jr.'s "I Have a Dream Speech" and many of his other revolutionary political philosophies and movements, see, for example, Tommie Shelby and Brandon M. Terry, eds., *To Shape a New World: Essays on the Political Philosophy of Martin Luther King, Jr.* (Cambridge, MA: Harvard University Press, 2018).

2. For illuminating discussions of Nyame's attributes, see Gyekye, *An Essay on African Philosophical Thought*; J. B. Danquah, *The Akan Doctrine of God: A Fragment of Gold Coast Ethics and Religion* (London: Lutterworth, 1944); Konadu, *The Akan Diaspora in the Americas*; and Opokuwaa, *The Quest for Spiritual Transformation.*

3. For brilliant discussions of these sorts of misrepresentation, misunder-

standing, and demonization of Akan and related religious and spiritual paths, see, for example, Bempah, *Akan Traditional Religion*; Ramsey, *The Spirits and the Law*; Crosson, *Experiments with Power*; Castor, *Spiritual Citizenship*; Beliso-de Jesús, *Electric Santería*; Apter, *Beyond Words*; Karen McCarthy Brown, *Mama Lola: A Vodou Priestess in Brooklyn* (Berkeley: University of California Press, 2001); Hucks, *Yoruba Traditions and African American Religious Nationalism*; Hucks, *Obeah, Orisa, and Religious Identity in Trinidad*; John S. Mbiti, *African Religions and Philosophy*. For a similar dialogue on formations of Afro-Atlantic culture and the mutually constitutive, dynamic interrelations, see J. Lorand Matory, "Afro-Atlantic Culture: On the Live Dialogue between Africa and the Americas," in *Africana: The Encyclopedia of the African and African American Experience*, ed. Kwame A. Appiah and Henry L. Gates (New York: Basic Civitas Books, 1999), 36–44; Matory, *Black Atlantic Religion*. For profound work that explores and theorizes the shifting interrelations of politics, spirituality, embodiment, and nationhood in the Democratic Republic of Congo, see Yolanda Covington-Ward, *Gesture and Power: Religion, Nationalism, and Everyday Performance in Congo* (Durham, NC: Duke University Press, 2016). For the case of Nigeria, see Ebenezer Obadare, *Pentecostal Republic: Religion and the Struggle for State Power in Nigeria* (London: Zed, 2018); Ruth Marshall, *Political Spiritualities: The Pentecostal Revolution in Nigeria* (Chicago: University of Chicago Press, 2009).

4. For very clear discussions of Nyame, see, for example, Gyekye, *An Essay on African Philosophical Thought*; Bempah, *Akan Traditional Religion*; Peter Kwasi Sarpong, *The Sacred Stools of the Akan* (Accra: Ghana Publishing Corporation, 1971); Peter Kwasi Sarpong, *Libation* (Accra: Anansesem, 1996); Anthony Ephirim-Donkor, *African Spirituality: On Becoming Ancestors* (Lanham, MD: University Press of America, 2011); Konadu, *Our Own Way in This Part of the World*. For related discussions, see also, for example, Madeline Manoukian, *Akan and Ga-Adangme Peoples of the Gold Coast* (London: Oxford University Press, 1950).

5. For extensive discussions of Bosum Dzemawodzi and Nana Yao Opare Dinizulu I's work in traditional African spirituality in the United States, see, for example, Nana Kwabena Brown, "North America, African Religion in"; Konadu, *The Akan Diaspora in the Americas*; Dinizulu, *The Akan Priests in America*; Opokuwaa, *The Quest for Spiritual Transformation*; McMillan, "Entering the Sacred Circle"; Boakyewa, "Nana Oparebea and the Akonnedi Shrine"; Bright, "The Quest to Legitimize the Akan Religion in America (Phase One)."

6. See, for example, discussions in Sam K. Akesson, "The Akan Concept of the Soul," *African Affairs* 64, no. 257 (1965): 280–91. This epistemology of life force running through the so-called object world is akin to many newer anthro-

pological works on alterity and multiple ontologies. See, for example, de la Cadena, *Earth Beings*; Escobar, *Pluriversal Politics*; Povinelli, *Geontologies*; and Carlo Severi, *Capturing Imagination: A Proposal for an Anthropology of Thought*, trans. Catherine V. Howard, Matthew Carey, Eric Bye, Ramon Fonkoue, and Joyce Suechun Cheng (Chicago: HAU Books, 2018). This notion of ritual objects charged with *sasa*—and with more specific spiritual energies of the *Abosom* and ancestors—is a more direct and literal concept of vital matter than that which is found in much fascinating new materialism and neo-vitalist social theory, such as Jane Bennett's works: *The Enchantment of Modern Life: Attachments, Crossings, and Ethics* (Princeton, NJ: Princeton University Press, 2016) and *Vibrant Matter: A Political Ecology of Things* (Durham, NC: Duke University Press, 2010).

7. Some forms of spiritual, ethical, and moral offenses are so serious that they are classified in Akan as *musuo*, harms that afflict the soul. In his remarkable new book, Ato Quayson has drawn a powerful analogy between this class of offenses and "the category of impediments to ethical choice in Aristotle's formulation of impediments to *eudaimonia*." See *Tragedy and Postcolonial Literature* (Cambridge: Cambridge University Press, 2021), 10. In his analogy, Quayson also draws on Kwame Gyekye's definition: "Kwame Gyekye has defined *musuo* in terms of 'extraordinary moral evils' akin to social taboos and he lists under them 'suicide, incest, having sexual intercourse in the bush, rape, murder, stealing things dedicated to the deities or ancestral spirits, etc.' All the transgressions Gyekye names fall squarely under the rubric of cultural taboos among the Akan, and his interests are in their socially oriented character rather than in the harmful effects they may have on the individual. Deep harms that impact directly on individuals must also fall under *musuo*, however, since it is an umbrella category in his description." See ibid., 10, citing Gyekye, *An Essay on African Philosophical Thought*, 131–33.

8. Lauren Coyle Rosen, *Fires of Gold: Law, Spirit, and Sacrificial Labor in Ghana* (Oakland: University of California Press, 2020).

9. Rosalind Morris, "The Ancestors Call from the Future: Genealogy, Ancestrality, Judgment," *Comparative Literature Studies* 60, no. 1 (2023): 31–72.

10. Clarke, *Affective Justice*.

CHAPTER 2

1. Okomfo Kwabena Duku cofounded a Caribbean jazz band that began in the 1980s on the campus of an HCBU (historically Black campus or university).

2. Coyle Rosen, *Fires of Gold*.

3. For rich discussions of Tano and other Abosom or divine spirits currently prominent in Southern Ghana and the diaspora, see, for example, Konadu, *The Akan Diaspora in the Americas*; Opokuwaa, *The Quest for Spiritual Transformation*; McMillan, "Entering the Sacred Circle"; Konadu, *Transatlantic Africa*; Konadu, *Our Own Way in This Part of the World*. For extensive discussions of Akan philosophies of being, time, and movement, see, for example, Gyekye, *An Essay on African Philosophical Thought*; Appiah, *In My Father's House*.

CHAPTER 3

1. For rich, illuminating anthropological and historical works on Ifá, Vodou, Santería, Candomblé, and other religions that have emerged from within African traditional religious practices in the Americas, in Africa, and elsewhere, see, for example, Ramsey, *The Spirits and the Law*; Castor, *Spiritual Citizenship*; Crosson, *Experiments with Power*; Brown, "North American, African Religion in"; Konadu, *The Akan Diaspora in the Americas*; Jacob K. Olupona, *The City of 201 Gods: Ile-Ife (Nigeria) in Time, Space and the Imagination* (Berkeley: University of California Press, 2011); Elizabeth Peréz, *Religion in the Kitchen: Cooking, Talking, and the Making of Black Atlantic Traditions* (New York: NYU Press, 2016); Palmié, "Africanisms"; Laurent Dubois, "The Citizen's Trance: The Haitian Revolution and the Motor of History," in *Magic and Modernity: Interfaces of Revelation and Concealment,* eds. Birgit Meyer and Peter Pels (Stanford, CA: Stanford University Press, 2003), 103–28; Beliso-de Jesús, *Electric Santería*; Brown, *Mama Lola*; Andrew Apter, "On African Origins: Creolization and *Connaissance* in Haitian Vodou," *American Ethnologist* 29, no. 2 (2002): 233–60; Andrew Apter, "Recasting Ifá: Historicity and Recursive Recollection in Ifá Divination Texts," in *Ifá Divination, Knowledge, Power, and Performance,* eds. Jacob K. Olupona and Rowland O. Abiodun (Bloomington: Indiana University Press, 2016), 43–49; Elina Inkeri Hartikainen, "Candomblé and the Academic's Tools: Religious Expertise and the Binds of Recognition in Brazil," *American Anthropologist* 121, no. 4 (2019): 815–29; Paul Christopher Johnson, *Secrets, Gossip, and Gods: The Transformation of Brazilian Candomblé* (Oxford: Oxford University Press, 2005); Paul Christopher Johnson, "Spirits and Things in the Making of the Afro-Atlantic World," in *Spirited Things: The Work of "Possession" in Afro-Atlantic Religions,* ed. Paul Christopher Johnson (Chicago: University of Chicago Press, 2014), 1–22; Stefania Capone Laffitte, *Searching for Africa in Brazil: Power and Tradition in Candomblé* (Durham, NC: Duke University Press, 2010). For an insightful piece on the fragmentary nature of narratives and anthropologies of

diasporas, see David Scott, "That Event, This Memory: Notes on the Anthropology of African Diasporas in the New World," *Diaspora* 1, no. 3 (1991): 261–84.

2. The preparation of food for religious ceremonies, in particular, often generates deep and multilayered affective charges, linking intensely personal experiences and archives of memory to broader collective memories and affective registers. For fascinating studies of these and related phenomena, see, for example, Peréz, *Religion in the Kitchen*; Napolitano, *Migrant Hearts and the Atlantic Return*; Crosson, *Experiments with Power*; Castor, *Spiritual Citizenship*; Palmié, *The Cooking of History*; and Sidney Mintz, *Sweetness and Power: The Place of Sugar in Modern History* (New York: Penguin, 1986).

3. In my use of "affective archives," I draw on work by Deborah Thomas, for whom affective archives are a central part of her Witnessing 2.0 project: "By focusing on the extent to which one recognizes the various ways we are implicated in the processes we address, Witnessing 2.0 both produces intimacies through the development of affective archives and reveals the ways we maintain the conjunctures of power within which we live." See Thomas, *Political Life in the Wake of the Plantation*, Kindle loc. 197. For other deep and illuminating studies on affect, affective registers, and affective embodiments, see, for, example, Clarke, *Affective Justice*; Stewart, *Ordinary Affects*; and de Abreu, *The Charismatic Gymnasium*.

4. Five is a pseudonym, used at his request.

CHAPTER 4

1. For powerful discussions of the revolts and their aftermaths, as well as their political, social, and spiritual dimensions, see Vincent Brown, *The Reaper's Garden: Death and Power in the World of Atlantic Slavery* (Cambridge, MA: Harvard University Press, 2008); Vincent Brown, *Tacky's Revolt: The Story of an Atlantic Slave War* (Cambridge, MA: Harvard University Press, 2020). For broader related discussions, see Zora Neale Hurston, *Tell My Horse: Voodoo and Life in Haiti and Jamaica* (1938; repr., New York: HarperCollins, 2008); Deborah A. Thomas, *Exceptional Violence: Embodied Citizenship in Transnational Jamaica* (Durham, NC: Duke University Press, 2011); Deborah A. Thomas, *Political Life in the Wake of the Plantation: Sovereignty, Witnessing, Repair* (Durham, NC: Duke University Press, 2019); and Deborah A. Thomas, "Time and the Otherwise: Plantations, Garrisons, and Being Human in the Caribbean," *Anthropological Theory* 16, nos. 2–3 (2016): 177–200. For other revelatory discussions of the strik-

ing silence on these and related revolts in many Eurocentric historical narratives, see, for example, Michel-Rolph Trouillot, *Silencing the Past: Power and the Production of History* (Boston: Beacon Press, 1995).

2. This conference, which I helped to organize, in collaboration with Okomfohema Botwe I, Nana Atei, and Osofo Yaw, featured priestesses and priests from the Akan sacred path who are based in the United States. It was titled "The Powers of African Spirituality in Global Consciousness: Light, Vision, and Truth" and was held in October 2019 on Princeton University's campus.

3. For partial collections of some Akan proverbs and parables, see, for example, Kwasi Konadu, *Transatlantic Africa* (New York: Diasporic Africa, 2018); Konadu, *Our Own Way in This Part of the World*; Konadu, *The Akan Diaspora in the Americas*; R. Sutherland Rattray, trans., *Ashanti Proverbs* (Oxford: Clarendon Press, 1916); Quayson, *Tragedy and Postcolonial Literature*; Johannes G. Platvoet, "*Nyame Ne Aberewa:* Towards a History of Akan Notions of 'God,'" *Ghana Bulletin of Theology* 4 (December 2012): 41–68; Opokuwaa, *Akan Protocol*; Opokuwaa, *The Quest for Spiritual Transformation*; Kofi A. Opoku, *West African Traditional Religion* (Accra: FEP, 1978) and Eva L. R. Meyerowitz, *The Sacred State of the Akan* (London: Faber and Faber, 1953). For important critiques of the colonial entanglements and other problems in the work of Rattray, see, for example, Theodore H. von Laue, "Anthropology and Power: R.S. Rattray Among the Ashanti," *African Affairs* 75, no. 298 (1976): 33–54.

CHAPTER 5

1. Travel to Ghana is very expensive and time-consuming for many shrine community members who live in the United States and elsewhere. Virtual openings may well thrive for years into the future, and it was an important matter for the elders and spirits to have blessed them. Traditionally, the Nana Asuo Gyebi festival, for example, has not been open online. Now people can virtually join part of the end of the Nana Asuo Gyebi festival for a modest registration fee or donation, enjoying talks, music, dancing, sacred songs, and interactions with the spiritualists online.

2. The book referenced may be one of several: R. Sutherland Rattray, *Ashanti* (Oxford: Clarendon Press, 1923); R. Sutherland Rattray, *Religion and Art in Ashanti* (Oxford: Clarendon Press, 1927); or R. Sutherland Rattray, *Ashanti Law and Constitution* (Oxford: Clarendon Press, 1929). See also R. Sutherland Rattray, trans. *Ashanti Proverbs*; R. Sutherland Rattray, *Akan-Ashanti Folk-Tales*

(Oxford: Clarendon Press, 1930); and R. Sutherland Rattray, *The Golden Stool of Ashanti: A Sacred Shrine Regarded as a Symbol of the Nation's Soul, and Never Lost or Surrendered, Its True History, a Romance of African Colonial Administration* (London: Illustrated London News, 1935). More generally, see Donald I. Ray, "Divided Sovereign: Traditional Authority and the State in Ghana," *Journal of Legal Pluralism and Unofficial Law* 28 (1996): 181–202; Theodore H. von Laue, "Anthropology and Power: R.S. Rattray Among the Ashanti"; Richard Rathbone, *Nkrumah and the Chiefs: The Politics of Chieftaincy in Ghana, 1951–1960* (Athens: Ohio University Press, 2000); Terence Ranger, "Invention of Tradition in Colonial Africa," in *The Invention of Tradition,* eds. Eric Hobsbawm and Terence Ranger (New York: Cambridge University Press, 1983), 211–62; Edwin W. Smith, "Religious Beliefs of the Akan," *Africa: Journal of the International African Institute* 15, no. 1 (1945): 23–29; Victoria B. Tashjian and Jean Allman, *"I Will Not Eat Stone": A Women's History of Colonial Asante* (Portsmouth, NH: Heinemann, 2000); Ivor Wilks, *Forests of Gold: Essays on the Akan and the Kingdom of Asante* (Athens: Ohio University Press, 1993); and Thomas C. McCaskie, *"Akwantemfi*—'In Mid Journey': An Asante Shrine Today and Its Clients," *Journal of Religion in Africa* 38, no. 1 (2008): 57–80.

3. For rich and extensive discussions, see Bempah, *Akan Traditional Religion;* Sarpong, *The Sacred Stools of the Akan;* Sarpong, *Libation;* Ephirim-Donkor, *African Spirituality;* Konadu, *Our Own Way in This Part of the World;* and Konadu, *The Akan Diaspora in the Americas.*

4. For revelatory work on these dimensions, see, for example, Piot, *Nostalgia for the Future;* Afe Adogame, ed. *The Public Face of African New Religious Movements in Diaspora: Imagining the Religious "Other"* (Farnham: Ashgate, 2014); Afe Adogame, Roswith Gerloff, and Klaus Hock, eds. *Christianity in Africa and the African Diaspora: The Appropriation of a Scattered Heritage* (New York: Continuum, 2008); Jesse Weaver Shipley, "Comedians, Pastors, and the Miraculous Agency of Charisma in Ghana," *Cultural Anthropology* 24, no. 3 (2009): 523–52; Birgit Meyer, "Commodities and the Power of Prayer: Pentecostalist Attitudes Towards Consumption in Contemporary Ghana," in *Globalization and Identity: Dialectics of Flow and Closure,* ed. Birgit Meyer and Peter Geschiere (Oxford: Oxford University Press, 1999), 151–76; Birgit Meyer, "The Power of Money: Politics, Occult Force, and Pentecostalism in Ghana," *African Studies Review* 41, no. 3 (1998): 15–37; and Bruno Reinhardt, "Atmospheric Presence: Reflections on 'Mediation' in the Anthropology of Religion and Technology," *Anthropological Quarterly* 93, no. 1 (2020): 1523–53.

CHAPTER 6

1. During this conversation, an interpreter helped us with translation between Nana Afoah Baakang's words, from her dialect of Twi, and our English, as was necessary.

CHAPTER 7

1. For recent coverage, see Dana Canedy, "Woman Who Accused Emmett Till Says She Didn't Want Him Dead in Memoir," *The Guardian,* July 14, 2022, https://www.theguardian.com/us-news/2022/jul/14/emmett-till-accuser-harm-memoir. For fuller accounts of the murder, see Devery S. Anderson, *Emmett Till: The Murder that Shocked the World and Propelled the Civil Rights Movement* (Jackson: University Press of Mississippi, 2015); Elliott J. Gorn, *Let the People See: The Story of Emmett Till* (Oxford: Oxford University Press, 2018); Timothy B. Tyson, *The Blood of Emmett Till* (New York: Simon & Schuster, 2017); and Dave Tell, *Remembering Emmett Till* (Chicago: University of Chicago Press, 2019).

2. For deep discussions of the film and its broader cultural and spiritual resonances, see, for example, Mark A. Reid, *Black Lenses, Black Voices: African American Film Now* (New York: Rowman & Littlefield, 2005); and Allyson Nadia Field, "To Journey Imperfectly: Black Cinema Aesthetics and the Filmic Language of *Sankofa*," *Framework* 55, no. 2 (2014): 171–90.

3. Reid, *Black Lenses, Black Voices,* 112.

CONCLUSION

1. McAllister and Napolitano, "Political Theology/Theopolitics," 7.1–7.16, 7.1.

2. Goodale and Zenker, eds., *Reckoning with Law in Excess.*

BIBLIOGRAPHY

Aborampa, Osei-Mensah. "Women's Roles in the Mourning Rituals of the Akan of Ghana." *Ethnology* 38, no. 3 (1999): 257–71.

Aderibigbe, Ibigbolade S., and Toyin Falola, eds. *The Palgrave Handbook of African Traditional Religion.* Cham: Palgrave Macmillan, 2022.

Adjaye, Jospeh K. *Boundaries of Self and Other in Ghanaian Popular Culture.* Westport, CT: Praeger, 2004.

Adogame, Afe, ed. *The Public Face of African New Religious Movements in Diaspora: Imagining the Religious "Other."* Farnham: Ashgate, 2014.

Adogame, Afe, Roswith Gerloff, and Klaus Hock, eds. *Christianity in Africa and the African Diaspora: The Appropriation of a Scattered Heritage.* New York: Continuum, 2008.

Agamben, Giorgio. *The Sacrament of Language: An Archaeology of the Oath (Homo Sacer II, 3).* Translated by Adam Kotsko. Stanford, CA: Stanford University Press, 2008.

Agrama, Hussein Ali. *Questioning Secularism: Islam, Sovereignty, and the Rule of Law in Egypt.* Chicago: University of Chicago Press, 2012.

Ahlman, Jeffrey. *Living with Nkrumahism: Nation, State, and Pan-Africanism in Ghana.* Athens: Ohio University Press, 2017.

Akesson, Sam K. "The Akan Concept of the Soul." *African Affairs* 64, no. 257 (1965): 280–91.

———. "The Secret of Akom: I." *African Affairs* 49, no. 196 (1950): 237–46.

———. "The Secret of Akom: II." *African Affairs* 49, no. 197 (1950): 325–33.

Akinyela, Makungu M. "Battling the Serpent: Nat Turner, Africanized Christianity, and a Black Ethos." *Journal of Black Studies* 33, no. 3 (2003): 255–80.

Akyeampong, Emmanuel. "*Ahenfo Nsa* (the 'Drink of Kings'): Dutch Schnapps and Ritual in Ghanaian History." In *Merchants, Missionaries, and Migrants: 300 Years of Dutch-Ghanaian Relations,* edited by Ineke van Kessel, 51–60. Karlsruhe: KIT, 2002.

———. *Drink, Power, and Cultural Change: A Social History of Alcohol in Ghana, c. 1800 to Recent Times.* Portsmouth, NH: Heinemann, 1996.

Allman, Jean, and John Parker. *Tongnaab: The History of a West African God.* Bloomington: Indiana University Press, 2005.

Amponsah, David Kofi. "Desirable Customs: A History of Indigenous Religion and the Making of Modern Ghana, c. 1800–1966." PhD diss., Harvard University, 2015.

———. "Kwame Nkrumah and the Politics of Indigenous Religion in Early Postcolonial Ghana." Paper presented at the Indigeneity, Religion, and the Public Sphere conference in Africa and the African Diaspora, Cambridge, MA, December 5–6, 2019.

Anderson, Devery S. *Emmett Till: The Murder that Shocked the World and Propelled the Civil Rights Movement.* Jackson: University Press of Mississippi, 2015.

Antwi, Eric Baffoe. "Creation in the Image of God: Human Uniqueness from the Akan Religious Anthropology to the Renewal of Christian Anthropology." PhD diss., Duquesne University, 2015.

Appiah, Kwame Anthony. *Experiments in Ethics.* Cambridge, MA: Harvard University Press, 2008.

———. *In My Father's House: Africa in the Philosophy of Culture.* New York: Oxford University Press, 1993.

Apter, Andrew. *Beyond Words: Discourse and Critical Agency in Africa.* Chicago: University of Chicago Press, 2007.

———. "History in the Dungeon: Atlantic Slavery and the Spirit of Capitalism in Cape Coast, Ghana." *American Historical Review* 122, no. 1 (2017): 23–54.

———. "On African Origins: Creolization and *Connaissance* in Haitian Vodou." *American Ethnologist* 29, no. 2 (2002): 233–60.

———. "Recasting Ifá: Historicity and Recursive Recollection in Ifá Divination Texts." In *Ifá Divination, Knowledge, Power, and Performance,* edited by Jacob K. Olupona and Rowland O. Abiodun, 43–49. Bloomington: Indiana University Press, 2016.

Apter, Andrew, and Lauren Derby, eds. *Activating the Past: History and Memory in the Black Atlantic World.* Newcastle upon Tyne: Cambridge Scholars, 2010.

Arhin, Kwame. *The Life and Work of Kwame Nkrumah.* Trenton, NJ: Africa World Press, 1993.

———. *The Political Systems of Ghana: Background to Transformations in Traditional Authority in the Colonial and Post-Colonial Periods.* Accra: Historical Society of Ghana, 2002.

———. *Political Systems of Ghana: Traditional Rule in Colonial and Postcolonial Ghana.* Accra: University of Ghana, 1994.

Assanful, Vincent. "'He Who Gives Power Takes Away Power': The Role of The *Ohemaa* in Akan Chieftancy." *Ghana Journal of Religion and Theology* 9, no. 1 (2019): 101–16.

Assimeng, Max. *Religion and Social Change in West Africa.* Accra: Woeli, 2010.

Austin, Gareth. *Labour, Land, and Capital in Ghana: From Slavery to Free Labour in Asante, 1807–1956.* Rochester, NY: University of Rochester Press, 2005.

Ayeboafo, Nana Akomfohene Korantema. *Celebrating the Life of Nana Okomfohene Akua Oparebea.* Philadelphia: StarSpirit Press, 2006.

Bachelard, Gaston. *The Poetics of Space.* Translated by Maria Jolas. 1958. Reprint, Boston: Beacon Press, 1969.

Bacigalupo, Ana Mariella. *Thunder Shaman: Making History with Mapuche Spirits in Chile and Patagonia.* Austin: University of Texas Press, 2016.

Baldwin, James. *The Fire Next Time.* 1963. Reprint, New York: Modern Library, 2021.

Barad, Karen. "Posthumanist Performativity: Toward an Understanding of How Matter Comes to Matter." *Signs* 28, no. 3 (2003): 801–31. https://doi.org/10.1086/345321.

Beliso-de Jesús, Aisha. *Electric Santería: Racial and Sexual Assemblages of Transnational Religion.* New York: Columbia University Press, 2015.

———. "Santería Copresence and the Making of African Diaspora Bodies." *Cultural Anthropology* 29, no. 3 (2014): 503–26.

Bempah, Kofi. *Akan Traditional Religion: The Truth and the Myths.* Charleston, SC: BookSurge, 2010.

Benjamin, Walter. *Illuminations: Essays and Reflections.* Edited by Hannah Arendt. Translated by Harry Zohn. New York: Schocken, 1969.

Bennett, Jane. *The Enchantment of Modern Life: Attachments, Crossings, and Ethics.* Princeton, NJ: Princeton University Press, 2016.

———. *Vibrant Matter: A Political Ecology of Things.* Durham, NC: Duke University Press, 2010.

Bernstein, Anya. "More Alive Than All the Living: Sovereign Bodies and Cosmic Politics in Buddhist Siberia." *Cultural Anthropology* 27, no. 2 (2012): 261–85.

————. *Religious Bodies Politic: Rituals of Sovereignty in Buryat Buddhism*. Chicago: University of Chicago Press, 2013.

Berry, Sara. *Chiefs Know Their Boundaries: Essays on Property, Power, and the Past in Asante, 1896–1996*. Santa Barbara, CA: ABC-CLIO, 2001.

Boahen, A. Adu. *African Perspectives on Colonialism*. Baltimore: Johns Hopkins University Press, 1987.

————. *Ghana: Evolution and Change in the Nineteenth and Twentieth Centuries*. London: Longman, 1975.

Boakyewa, Okomfo Ama. "Nana Oparebea and the Akonnedi Shrine: Cultural, Religious and Global Agents." PhD diss., Indiana University, 2014.

Bocarejo, Diana. "Cultivating Justice Beyond Law." *PoLAR: Political and Legal Anthropology Review* 43, no. 2 (2020): 304–318.

Boddy, Janice. "Spirit Possession Revisited: Beyond Instrumentality." *Annual Review of Anthropology* 23 (1994): 407–34.

Bourdieu, Pierre. *Language and Symbolic Power*. Edited by Gino Raymond and Matthew Adamson. Translated by Gino Raymond and Matthew Adamson. Cambridge: Polity Press, 1991.

Bright, Doris V. "The Quest to Legitimize the Akan Religion in America (Phase One): The Akonedi Shrine, Larteh, Ghana, and the Bosum Dzemawodzi." PhD diss., the Union Graduate School, 1977.

Brokensha, David W. *Social Change at Larteh, Ghana*. Oxford: Oxford University Press, 1966.

Brookman-Amissah, Joseph. "Akan Proverbs about Death." *Anthropos* 81, nos. 1/3 (1986): 75–85.

Brown, Karen McCarthy. *Mama Lola: A Vodou Priestess in Brooklyn*. Berkeley: University of California Press, 2001.

Brown, Nana Kwabena. "North America, African Religion in." In *Encyclopedia of African Religion*, edited by Molefi Kete Asante and Ama Mazama, 456–60. Vol. 2. London: SAGE, 2008.

Brown, Vincent. *The Reaper's Garden: Death and Power in the World of Atlantic Slavery*. Cambridge, MA: Harvard University Press, 2008.

————. *Tacky's Revolt: The Story of an Atlantic Slave War*. Cambridge, MA: Harvard University Press, 2020.

Buah, F. K. *A History of Ghana*. London: Macmillan, 1980.

Bulkeley, Kelly. "Dreaming as a Spiritual Practice." *Anthropology of Consciousness* 7, no. 2 (1996): 1–15.

Burckhardt, Titus. *Alchemy: Science of the Cosmos, Science of the Soul*. Louisville, KY: Fons Vitae, 1997.

Busia, Kofi A. *The Position of the Chief in the Modern Political System of Ashanti.* Oxford: Oxford University Press, 1951.

Butler, Judith. *The Psychic Life of Power: Theories in Subjection.* Stanford, CA: Stanford University Press, 1997.

Butticci, Annalisa. *African Pentecostals in Catholic Europe: The Politics of Presence in the Twenty-First Century.* Cambridge, MA: Harvard University Press, 2016.

Buyandelger, Manduhai. *Tragic Spirits: Shamanism, Memory, and Gender in Contemporary Mongolia.* Chicago: University of Chicago Press, 2013.

Campt, Tina. *A Black Gaze: Artists Changing How We See.* Cambridge, MA: MIT Press, 2021.

Canedy, Dana. "Woman Who Accused Emmett Till Says She Didn't Want Him Dead in Memoir." *The Guardian,* July 14, 2022. https://www.theguardian.com/us-news/2022/jul/14/emmett-till-accuser-harm-memoir.

Capone Laffitte, Stefania. *Searching for Africa in Brazil: Power and Tradition in Candomblé.* Durham, NC: Duke University Press, 2010.

Castor, N. Fadeke. "Shifting Multicultural Citizenship: Trinidad Orisha Opens the Road." *Cultural Anthropology* 28, no. 3 (2013): 475–89.

———. *Spiritual Citizenship: Transnational Pathways from Black Power to Ifá in Trinidad.* Durham, NC: Duke University Press, 2017.

Cavanaugh, William T. *Theopolitical Imagination.* London: T&T Clark, 2002.

Césaire, Aimé. *Discourse on Colonialism.* Translated by Joan Pinkham. 1955. Reprint, New York: Monthly Review Press, 2000.

———. *Notebook of a Return to My Native Land.* Edited by Mireille Rosello. Translated by Mireille Rosello and Annie Pritchard. 1947. Reprint, Hexham: Bloodaxe, 1995.

Chakrabarty, Dipesh. *Provincializing Europe: Postcolonial Thought and Historical Difference.* Princeton, NJ: Princeton University Press, 2000.

Chalfin, Brenda. *Neoliberal Frontiers: An Ethnography of Sovereignty in West Africa.* Chicago: University of Chicago Press, 2010.

Chin, Elizabeth, ed. *Katherine Dunham: Recovering an Anthropological Legacy, Choreographing Ethnographic Futures.* Santa Fe, NM: SAR Press, 2015.

Christaller, Johann Gottlieb. *A Collection of Three Thousand and Six Hundred Tshi Proverbs.* Basel: Basel Missionary Society, 1879.

Clarke, Kamari Maxine. *Affective Justice: The International Criminal Court and the Pan-Africanist Pushback.* Durham, NC: Duke University Press, 2019.

———. *Mapping Yoruba Networks: Power and Agency in the Making of Transnational Communities.* Durham, NC: Duke University Press, 2004.

Clarke, P. B. *West Africa and Christianity: A Study of Religious Development from the 15th to 20th Century.* London: Edward Arnold, 1986.

Coetzee, P. H., and A. P. J. Roux, eds. *The African Philosophy Reader.* 2nd ed. New York: Routledge, 2004.

Cole, Catherine M. *Ghana's Concert Party Theatre.* Bloomington: Indiana University Press, 2001.

Cole, Teju. *Black Paper: Writing in a Dark Time.* Chicago: University of Chicago Press, 2021.

Coleman, Simon, Rosalind I. J. Hackett, and Joel Robbins, eds. *The Anthropology of Global Pentecostalism and Evangelicalism.* New York: NYU Press, 2015.

Coleman-Tobias, Meredith F. "Audre and Africa: Reconsidering Lorde's Rites/Rights." *Journal of Interreligious Studies* 23 (2018): 68–74.

Cooper, Frederick. *Africa in the World: Capitalism, Empire, Nation-State.* Cambridge, MA: Harvard University Press, 2014.

Covington-Ward, Yolanda. *Gesture and Power: Religion, Nationalism, and Everyday Performance in Congo.* Durham, NC: Duke University Press, 2016.

Cox, Aimee Meredith. "The Body and the City Project: Young Black Women Making Space, Community, and Love in Newark, New Jersey." *Feminist Formations* 26, no. 3 (2014): 1–28.

———. "In the Dunham Way: Sewing (Sowing) the Seams of Dance, Anthropology, and Youth Arts Activism." In *Katherine Dunham: Recovering an Anthropological Legacy, Choreographing Ethnographic Futures,* edited by Elizabeth Chin, 127–144. Santa Fe, NM: SAR Press, 2015.

———. *Shapeshifters: Black Girls and the Choreography of Citizenship.* Durham, NC: Duke University Press, 2015.

Coyle Rosen, Lauren. *At the Altar of the Winds.* Washington, DC: Seven Lighthouses, 2023.

———. "The Birth of the Labor Bureau: Surveillance, Pacification, and the Statistical Objectivity Metanarrative." *Rethinking Marxism* 22 (2010): 544–68.

———. "Composer Hannibal Lokumbe on the Illusions of Time and John Coltrane's Visionary Sheets of Sound." *The Spiritual Muses,* 2024. https://www.thespiritualmuses.com/blogs/composer-and-musician-hannibal-lokumbe-on-the-illusions-of-time-and-john-coltranes-visionary-sheets-of-sound.

———. "Copresent Jurisdictions: Spirits, Theopolitics, and the Rise of Akan Spirituality in the United States." *PoLAR: Political and Legal Anthropology Review* 47, no. 1 (2024): 76–87. https://anthrosource.onlinelibrary.wiley.com/doi/10.1111/plar.12568.

———. "Fallen Chiefs and Sacrificial Mining in Ghana." In *The Politics of Custom: Chiefs, Capital, and Culture in Contemporary Africa*, eds. John L. Comaroff and Jean Comaroff, 247–278. Chicago: University of Chicago Press, 2018.

———. *Fires of Gold: Law, Spirit, and Sacrificial Labor in Ghana.* Oakland: University of California Press, 2020.

———. "Mining Rituals in Vital Spaces: The Cosmopolitics of Gold and the Precarity of Mine Closure in Ghana." *Ethnos: Journal of Anthropology* (2023). Accessed March 5, 2024. https://www.tandfonline.com/doi/abs/10.1080/001 41844.2023.2288535.

———. *Seven Tones of Time.* Washington, DC: Seven Lighthouses, 2023.

———. *Sky Ensouled.* Washington, DC: Seven Lighthouses, 2023.

———. *Solarium.* Washington, DC: Seven Lighthouses, 2024.

———. "The Spiritless Rose in the Cross of the Present: Retracing Hegel in Adorno's *Negative Dialectics* and Related Lectures." *Telos* 155 (2011): 39–61.

———. *Storms of Silent Wings.* Washington, DC: Seven Lighthouses, 2023.

———. "Tender Is the Mine: Law, Shadow Rule, and the Public Gaze in Ghana." In *Corporate Social Responsibility? Human Rights in the New Global Economy*, edited by Charlotte Walker-Said and John Kelly, 297–317. Chicago: University of Chicago Press, 2015.

———. *A Thousand Lit Streams.* Washington, DC: Seven Lighthouses, 2023.

———. *Veils of Apollo.* Washington, DC: Seven Lighthouses, 2024.

Coyle Rosen, Lauren, and J. Brent Crosson. "Conversation on *Fires of Gold*," *Religiology* (2021). https://sites.utexas.edu/religiology/2021/02/24/conversation-with-lauren-coyle-rosen/.

Coyle Rosen, Lauren, and Hannibal Lokumbe. *Hannibal Lokumbe: Spiritual Soundscapes of Music, Life, and Liberation.* New York: Columbia University Press, 2024.

Coyle Rosen, Lauren, Nate Ela, and Zinaida Miller. "Introduction: Reveling in Resistance, Imagining Reconstruction," *Unbound: Harvard Journal of the Legal Left* 3 (2007): i–v.

Coyle Rosen, Lauren, and Princeton University Humanities Council. "Retrospective Reads: *Fires of Gold*" (2021). https://humanities.princeton.edu/2021/04 /01/retrospective-reads-fires-of-gold-by-lauren-coyle-rosen/. Last accessed March 5, 2024.

Crapanzano, Vincent. *Imaginative Horizons: An Essay in Literary-Philosophical Anthropology.* Chicago: University of Chicago Press, 2010.

Crosson, J. Brent. *Experiments with Power: Obeah and the Remaking of Religion in Trinidad.* Chicago: University of Chicago Press, 2020.

Csordas, Thomas J. *Body/Meaning/Healing.* New York: Palgrave Macmillan, 2002.

———. "Introduction: Modalities of Transnational Transcendence." In *Transnational Transcendence: Essays on Religion and Globalization,* edited by Thomas J. Csordas, 1–30. Berkeley: University of California Press, 2009.

Daniel, Yvonne. *Dancing Wisdom: Embodied Knowledge in Haitian Vodou, Cuban Yoruba, and Bahian Candomblé.* Champaign: University of Illinois Press, 2005.

Danquah, J. B., ed. *The Akan Doctrine of God: A Fragment of Gold Coast Ethics and Religion.* London: Lutterworth, 1944.

———. *Cases in Akan Law.* London: G. Routledge & Sons, 1928.

Das, Joanna Dee. *Katherine Dunham: Dance and the African Diaspora.* New York: Oxford University Press, 2017.

Davidson, Basil. *Black Star: A View of the Life and Times of Kwame Nkrumah.* 1973. Reprint, Oxford: James Currey, 2007.

Davis, Angela Y. *Women, Race, & Class.* New York: Knopf Doubleday, 2011.

Dawdy, Shannon Lee. *American Afterlives: Reinventing Death in the Twenty-First Century.* Princeton, NJ: Princeton University Press, 2021.

De Boeck, Filip, and Marie-Françoise Plissart. *Kinshasa: Tales of the Invisible City.* Leuven: Leuven University Press, 2014.

de la Cadena, Marisol. *Earth Beings: Ecologies of Practice Across Andean Worlds.* Durham, NC: Duke University Press, 2015.

———. "Indigenous Cosmopolitics in the Andes: Conceptual Reflections Beyond 'Politics.'" *Cultural Anthropology* 25, no. 2 (2010): 334–70.

de la Cadena, Marisol, and Mario Blaser, eds. *A World of Many Worlds.* Durham, NC: Duke University Press, 2018.

Deleuze, Gilles, and Felix Guattari. *A Thousand Plateaus: Capitalism and Schizophrenia.* Translated by Brian Massumi. Minneapolis: University of Minnesota Press, 1987.

Deren, Maya. *Divine Horsemen: The Living Gods of Haiti.* Kingston, NY: McPherson, 1983.

Despret, Vinciane. *Our Grateful Dead: Stories of Those Left Behind.* Translated by Stephen Muecke. Minneapolis: University of Minnesota Press, 2021.

Di Franco, Ani, and Lauren Coyle Rosen. *The Spirit of Ani: Reflections on Spirituality, Feminism, Music, and Freedom.* Forthcoming. Full manuscript on file with authors.

Dickson, Kwamina B. *A Historical Geography of Ghana.* London: Cambridge University Press, 1969.

Dinizulu I, Nana Yao Opare. *The Akan Priests in America.* Long Island City, NY: Aims of Modzawe, 1974.

Drabinski, John. *Glissant and the Middle Passage: Philosophy, Beginning, Abyss.* Minneapolis: University of Minnesota Press, 2019.

Dubois, Laurent. "The Citizen's Trance: The Haitian Revolution and the Motor of History." In *Magic and Modernity: Interfaces of Revelation and Concealment,* edited by Birgit Meyer and Peter Pels, 103–28. Stanford, CA: Stanford University Press, 2003.

Du Bois, W.E.B. *Darkwater: Voices from Within the Veil.* 1920. Reprint, London: Verso. 2021.

———. "The Princess Steel." *PMLA* 130, no. 3 (2015): 819–29.

———. *The World and Africa, and Color and Democracy.* Edited by Henry Louis Gates, Jr. New York: Oxford University Press, 2007.

Dunham, Katherine. *Island Possessed.* 1969. Reprint, New York: Doubleday, 2012.

———. *Journey to Accompong.* 1946. Reprint, Whitefish, MT: Literary Licensing, 2013.

Eboyi-Anza, F.K. *The Akan Concept of Man (Nzema Case Study).* Accra: New Times, 1997.

Ebron, Paulla. *Performing Africa.* Princeton, NJ: Princeton University Press, 2009.

———. "Slavery and Transnational Memory: The Making of New Publics." In *Transnational Memory: Circulation, Articulation, Scales,* edited by Chiara De Cesari and Ann Rigney, 147–68. Boston: Walter de Gruyter, 2014.

Engelke, Matthew. *A Problem of Presence: Beyond Scripture in an African Church.* Berkeley: University of California Press, 2007.

Ephirim-Donkor, Anthony. *African Personality and Spirituality: The Role of Abosom and Human Essence.* Lanham, MD: Lexington Books, 2015.

———. *African Spirituality: On Becoming Ancestors.* Lanham, MD: University Press of America, 2011.

———. "Akom: The Ultimate Mediumship Experience Among the Akan." *Journal of the American Academy of Religion* 76 (2008): 54–81.

Escobar, Arturo. *Designs for the Pluriverse: Radical Interdependence, Autonomy, and the Making of Worlds.* Durham, NC: Duke University Press, 2018.

———. *Pluriversal Politics: The Real and the Possible.* Durham, NC: Duke University Press, 2020.

Eshun, Ekow. *Black Gold of the Sun: Searching for Home in England and Africa.* New York: Penguin Books, 2006.

Etikpah, Samuel Edukubile. "The Kundum Festival in Ghana: Ritual Interaction with the Nonhuman among the Akan." *Journal of Africana Religions* 3, no. 4 (2015): 343–96.

Evans-Anfom, E. *Traditional Medicine in Ghana: Practices, Problems, and Prospects.* Accra: J. B. Danquah Memorial Lectures, 1986.

Eze, Emmanuel Chukwudi, ed. *African Philosophy: An Anthology.* Cambridge, MA: Blackwell, 1997.

Faudree, Paja. *Singing for the Dead: The Politics of Indigenous Revival in Mexico.* Durham, NC: Duke University Press, 2013.

Fedele, Anna, and Ruy Llera Blanes, eds. *Encounters of Body and Soul in Contemporary Religious Practices: Anthropological Reflections.* New York: Berghahn, 2011.

Feeley-Harnik, Gillian. "Issues of Divine Kingship." *Annual Review of Anthropology* 14 (1985): 273–313.

Ferguson, James. *Give a Man a Fish: Reflections on the New Politics of Distribution.* Durham, NC: Duke University Press, 2015.

———. *Global Shadows: Africa in the Neoliberal World Order.* Durham, NC: Duke University Press, 2006.

Ferme, Mariane C. *Out of War: Violence, Trauma, and the Political Imagination in Sierra Leone.* Oakland: University of California Press, 2018.

———. *The Underneath of Things: Violence, History and the Everyday in Sierra Leone.* Berkeley: University of California Press, 2001.

Field, Allyson Nadia. "To Journey Imperfectly: Black Cinema Aesthetics and the Filmic Language of *Sankofa.*" *Framework* 55, no. 2 (2014): 171–190.

Fischer, Michael. *Emergent Forms of Life and the Anthropological Voice.* Durham, NC: Duke University Press, 2003.

Fisher, Robert B. *West African Religious Traditions: Focus on the Akan of Ghana.* New York: Orbis, 1998.

Fortes, Meyer. *Time and Social Structure and Other Essays.* New York: Humanities, 1970.

Foucault, Michel. *Ethics: Subjectivity and Truth.* Edited by Paul Rabinow. New York: New Press, 1997.

Frigerio, Alejandro. "Reafricanization in Secondary Religious Diasporas: Constructing a World Religion." *Civilisations* 51 (2004): 39–60.

Fuentes, Marisa J. *Dispossessed Lives: Enslaved Women, Violence, and the Archive.* Philadelphia: University of Pennsylvania Press, 2016.

Gaines, Kevin. *American Africans in Ghana: Black Expatriates and the Civil Rights Era.* Chapel Hill: University of North Carolina Press, 2006.

Galinier, Jacques, Aurore Modod Becquelin, Guy Bordin, Laurent Fontaine, Francine Fourmaux, Juliette Roullet Ponce, Piero Salzarulo, Philippe Simonnot, Michéle Therrien, and Iole Zilli. "Anthropology of the Night: Cross-Disciplinary Investigations." *Current Anthropology* 51, no. 6 (2010): 819–47.

Garrard, Timothy F. *Akan Weights and the Gold Trade.* New York: Longman, 1980.

Geertz, Clifford. "Local Knowledge: Fact and Law in Comparative Perspective." In *Local Knowledge: Further Essays in Interpretive Anthropology,* 167–234. 1983. Reprint, New York: Basic Books, 2000.

Ghana Tourism Authority. "Year of Return, Ghana 2019." Last modified October 24, 2021. https://visitghana.com/events/year-of-return-ghana-2019/.

Gilbert, Michelle. "Akan Religion." In *Encyclopedia of Religion.* https://www .encyclopedia.com/environment/encyclopedias-almanacs-transcripts-and-maps/akan-religion. Last accessed March 5, 2024.

Gilroy, Paul. *Postcolonial Melancholia.* New York: Columbia University Press, 2005.

Glaude, Jr., Eddie S. *Exodus!: Religion, Race, and Nation in Early Nineteenth-Century Black America.* Chicago: University of Chicago Press, 2000.

———. *An Uncommon Faith: A Pragmatic Approach to the Study of African American Religion.* Athens: University of Georgia Press, 2018.

Globus, Gordon G. "Some Philosophical Implications of Dream Existence." *Anthropology of Consciousness* 5, no. 3 (1994): 24–27.

Goldberg, David T. *The Racial State.* New York: Wiley-Blackwell, 2002.

Goldschmidt, Henry, and Elizabeth McAlister, eds. *Race, Nation, and Religion in the Americas.* New York: Oxford University Press, 2004.

Goodale, Mark. *A Revolution in Fragments: Traversing Scales of Justice, Ideology, and Practice in Bolivia.* Durham, NC: Duke University Press, 2019.

Goodale, Mark, and Olaf Zenker, eds., *Reckoning with Law in Excess: Mobilization, Confrontation, Refusal.* Cambridge: Cambridge University Press, 2024.

Gordon, David M. *Invisible Agents: Spirits in a Central African History.* Athens: Ohio University Press, 2012.

Gordon, Edmund T., and Mark Anderson. "The African Diaspora: Toward an Ethnography of Diasporic Identification." *Journal of American Folklore* 112, no. 445 (1999): 282–96.

Gorn, Elliott J. *Let the People See: The Story of Emmett Till.* Oxford: Oxford University Press, 2018.

Gott, Suzanne. "Native Gold, Precious Beads and the Dynamics of Concealed Power in Akan Beliefs and Practices." *Etnofoor* 25, no. 1 (2013): 48–77.

Graham, Laura R. *Performing Dreams: Discourses of Immortality among the Xavante of Central Brazil.* Austin: University of Texas Press, 1995.

Greene, Sandra. *Sacred Sites and the Colonial Encounter: A History of Meaning and Memory in Ghana.* Bloomington: Indiana University Press, 2002.

Greenhouse, Carol. "Just in Time: Temporality and the Cultural Legitimation of Law." *Yale Law Journal* 98, no. 8 (1989): 1631–51.

Guedj, Pauline. "Diaspora: Re-Africanization." In *New Encyclopedia of Africa*, edited by John Middleton and Joseph Calder Miller, 890. Vol. 2. Boston: Gale, 2007.

———. "The Transnationalization of the Akan Religion: Religion and Identity among the US African American Community." *Religions* 6, no. 1 (2015): 24–39.

Gyekye, Kwame. *An Essay on African Philosophical Thought: The Akan Conceptual Scheme*. Revised edition. Philadelphia: Temple University Press, 1995.

Hackett, Rosalind I.J. *New Media and Religious Transformations in Africa*. Bloomington: Indiana University Press, 2015.

Hage, Ghassan. *Alter-Politics: Critical Thought and the Globalization of the Colonial-Settler Condition*. Melbourne: Melbourne University Press, 2015.

Hale, Frederick. "Akan Funeral Practices in Samuel Asare Konadu's 'Ordained by the Oracle.'" *Journal for the Study of Religion* 9, no. 2 (1996): 21–40.

Hall, Stuart. *Selected Writings on Race and Difference*. Edited by Paul Gilroy and Ruth Wilson Gilmore. Durham, NC: Duke University Press, 2021.

Hansen, Thomas Blom, and Finn Stepputat. "Sovereignty Revisited." *Annual Review of Anthropology* 35 (2006): 295–315.

Haraway, Donna. "Anthropocene, Capitalocene, Plantationocene, Chthulucene: Making Kin." *Environmental Humanities* 6, no. 1 (2015): 159–65. https://www.environmentandsociety.org/mml/anthropocene-capitalocene-plantationocene-chthulucene-making-kin.

Harding, Rachel Elizabeth. "É a Senzala: Slavery, Women, and Embodied Knowledge in Afro-Brazilian Candomblé." In *Women and Religion in the African Diaspora: Knowledge, Power, and Performance*, edited by R. Marie Griffith and Barbara Dianne Savage, 26–46. Baltimore: Johns Hopkins University Press, 2006.

Harman, Graham. *Weird Realism: Lovecraft and Philosophy*. Alresford: Zero Books, 2012.

Hartikainen, Elina Inkeri. "Candomblé and the Academic's Tools: Religious Expertise and the Binds of Recognition in Brazil." *American Anthropologist* 121, no. 4 (2019): 815–29.

Hartman, Saidiya. *Lose Your Mother: A Journey Along the Atlantic Slave Route*. New York: Farrar, Straus, and Giroux, 2008.

———. *Scenes of Subjection: Terror, Slavery, and Self-Making in Nineteenth-Century America*. New York: Oxford University Press, 1997.

Harvey, David. *A Brief History of Neoliberalism*. Oxford: Oxford University Press, 2007.

Harvey, Marcus L. "From the Sacred Sound of the Conch Shell to the Cemetery Dance: Reimagining an Africana Festival Created in a Southern Appalachian City." Special issue, "Race and Religion: New Approaches to African American Religions," *Religions* 8, no. 8 (2017): 1–30.

———. "Gnostic and Epistemological Themes in African Traditional Religion." In *The Palgrave Handbook of African Traditional Religion*, 535–546. Cham: Palgrave Macmillan, 2022.

———. "'Hard Skies' and Bottomless Questions: Zora Neale Hurston's *Their Eyes Were Watching God* and Epistemological 'Opacity' in Black Religious Experience." *Journal of Africana Religions* 4, no. 2 (2016): 186–214.

———. "Medial Deities and Relational Meanings: Tracing Elements of an Akan Grammar of Knowing." *Journal of Africana Religions* 3, no. 4 (2015): 397–441.

Heo, Angie. "The Divine Touchability of Dreams." In *Sensational Religion: Sensory Cultures in Material Practice*, edited by Sally M. Promey, 435–40. New Haven, CT: Yale University Press, 2014.

Hobsbawm, Eric. "Introduction: Inventing Traditions." In *The Invention of Tradition*, edited by Eric Hobsbawm and Terence Ranger, 1–14. New York: Cambridge University Press, 1983.

Hord, Fred Lee, and Jonathan Scott Lee, eds. *I Am Because We Are: Readings in Africana Philosophy*. Amherst: University of Massachusetts Press, 2016.

Howes, David, ed. *The Varieties of Sensory Experience: A Sourcebook in the Anthropology of the Sense*. Toronto: University of Toronto Press, 1991.

Hucks, Tracey E. "'I Smoothed the Way, I Opened Doors': Women in the Yoruba-Orisha Tradition of Trinidad." In *Women and Religion in the African Diaspora: Knowledge, Power, and Performance*, edited by R. Marie Griffith and Barbara Dianne Savage, 48–71. Baltimore: Johns Hopkins University Press, 2006.

———. *Obeah, Orisa, and Religious Identity in Trinidad*. Vol. 1, *Obeah: Africans in the White Colonial Imagination*. Durham, NC: Duke University Press, 2022.

———. *Yoruba Traditions and African American Religious Nationalism*. Albuquerque: University of New Mexico Press, 2012.

Hurston, Zora Neale. *Tell My Horse: Voodoo and Life in Haiti and Jamaica*. 1938. Reprint, New York: HarperCollins, 2008.

Itzhak, Nofit. "Making Selves and Meeting Others in Neo-Shamanic Healing." *Ethos* 43, no. 3 (2015): 286–310.

Jackson, Jeanne-Marie. *The African Novel of Ideas: Philosophy and Individualism in the Age of Global Writing.* Princeton, NJ: Princeton University Press, 2021.

Jakobsen, Merete Demant. *Shamanism: Traditional and Contemporary Approaches to the Mastery of Spirits and Healing.* New York: Berghahn, 1999.

James, C. L. R. *Nkrumah and the Ghana Revolution.* Westport, CT: L. Hill, 1977.

James, William. *The Varieties of Religious Experience: A Study in Human Nature.* 1902. Reprint, Lexington, KY: Seven Treasures, 2009.

Johnson, Paul Christopher. "An Atlantic Genealogy of 'Spirit Possession.'" *Comparative Studies in Society and History* 53, no. 2 (2011): 393–425.

———. *Diaspora Conversions: Black Carib Religion and the Recovery of Africa.* Berkeley: University of California Press, 2007.

———. *Secrets, Gossip, and Gods: The Transformation of Brazilian Candomblé.* Oxford: Oxford University Press, 2005.

———. "Spirits and Things in the Making of the Afro-Atlantic World." In *Spirited Things: The Work of "Possession" in Afro-Atlantic Religions,* edited by Paul Christopher Johnson, 1–22. Chicago: University of Chicago Press, 2014.

———. "Translating Spirits: Medical-Ritual Healing and Law in Brazil and the Broader Afro-Atlantic World." *Osiris* 36 (2021): 27–45.

Johnson, Walter. *River of Dark Dreams: Slavery and Empire in the Cotton Kingdom.* Cambridge, MA: Harvard University Press, 2013.

Jones, Graham. "A Diplomacy of Dreams: Jean Rouch and Decolonization." *American Anthropologist* 107, no. 1 (2008): 118–20.

José de Abreu, Maria. "Acts Is Acts: Tautology and Theopolitical Form," *Social Analysis* 64, no. 4 (2020): 42–59.

———. *The Charismatic Gymnasium: Breath, Media, and Religious Revivalism in Contemporary Brazil.* Durham, NC: Duke University Press, 2021.

Kalu, Ogbu. *African Pentecostalism: An Introduction.* Oxford: Oxford University Press, 2008.

Keane, Webb. *Ethical Life: Its Natural and Social Histories.* Princeton, NJ: Princeton University Press, 2016.

Kelley, Robin D. G. *Freedom Dreams: The Black Radical Imagination.* Boston: Beacon Press, 2002.

Kertzer, David I. *Ritual, Politics, and Power.* New Haven, CT: Yale University Press, 1988.

King, Martin Luther, Jr. *I Have a Dream: Writings and Speeches That Changed the World, Special 75th Anniversary Edition.* San Francisco: HarperOne, 2003.

Klein, Norman A. "Toward a New Understanding of Akan Origins." *Africa* 66, no. 2 (1996): 248–73.

Klima, Alan. *Ethnography #9.* Durham, NC: Duke University Press, 2019.

Kohn, Eduardo. *How Forests Think: Toward an Anthropology Beyond the Human.* Berkeley: University of California Press, 2013.

Konadu, Kwasi. *The Akan Diaspora in the Americas.* New York: Oxford University Press, 2010.

———. "The Calendrical Factor in Akan History." *International Journal of African Historical Studies* 45, no. 2 (2012): 217–46.

———. *Our Own Way in This Part of the World: Biography of an African Community, Culture, and Nation.* Durham, NC: Duke University Press, 2019.

———. *Transatlantic Africa.* New York: Diasporic Africa, 2018.

Konadu, Kwasi, and Clifford C. Campbell, eds. *The Ghana Reader: History, Culture, Politics.* Durham, NC: Duke University Press, 2016.

Kothari, Ashish, Ariel Salleh, Arturo Escobar, Federico Demaria, and Alberto Acosta. *Pluriverse: A Post-Development Dictionary.* New Delhi: Tulika, 2019.

Krippner, Stanley. "Waking Life, Dream Life, and the Construction of Reality." *Anthropology of Consciousness* 5, no. 3 (1994): 17–24.

Opoku, John Yaw. *Spirituality and Healing: Impacts on the Akan in Ghana.* Maastricht: Shaker, 2016.

La Fontaine, Jean S. *Initiation: Ritual Drama and Secret Knowledge Across the World.* Manchester: Manchester University Press, 1986.

———. *Person and Individual: Some Anthropological Reflections.* Cambridge: Cambridge University Press, 1985.

Lambek, Michael. "Spirit Possession/Spirit Succession: Aspects of Social Continuity among Malagasy Speakers in Mayotte." *American Ethnologist* 15, no. 4 (1988): 710–31.

Lan, David. *Guns and Rain: Guerillas and Spirit Mediums in Zimbabwe.* Berkeley: University of California Press, 1985.

Langwick, Stacey. *Bodies, Politics, and African Healing: The Matter of Maladies in Tanzania.* Bloomington: Indiana University Press, 2011.

Lanternari, Vittorio. "Dreams and Visions from the Spiritual Churches of Ghana." *Paideuma* 24 (1978): 85–102.

Larsen, Kjersti. "Bodily Selves: Identity and Shared Realities Among Humans and Spirits in Zanzibar." *Journal of Religion in Africa* 44, no. 1 (2014): 5–27.

Le Breton, David. *Sensing the World: An Anthropology of the Senses.* Translated by Carmen Ruschiensky. New York: Bloomsbury Academic, 2017.

Lincoln, C. Eric, and Lawrence H. Mamiya. *The Black Church in the African American Experience.* Durham, NC: Duke University Press, 1990.

Lock, Margaret. "Cultivating the Body: Anthropology and Epistemologies of Bodily Practice and Knowledge." *Annual Review of Anthropology* 22 (1993): 133–55.

Lomnitz, Claudio. *Death and the Idea of Mexico*. New York: Zone Books, 2005.

———. *Deep Mexico, Silent Mexico: An Anthropology of Nationalism*. Minneapolis: University of Minnesota Press, 2001.

———. *Nuestra América: My Family in the Vertigo of Translation*. New York: Other Press, 2021.

———. *The Return of Comrade Ricardo Flores Magón*. New York: Zone Books, 2014.

Lugira, Aloysius Muzzanganda. *African Traditional Religion*. New York: Infobase, 2009.

Lund, Christian, ed. *Twilight Institutions: Public Authority and Local Politics in Africa*. Hoboken, NJ: Wiley-Blackwell, 2007.

Mageo, Jeannette, and Robin E. Sheriff, eds. *New Directions in the Anthropology of Dreaming*. New York: Routledge, 2021.

Mamdani, Mahmood. *Citizen and Subject: Contemporary Africa and the Legacy of Late Colonialism*. Princeton, NJ: Princeton University Press, 1996.

Manning, Erin. *Relationscapes: Movement, Art, Philosophy*. Cambridge, MA: MIT Press, 2009.

Manning, Erin, and Brian Massumi. *Thought in the Act: Passages in the Ecology of Experience*. Minneapolis: University of Minnesota Press, 2014.

Manoukian, Madeline. *Akan and Ga-Adangme Peoples of the Gold Coast*. London: Oxford University Press, 1950.

Marshall, Ruth. *Political Spiritualities: The Pentecostal Revolution in Nigeria*. Chicago: University of Chicago Press, 2009.

Masquelier, Adeline. *Prayer Has Spoiled Everything: Possession, Power, and Identity in an Islamic Town of Niger*. Durham, NC: Duke University Press, 2001.

Masuzawa, Tomoko. *The Invention of World Religions: Or, How European Universalism Was Preserved in the Language of Pluralism*. Chicago: University of Chicago Press, 2005.

Matory, J. Lorand. "Afro-Atlantic Culture: On the Live Dialogue between Africa and the Americas." In *Africana: The Encyclopedia of the African and African American Experience*, edited by Kwame A. Appiah and Henry L. Gates, 36–44. New York: Basic Civitas Books, 1999.

———. *Black Atlantic Religion: Tradition, Transnationalism, and Matriarchy in the Afro-Brazilian Candomblé*. Princeton, NJ: Princeton University Press, 2005.

Mazzarella, William. "Affect: What Is It Good for?" In *Enchantments of Modernity: Empire, Nation, Globalization*. Edited by Saurabh Dube, 291–309. New York: Routledge, 2009.

Mbiti, John S. *African Religions and Philosophy*. Oxford: Heinemann, 1999.

———. *Concepts of God in Africa*. New York: Praeger, 1970.

McAlister, Elizabeth. *Rara! Vodou, Power, and Performance in Haiti and Its Diaspora*. Berkeley: University of California Press, 2002.

McAllister, Carlota. "No One Can Hold It Back: The Theopolitics of Water and Life in Chilean Patagonia Without Dams." *Social Analysis* 64, no. 4 (2020): 121–39.

McAllister, Carlota, and Valentina Napolitano. "Political Theology/Theopolitics: The Thresholds and Vulnerabilities of Sovereignty." *Annual Review of Anthropology* 50 (2021): 7.1–7.16.

McCaskie, Thomas C. "*Akwantemfi*—'In Mid Journey': An Asante Shrine Today and Its Clients." *Journal of Religion in Africa* 38, no. 1 (2008): 57–80.

McMillan, Angela T. "Entering the Sacred Circle: A History of the Akan Spiritual Tradition in the United States, 1965–2015." PhD diss., Howard University, 2015.

Memmi, Albert. *The Colonizer and the Colonized*. 1965. Reprint, Boston: Beacon, 1995.

Meriwether, James H. *Proudly We Can Be Africans: Black Americans and Africa, 1935–1961*. Durham, NC: University of North Carolina Press, 2009.

Merleau-Ponty, Maurice. *Phenomenology of Perception*. Translated by Colin Smith. London: Routledge, 1962.

Merry, Sally Engle. *Colonizing Hawai'i: The Cultural Power of Law*. Princeton, NJ: Princeton University Press, 2000.

Meyer, Birgit. "Commodities and the Power of Prayer: Pentecostalist Attitudes Towards Consumption in Contemporary Ghana." In *Globalization and Identity: Dialectics of Flow and Closure*, 151–76, edited by Birgit Meyer and Peter Geschiere (Oxford: Oxford University Press, 1999).

———. "The Power of Money: Politics, Occult Force, and Pentecostalism in Ghana," *African Studies Review* 41, no. 3 (1998): 15–37.

———. *Translating the Devil: Religion and Modernity among the Ewe in Ghana*. Edinburgh: Edinburgh University Press for the International African Institute, 1999.

Meyerowitz, Eva L. R. "The Akan and Ghana." *Man* 57, no. 6 (1957): 83–88.

———. "Concepts of the Soul Among the Akan of the Gold Coast." *Africa* 21, no. 1 (1951): 24–31.

————. "A Note on the Origins of Ghana." *African Affairs* 51, no. 205 (1952): 319–23.

————. *The Sacred State of the Akan.* London: Faber and Faber, 1953.

Mignolo, Walter D., and Catherine E. Walsh. *On Decoloniality: Concepts, Analytics, Praxis.* Durham, NC: Duke University Press, 2018.

Mintz, Sidney. *Sweetness and Power: The Place of Sugar in Modern History.* New York: Penguin, 1986.

Mittermaier, Amira. *Dreams that Matter: Egyptian Landscapes of the Imagination.* Berkeley: University of California Press, 2010.

Morris, Rosalind. "The Ancestors Call from the Future: Genealogy, Ancestrality, Judgment." *Comparative Literature Studies* 60, no. 1 (2023): 31–72.

————. *In the Place of Origins: Modernity and Its Mediums in Northern Thailand.* Durham, NC: Duke University Press, 2000.

Morrison, Toni. Foreword to *The Harlem Book of the Dead,* by James Van Der Zee, Owen Dodson, and Camille Billops. Dobbs Ferry, NY: Morgan & Morgan, 1978.

Mudimbe, Valentin Y. *The Invention of Africa: Gnosis, Philosophy, and the Order of Knowledge.* Bloomington: Indiana University Press, 1988.

Napolitano, Valentina. *Migrant Hearts and the Atlantic Return: Transnationalism and the Roman Catholic Church.* New York: Fordham University Press, 2015.

————. "On the Touch-Event: Theopolitical Encounters." *Social Analysis* 64, no. 4 (2020): 81–99.

Nketia, J. H. *Funeral Dirges of the Akan.* Accra: Achimota, 1955.

Nkrumah, Kwame. *Africa Must Unite.* London: Heinemann, 1963.

————. *Ghana: The Autobiography of Kwame Nkrumah.* New York: International Publishers, 1957.

————. *Neo-colonialism: The Last Stage of Imperialism.* New York: International Publishers, 1965.

O'Neill, Kevin Lewis. *City of God: Christian Citizenship in Postwar Guatemala.* Berkeley: University of California Press, 2010.

Obadare, Ebenezer. *Pentecostal Republic: Religion and the Struggle for State Power in Nigeria.* London: Zed, 2018.

Oduyoye, Mercy Amba. "The African Experience of God through the Eyes of an Akan Woman." *CrossCurrents* 47, no. 4 (1997): 493–504.

Oduyoye, Modupe. "Man's Self and Its Spiritual Double." In *Traditional Religion in West Africa,* edited by E. A. Ade Adegbola, 150–69. Ibadan: Daystar, 1983.

Ogunnaike, Oludamini. "African Philosophy Reconsidered: Africa, Religion, Race, and Philosophy." *Journal of Africana Religions* 5, no. 2 (2017): 181–216.

Olaniyan, Tejumola, ed. *State and Culture in Postcolonial Africa: Enchantings.* Bloomington: Indiana University Press (2017).

Olaniyan, Tejumola, and Ato Quayson, eds. *African Literature: An Anthology of Criticism and Theory.* Malden, MA: Blackwell, 2007.

Olaniyan, Tejumola, and James H. Sweet, eds. *The African Diaspora and the Disciplines.* Bloomington: Indiana University Press, 2010.

Olupona, Jacob K., ed. *African Spirituality: Forms, Meanings, and Expressions.* New York: Crossroads, 2000.

———, ed. *African Traditional Religion in Contemporary Society.* New York: Paragon House, 1991.

———. *The City of 201 Gods: Ile-Ife (Nigeria) in Time, Space and the Imagination.* Berkeley: University of California Press, 2011.

———. "Thinking Globally About African Religion." In *The Oxford Handbook of Global Religions,* edited by Mark Juergensmeyer, 527–36. Oxford: Oxford University Press, 2006.

Opoku, Kofi A. *West African Traditional Religion.* Accra: FEP, 1978.

Opokuwaa, Nana Akua Kyerewaa. *Akan Protocol: Remembering the Traditions of Our Ancestors.* Lincoln, NE: iUniverse, 2005.

———. *The Quest for Spiritual Transformation: Introduction to Traditional Akan Religion, Rituals, and Practices.* Lincoln, NE: iUniverse, 2005.

Oredein, Oluwatomisin. "'Reminders of What Once Was': The Ethics of Mercy Amba Oduyoye." In *The Palgrave Handbook of African Social Ethics,* edited by Nimi Wariboko and Toyin Falola, 605–22. London: Palgrave Macmillan, 2020.

Ortner, Sherry. *Anthropology and Social Theory: Culture, Power, and the Acting Subject.* Durham, NC: Duke University Press, 2006.

Palmié, Stephan. "Africanisms." *African Diaspora* 11 (2018): 17–34.

———. *The Cooking of History: How Not to Study Afro-Cuban Religion.* Chicago: University of Chicago Press, 2013.

Paquette, Danielle. "Ghana to Black Americans: Come Home. We'll Help You Build a Life Here." *Washington Post,* July 4, 2020.

Parish, Jane. "Beyond Occult Economies: Akan Spirits, New York Idols, and Detroit Automobiles." *HAU: Journal of Ethnographic Theory* 5, no. 2 (2015): 101–20.

———. "The Dynamics of Witchcraft and Indigenous Shrines Among the Akan." *Africa* 69, no. 3 (1999): 426–48.

Parker, John. "Witchcraft, Anti-Witchcraft and Trans-Regional Ritual Innovation in Early Colonial Ghana: Sakrabundi and Aberewa, 1889–1910." *Journal of African History* 45, no. 3 (2004): 393–420.

Parrinder, Geoffrey. *West African Religions.* 2nd ed. London: Epworth Press, 1961.

Peréz, Elizabeth. *Religion in the Kitchen: Cooking, Talking, and the Making of Black Atlantic Traditions.* New York: NYU Press, 2016.

Perry, Imani. *South to America: A Journey Below the Mason-Dixon to Understand the Soul of a Nation.* New York: Ecco, 2022.

Pierre, Jemima. *The Predicament of Blackness: Postcolonial Ghana and the Politics of Race.* Chicago: University of Chicago Press, 2012.

Pierre, Jemima, and Jesse Weaver Shipley. "African/Diaspora History: W. E. B. Dubois and Pan-Africanism in Ghana." In *Ghana in Africa and the World: Essays in Honor of Adu Boahen,* edited by Toyin Falola, 731–53. Trenton, NJ: Africa World Press, 2003.

Piot, Charles. *Nostalgia for the Future: West Africa After the Cold War.* Chicago: University of Chicago Press, 2010.

Pitts, Jonathan M. "West African Religions Are on the Rise in Maryland as Practitioners Connect with Roots." *Washington Post,* 6 April 2019.

Platvoet, Johannes G. "Does God have a Body?: On the Materiality of Akan Spirituality." In *Unterwegs: Neue Pfade in der Religionswissnschaft/New Paths in the Study of Religions; Festschrift in Honour of Michael Pye on His 65th Birthday,* edited by Christoph Kleine, Monika Schrimpf, and Katja Triplett, 175–196. Munich: Biblion Verlag, 2004.

———. "*Nyame Ne Aberewa:* Towards a History of Akan Notions of 'God.'" *Ghana Bulletin of Theology* 4 (December 2012): 41–68.

Povinelli, Elizabeth. *Geontologies: A Requiem to Late Liberalism.* Durham, NC: Duke University Press, 2016.

Puett, Michael. "Economies of Ghosts, Gods, and Goods: The History and Anthropology of Chinese Temple Networks." In *Radical Egalitarianism: Local Realities, Global Relations,* edited by Felicity Aulino, Mirian Goheen, and Stanley S. Tambiah, 91–100. New York: Fordham University Press, 2013.

———. *To Become a God: Cosmology, Sacrifice, and Self-Divinization in Early China.* Cambridge, MA: Harvard-Yenching Institute Monograph, 2004.

Quayson, Ato. *Tragedy and Postcolonial Literature.* Cambridge: Cambridge University Press, 2021.

Raboteau, Albert J. *Canaan Land: A Religious History of African Americans.* Oxford: Oxford University Press, 2001.

———. *A Fire in the Bones: Reflections on African-American Religious History.* Boston: Beacon Press, 1996.

———. *Slave Religion: The "Invisible Institution" in the Antebellum South.* Oxford: Oxford University Press, 2004.

Ralph, Michael, and Lauren Coyle Rosen. "Resource Curse?" *Transition* 107 (2012): 151–159.

Ramsey, Kate. "Katherine Dunham and the Folklore Performance Movement in Post-US Occupation Haiti." In *Katherine Dunham: Recovering an Anthropological Legacy, Choreographing Ethnographic Futures,* edited by Elizabeth Chin, 51–72. Santa Fe, NM: SAR Press, 2015.

———. "Powers of Imagination and Legal Regimes against 'Obeah' in the Late Eighteenth- and Early Nineteenth-Century British Caribbean." *Osiris* 36 (2021): 46–63.

———. *The Spirits and the Law: Vodou and Power in Haiti.* Chicago: University of Chicago Press, 2011.

———. "Vodou, History, and New Narratives." *Transition* 111 (2013): 31–41.

Ranger, Terence. "Invention of Tradition in Colonial Africa." In *The Invention of Tradition,* edited by Eric Hobsbawm and Terence Ranger, 211–62. New York: Cambridge University Press, 1983.

Rathbone, Richard. *Nkrumah and the Chiefs: The Politics of Chieftaincy in Ghana, 1951–1960.* Athens: Ohio University Press, 2000.

Rattray, R. Sutherland. *Akan-Ashanti Folk-Tales.* Oxford: Clarendon Press, 1930.

———. *Ashanti.* Oxford: Clarendon Press, 1923.

———. *Ashanti Law and Constitution.* Oxford: Clarendon Press, 1929.

———, trans. *Ashanti Proverbs.* Oxford: Clarendon Press, 1916.

———. *The Golden Stool of Ashanti: A Sacred Shrine Regarded as a Symbol of the Nation's Soul, and Never Lost or Surrendered, Its True History, a Romance of African Colonial Administration.* London: Illustrated London News, 1935.

———. *Religion and Art in Ashanti.* Oxford: Clarendon Press, 1927.

Ray, Donald I. "Divided Sovereign: Traditional Authority and the State in Ghana." *Journal of Legal Pluralism and Unofficial Law* 28 (1996): 181–202.

Reid, Mark A. *Black Lenses, Black Voices: African American Film Now.* Lanham, MD: Rowman & Littlefield, 2005.

Reinhardt, Bruno. "Atmospheric Presence: Reflections on 'Mediation' in the Anthropology of Religion and Technology." *Anthropological Quarterly* 93, no. 1 (2020): 1523–53.

Richards, Sandra. "What Is to Be Remembered? Tourism to Ghana's Slave Castle-Dungeons." *Theatre Journal* 47, no. 4: 617–37.

Richland, Justin. *Cooperation Without Submission: Indigenous Jurisdictions in Native Nation-US Engagements*. Chicago: University of Chicago Press, 2021.

Robbins, Joel. "What Is the Matter with Transcendence? On the Place of Religion in the New Anthropology of Ethics." *Journal of the Royal Anthropological Institute* 22, no. 4 (2016): 767–81.

Roberts, Donna, and Donna Read, dirs. *Yemanjá: Wisdom from the African Heart of Brazil*. Project Zula, 2015. 53 min. https://vimeo.com/ondemand/yemanja.

Robinson, Cedric J. *On Racial Capitalism, Black Internationalism, and Cultures of Resistance*. Edited by H. L. T. Quan. London: Pluto, 2019.

Robotham, Donald Keith. "Transnationalism in the Caribbean: Formal and Informal." *American Ethnologist* 25, no. 2 (1998): 307–21.

Rodney, Walter. "African History in the Service of the Black Liberation." *Small Axe* 10 (2001): 66–80.

Romberg, Raquel. *Healing Dramas: Divination and Magic in Modern Puerto Rico*. Austin: University of Texas Press, 2009.

Rose, Gillian. *Mourning Becomes the Law: Philosophy and Representation*. Cambridge: Cambridge University Press, 1996.

Rucker, Walter C. *Gold Coast Diasporas: Identity, Culture, and Power*. Bloomington: Indiana University Press, 2015.

Sahlins, Marshall. *The New Science of the Enchanted Universe: An Anthropology of Most of Humanity*. Princeton, NJ: Princeton University Press, 2022.

Santo, Diana Espirito. "Making Dreams: Spirits, Visions, and the Ontological Effects of Dream Knowledge in Cuban Espiritismo." *Suomen Antropologi* 34, no. 3 (2009): 6–24.

Sarpong, Peter Kwasi. *Libation*. Accra: Anansesem, 1996.

———. *The Sacred Stools of the Akan*. Accra: Ghana Publishing Corporation, 1971.

Sarr, Felwine. *Afrotopia*. Translated by Drew S. Burk and Sarah Jones-Boardman. Minneapolis: University of Minnesota Press, 2020.

Savage, Barbara Dianne. *Your Spirits Walk Beside Us: The Politics of Black Religion*. Cambridge, MA: Belknap Press of Harvard University Press, 2008.

Scherz, China, George Mpanga, and Sarah Namirembe. *Higher Powers: Alcohol and After in Uganda's Capital City*. Oakland: University of California Press, 2024.

Schwartz, Peggy, and Murray Schwartz. *The Dance Claimed Me: A Biography of Pearl Primus*. New Haven, CT: Yale University Press, 2012.

Scott, David. "That Event, This Memory: Notes on the Anthropology of African Diasporas in the New World." *Diaspora* 1, no. 3 (1991): 261–84.

Sedgwick, Eve Kosofsky. "Paranoid Reading and Reparative Reading: Or, You're So Paranoid, You Probably Think This Introduction Is About You."

In *Novel Gazing: Queer Readings in Fiction,* edited by Eve Kosofsky Sedgwick, 1–40. Durham, NC: Duke University Press.

Sernett, Milton C., ed. *African American Religious History: A Documentary Witness.* Durham, NC: Duke University Press, 2000.

Severi, Carlo. *Capturing Imagination: A Proposal for an Anthropology of Thought,* translated by Catherine V. Howard, Matthew Carey, Eric Bye, Ramon Fonkoue, and Joyce Suechun Cheng. Chicago: HAU Books, 2018.

Shabazz, Mensimah. "Traditional Medicine and Healing Practices of the Akan of Ghana: Understanding Akan Spirituality, Mysticism, and Concept of Grace." PhD diss., California Institute of Integral Studies, 2018.

Sharpe, Christina. *In the Wake: On Blackness and Being.* Durham, NC: Duke University Press, 2016.

Shaw, Rosalind. *Memories of the Slave Trade: Ritual and the Historical Imagination in Sierra Leone.* Chicago: University of Chicago Press, 2002.

Shelby, Tommie, and Brandon M. Terry, eds. *To Shape a New World: Essays on the Political Philosophy of Martin Luther King, Jr.* Cambridge, MA: Harvard University Press, 2018.

Shipley, Jesse Weaver. "Comedians, Pastors, and the Miraculous Agency of Charisma in Ghana." *Cultural Anthropology* 24, no. 3 (2009): 523–52.

Shipley, Jesse Weaver, and Jemima Pierre. "The Intellectual and Pragmatic Legacy of Du Bois's Pan-Africanism in Contemporary Ghana." In *Re-Cognizing W. E. B. Du Bois in the Twenty-First Century: Essays on W. E. B. Du Bois,* edited by Mary Keller and Chester J. Fontenot, 61–87. Macon, GA: Mercer University Press, 2007.

Shumway, Rebecca. "The Fante Shrine of Nananom Mpow and the Atlantic Slave Trade in Southern Ghana." *International Journal of African Historical Studies* 44, no. 1 (2011): 27–44.

Simone, AbdouMaliq. *Improvised Lives: Rhythms of Endurance in an Urban South.* New York: Polity, 2018.

Smith, Edwin W., ed. *African Ideas of God.* London: Edinburgh House, 1950.

Smith, Edwin W. "Religious Beliefs of the Akan." *Africa: Journal of the International African Institute* 15, no. 1 (1945): 23–29.

Smith, James H. *The Eyes of the World: Mining the Digital Age in the Eastern DR Congo.* Chicago: University of Chicago Press, 2021.

Smith, James H., and Rosalind I. J. Hackett, eds. *Displacing the State: Religion and Conflict in Neoliberal Africa.* South Bend, IN: University of Notre Dame Press, 2011.

Soothill, Jane E. *Gender, Social Change, and Spiritual Power: Charismatic Christianity in Ghana*. Leiden: Brill, 2007.

Stengers, Isabelle. "A Cosmopolitical Proposal." In *Making Things Public: Atmospheres of Democracy*, edited by Bruno Latour and Peter Weibel, 994–1003. Cambridge, MA: MIT Press, 2005.

Stewart, Charles. *Dreaming and Historical Consciousness in Island Greece*. Chicago: University of Chicago Press, 2017.

Stewart, Kathleen. "In the World that Affect Proposed." *Cultural Anthropology* 32, no. 2 (2017): 192–98. https://journal.culanth.org/index.php/ca/article/view/ca32.2.03/148.

———. *Ordinary Affects*. Durham, NC: Duke University Press, 2007.

Strange, Stuart E. "The Dialogical Collective: Mediumship, Pain, and the Interactive Creation of Ndyuka Maroon Subjectivity." *Journal of the Royal Anthropological Institute* 22, no. 3 (2016): 516–33.

Sweet, James. *Domingos Álvares, African Healing, and the Intellectual History of the Atlantic World*. Chapel Hill: University of North Carolina Press, 2011.

———. *Recreating Africa: Culture, Kinship, and Religion in the African-Portuguese World, 1441–1770*. Chapel Hill: University of North Carolina Press, 2004.

Talton, Ben. *Politics of Social Change in Ghana: The Konkomba Struggle for Political Equality*. New York: Palgrave Macmillan, 2010.

Talton, Ben, and Quincy Mills, eds. *Black Subjects in Africa and Its Diasporas: Race and Gender in Research and Writing*. New York: Palgrave Macmillan, 2011.

Tashjian, Victoria B., and Jean Allman. *"I Will Not Eat Stone": A Women's History of Colonial Asante*. Portsmouth, NH: Heinemann, 2000.

Taussig, Michael. *What Color Is the Sacred?* Chicago: University of Chicago Press, 2010.

Taylor, Charles. *A Secular Age*. Cambridge, MA: Harvard University Press, 2007.

Tedlock, Barbara, ed. *Dreaming: Anthropological and Psychological Interpretations*. New York: Cambridge University Press, 1987.

Tell, Dave. *Remembering Emmett Till*. Chicago: University of Chicago Press, 2019.

Thomas, Deborah A. *Exceptional Violence: Embodied Citizenship in Transnational Jamaica*. Durham, NC: Duke University Press, 2011.

———. *Political Life in the Wake of the Plantation: Sovereignty, Witnessing, Repair*. Durham, NC: Duke University Press, 2019.

———. "Time and the Otherwise: Plantations, Garrisons, and Being Human in the Caribbean." *Anthropological Theory* 16, nos. 2–3 (2016): 177–200.

Thomas, Deborah A., and M. Kamari Clarke. "Globalization and Race: Structures of Inequality, New Sovereignties, and Citizenship in a Neoliberal Era." *Annual Review of Anthropology* 42 (2013): 305–25.

Tilley, Helen. "Traditional Medicine Goes Global: Pan-African Precedents, Cultural Decolonization, and Cold War Rights/Properties." *Osiris* 36 (2021): 132–59.

Trouillot, Michel-Rolph. *Silencing the Past: Power and the Production of History.* Boston: Beacon Press, 1995.

Trumbore, Dave. "'Black Panther': What Is the Heart-Shaped Herb and What Does It Do?" *Collider,* February 19, 2018.

Tsing, Anna L. *The Mushroom at the End of the World: On the Possibility of Life in Capitalist Ruins.* Princeton, NJ: Princeton University Press, 2015.

Ture, Kwame, and Charles V. Hamilton. *Black Power: Politics of Liberation in America.* New York: Vintage, 2011.

Turner, Victor. "Images of Anti-Temporality: An Essay in the Anthropology of Experience." *Harvard Theological Review* 75, no. 2 (1982): 243–65.

Tyson, Timothy B. *The Blood of Emmett Till.* New York: Simon & Schuster, 2017.

Vasquez, Manuel A., and Marie F. Marquardt. *Globalizing the Sacred: Religion Across the Americas.* New Brunswick, NJ: Rutgers University Press, 2003.

von Laue, Theodore H. "Anthropology and Power: R. S. Rattray Among the Ashanti." *African Affairs* 75, no. 298 (1976): 33–54.

Walker, Alice. *We Are the Ones We Have Been Waiting For: Inner Light in a Time of Darkness.* New York: New Press, 2021.

Walters, Ronald. *Pan Africanism in the African Diaspora: An Analysis of Modern Afrocentric Political Movements.* Detroit: Wayne State University Press, 1993.

Weber, Max. *The Vocation Lectures.* Edited by David Owen and Tracy Strong. Translated by Rodney Livingstone. 1919. Reprint, Indianapolis: Hackett, 2004.

Weidman, Amanda. "Anthropology and Voice." *Annual Review of Anthropology* 43 (2014): 37–51.

West, Cornel, and Christa Buschendorf. *Black Prophetic Fire.* Boston: Beacon Press, 2014.

West, Harry G. *Kupilikula: Governance and the Invisible Realm in Mozambique.* Chicago: University of Chicago Press, 2005.

Wilks, Ivor. *Forests of Gold: Essays on the Akan and the Kingdom of Asante.* Athens: Ohio University Press, 1993.

Winchell, Mareike. *After Servitude: Elusive Property and the Ethics of Kinship in Bolivia.* Oakland: University of California Press, 2022.

INDEX

Abosom (sing., Obosom; exalted divine spirits): ancestor spirits in spiritual realm of, 80; ancestor spirits utilized by, to send messages to people, 80; announcing optimal time and space for conferral of higher spiritual knowledge, 58; approval of resolutions in formal adjudication of conflicts, 113; children born interlaced with, 94; as children of God, 128; children of spiritualists as belonging to, 74–75; communicating and working amongst each other to address issues or aims, 28, 112, 144; constellations of subjectivity among, 63; definition of, 1, 16; details of problem solving not necessarily shared with spiritualists, 28–29, 41, 63–64; explaining deeper meanings of experiences, 58; fire as element, 38; free will of humans not controlled by, 70–71, 136; Ghanaian fear of and prohibitions on practice of, 135, 137; Guan and Akan people both welcomed by, 145; the hierarchy of shrine spirits, 123, 133, 140; and history of the two shrines in Larteh, 123, 133; the Holy Ghost of Christianity related to, 157; interrelation with exalted spirits from other traditions, 31, 63, 93; as jurisdiction of the spiritualists, 135; marriage blessing by, 102–104; as messengers or helpers to Nyame (God), 16, 70, 128, 157; negative perceptions and misunderstandings of, 16–17, 135, 137; *Osofo* relationship to, 106; as positive forces aligned with the laws of Light, 16–17; as protecting from spiritual attacks, 16–17, 34, 47; spiritualists as conduit for healing by, 71; surrender to the guidance of, 110–111, 113, 156; truth revealed by, 135; water as element, 38, 55, 61–62. *See also* communication with spirits; dreams; feeding the spirits; festivals; marriage, spiritual; possession by spirits; signs sent by the spirits; spatiotemporal assemblages of copresences; spiritual laws and ethical principles

Adade. *See* Nana Adade Kofi (Obosom)

affective archives of the researcher, 97,
184n3
Africa, Akan tradition spreading
within, 126
African Americans: DNA testing to
pinpoint ancestral origins, 20; and
empowerment movements of the
1960s and 1970s, 4–5, 146–147,
148–152; freedom fighters, 17–18, 37,
102, 150, 151; as identity of
interlocutors, 3; racist violence
against, 149–151; use of term, 171n1.
See also enslavement
African diasporans: as descent of
interlocutors, 3; use of term, 171n1.
See also Caribbean origins
African rites of passage and naming
ceremonies: Budd Boyz, Inc. a.k.a.
BBiBrotherhood Stool (nonprofit),
105; churches adopting, 20, 48; day
names given in Soul Journey, 22. See
also Soul Journey, Inc.
African spiritual traditions: Hawai'ian
traditions and, 38; importance of
teaching positive view of, 147–148;
interfaith programming (African
Traditional Spiritual Coalition), 5,
117, 164; interrelations among exalted
spirits from different traditions, 31,
63, 93; Okomfokese and the broader
culture of, 153, 157, 158; one supreme
creator as common to, 17, 109, 180n1;
and religion among the enslaved, 4,
157, 173–174n6; "traditional" used as
term to distinguish Christianity and
Islam from, 120, 174–175n7. See also
Akan spiritual path; Nyame (God,
Source); spirituality and religion;
other specific traditions
African Traditional Spiritual
Coalition (Washington, DC), 5, 117,
164
"after law" moment. See post-
juristocratic transition ("after law"
moment)

Akan (pure), 41
Akan language. See Twi (Akan)
language
Akan people: history of the Guan
people and, 118–120, 122–123, 144;
majority belong to Christian
churches, 134–135; as matrilineal,
118; Nana Oparebea's ancestry in,
133, 144–145. See also Ghana
Akan shrine communities: overview, 4;
fundraising, 24–25, 145; improvements
to infrastructure in Ghana, 132, 145,
158; responsibility to help others,
particularly elders, 27–28, 112. See also
Akonnedi Shrine (aka Nana Panyin
Shrine) (Larteh, Ghana); Asuo
Gyebi shrine (Larteh, Ghana);
copresent jurisdictions; elders;
formal adjudication process for
spiritual offenses or violations;
spiritual consultations; spiritual
laws and ethical principles;
spiritual purification
—IN THE UNITED STATES:
authorization and support by Nana
Oparebea to establish and grow,
2–3, 20, 22, 123–124, 147, 171n2; and
the civil rights and other
empowerment movements of the
1960s and 1970s, 4–5, 146–147,
148–152; and the general growth of
African or African-related spiritual
paths, 5; number of priestesses and
priests in, 5; Okomfokese on the
significant work required to
establish and maintain, 158–159;
regional promotion of the Akan
spiritual order, 146, 159. See also
Akan Spiritual Order (ASUO)
shrine (Maryland); Bosum
Dzemawodzi shrine house (New
York City); Obaatanpa N'Abosum
Fie shrine house (New York City);
transnational connection of Akan
spiritual community

Akan Spiritual Order (ASUO) shrine (Maryland): *akwasidae* ceremonies (Sundays), 87, 88; authorization by Nana Oparebea, 20, 22; Nana Atei as second lieutenant and Ankobeahema of, 23, 55, 78–79, 81, 112; and the Obaatanpa House of Hope, Inc. (umbrella organization), 146, 159; Okomfohema Botwe I as founding queen mother and chief priestess of, 5, 20, 22, 153; Okomfokese as first lieutenant for, 146; as site of research, 5. *See also* Akan shrine communities; Soul Journey, Inc. (Washington, DC)

Akan spiritual path: the elders as gateway to, 29–30; importance of teaching positive view of, 147–148; increasingly global presence of, 37; as incrementally revealed, 27; as less well-known than other West African traditions in the US, 4, 173–174n6; lifeforce in ritual objects and nonhuman beings, 32, 128, 181–182n6; Nana Oparebea as intensifying Akan influence over, 145; and the power of what is not said or shared, 10, 110, 143; ritual objects, 32, 134, 181–182n6; the spiritual and physical realms interwoven as one, 5; as traditional, definition of, 120, 174–175n7. *See also* Abosom; Akan shrine communities; analogies with Akan spirituality; ancestor spirits; ancestral worship; call to serve; ceremonies; communication with spirits; constellations of subjectivity; copresent jurisdictions; elders; flow; free will; gift-giving protocols; graduation of trainees (*akomfowaa*); hope; justice; misunderstandings of Akan spirituality; Nyame (God, Source); reincarnation; spiritual healing process; spiritual laws and

ethical principles; spiritual purification; surrender; training

Akom ceremonies: annual public ceremony held by Okomfokese/Obaatanpa shrine, 158; children "playing Akom," 99; Freedom Friday at Elmina Castle, Ghana, 1–2. *See also* ceremonies; virtual ceremonial spaces

akomfo (sing., *okomfo*: graduated priestesses and priests), 2, 83

akomfowaa (sing., *okomfowaa*: trainees), 83. *See also* graduation of trainees (*akomfowaa*); training

Akonnedi (Obosom). *See* Nana Panyin (Obosom), a.k.a. Akonnedi

Akonnedi Shrine (a.k.a. Nana Panyin Shrine) (Larteh, Ghana): chiefship call to (Ghana), 106; final graduation approvals held at, 96; as geographically upper shrine, 3; herbalist training of Osofo Yaw, 106; hierarchy of Abosom and, 123, 133, 140; history of formation of two shrines in Larteh, 123, 133; Nana Afoah Baakang at, 139, 141, 142; Nana Oparebea as chief priestess of, 2–3, 123–124, 133, 141, 142, 145, 171n2; official historian appointed for, 25; Okomfohema Panyin Nana Ama Ansaah as queen mother of, 139, 142. *See also* Akan shrine communities

Akuapem Association, 41

Akuapem people, 118, 120, 122–123, 153

Akufo-Addo, president of Ghana, 1, 160

akwasidae ceremonies, 87, 88

analogies with Akan spirituality. *See* Christianity—analogies with; legal analogies; medical analogies

ancestors, cherished: apparitions of, and the call, 87–88; invoked to begin ceremonies, 102; *odwira* festivals to strengthen ties to, 32–33 ancestor spirits: the Abosom as sending message to people through, 80; as "calling from the future," 51–52; and the Freedom Friday celebration of Great Return, 2; and the power of positive connectedness, 50–51, 54; spiritual plane of, as in realm with the Abosom, 80; talking with spiritualists to guide professional services for family members, 73, 81; who were enslaved, as guides, 50. *See also* Abosom; communication with spirits; possession

ancestral family lines: enslaved ancestors of African American spiritualists, 50, 64–65, 67, 107; healers or *akomfo* in, 26, 83, 144; interrelatedness of, 79; reconnection to African traditions and, 52

ancestral origins: divinations for, 65; DNA testing for, 20

ancestral worship: as common cultural practice in Ghana, 134–135; consequences of neglecting, 134; as imperative for chiefs and queen mothers, 134, 135; as imperative for spiritualists, 135; noble ancestors, defined, 134; ritual objects and offerings of food and drink, 134

Angola, 79

animals, spiritual affinity with, 60

Ankobeahema, as title, 23, 55

Ansah, Yaa, 67, 74, 75, 86

anthropology: collaborative ethnography and decolonization of knowledge, 12–13; and theopolitics, 176–177n12; tradition as term, vs. Akan spiritualists' term, 174–175n7. *See also* methodology

Aristotle, 182n7

Aruba, 61

Asase Yaa (Great Earth, the Great Mother), 102, 128

asceticism, 125. *See also* spiritual purification

Asuo Gyebi shrine (Larteh, Ghana): commemorative statue of Nana Oparebea, 22, 124, 158; enstooled husband of Okomfohema Botwe I (Nana Adu Richardson), 23–24, 102, 140; family responsible for business management of, 23–24, 139; as geographically lower shrine, 3; history of formation of two shrines in Larteh, 123, 133; improvement of infrastructure at, 145, 158; Nana Afoah Baakang as eldest priestess of, 1, 95, 139; Nana Atei enstooled as Ankobeahema, 23, 55; Nana Oparebea as chief priestess of, 124, 129–131; Nana Oparebea's work with Okomfohema Botwe I during life, 22, 120; Dr. Kwame Nkrumah and, 124; official historian appointed for, 25; Okomfohema Botwe I as enstooled queen mother and chief priestess of, 3, 5, 18, 19, 22, 23, 121, 139; Okomfohene Yirenkyi I as enstooled chief priest of, 23, 116, 121, 132, 139; Okomfohene Yirenkyi I as Okomfo serving Nana Oparebea for eleven years, 120, 121, 130–131; as site of research, 5. *See also* Akan shrine communities; graduation of trainees (*akomfowaa*); methodology—research trip to Larteh, Ghana

Baakan, as title, 92, 146

Babalawo, 84

Bacarejo, Diana, 7

Baptist church, 18, 86

Beliso-de Jesús, Aisha, copresences, 6

Benin, 84

Black History Month, 48

Black Lives Matter movement, 163

Black Panther (film), 32–33

Black Panthers, 149

Black Power movement, 149
Boamah, Kwabena (Alex), 25
Bosum Dzemawodzi shrine house
(New York City), 19; as first Akan
shrine house in the US, 2–3, 19, 147,
172n3; Nana Yao Opare Dinizulu I
as founder and leader, 2, 152;
Okomfohema Botwe I as part of,
19–20, 146–147; Okomfokese's
involvement with, 146–147, 152;
Yoruba as initial tradition of, 19–20.
See also Akan shrine communities;
Nana Yao Opare Dinizulu I
Brown, James, "Say It Loud, I'm Black
and I'm Proud," 149
Budd Boyz, Inc. a.k.a. BBiBrotherhood
Stool (nonprofit), 105
Buddha, 46, 53

call to serve: by apparitions of
cherished ancestors, 87–88; by
appearance of Obosom as stranger,
122; and challenges at home and/or
work, 58, 86, 87, 88–89; deep
knowing of inner truth as validation
of, 64; directly by Obosom, 122,
129–130, 142, 148; dreams as source
of, 23, 65–66, 77–78, 132, 152, 172n5;
easy transitions, 26–27; fainting as
first indication of, 142; and fear of
the rigors of training and life as an
okomfo, 57–58; free will and choice
to accept, 78; meaningfulness of, 155,
157; signs and affirmations sent by
the spirits for, 64, 86–89, 92, 130, 142;
and the spiritual principle that
challenges in life may only be
understood in retrospect, 58;
surrender to, 58, 67; tragic
experiences and surrender to, 58. *See
also* graduation of trainees
(*akomfowaa*); training
Candomblé, 4
Cape Coast Castle, Reverential Night
ceremony (Ghana), 172n4

Caribbean origins: ancestral, of Osofo
Yaw (Nana Osofo Yaw Nkrumah),
106–107, 108; of Nana Atei, 23, 59–60,
64, 65, 67, 76, 77; of Okomfowaa
(then Okomfo) Abena Baakan, 86
Castor, N. Fadeke, 11–12
Catholicism, interrelation of exalted
spirits and, 31
ceremonies: *akwasidae* ceremonies
(Sundays at ASUO), 87, 88; chiefship
installations, 106; food preparation
for, generally, 184n2; graduation
food preparation ritual, 96, 101,
184n2; graduation welcome, 95–96;
invocation of spiritual lineage, 102;
kneeling and hand gesture, 95;
marriage blessing, 101–104; opening
and closing of a formal
conversation, 122, 128, 132; thanking
of Abosom and ancestors, 103–104.
See also African rites of passage and
naming ceremonies; Akom
ceremonies; chants and lyrics;
clothing; drums and drumming;
festivals; libation pouring; virtual
ceremonial spaces
challenges, overcoming: of being born
into human form, 29; the call issued
among work/life challenges, 58, 86,
87, 88–89; children of spiritualists
and, 74–75; and the constellation of
subjectivity, expansion of, 68, 100;
environmental spiritual imprints,
39–40, 46; graduation as priestesses
and priests and, 100; lessons
replicated until the person learns,
111, 113; the *okra* (divine soul) as
aiding, 46; seeking a husband or
wife, 69–70; spiritual lessons
accepted in a future life, 37;
spiritual lessons may only be
understood in retrospect, 58, 68; in
training, 68. *See also* education of
people who seek help, as obligation;
justice; mental health issues;

challenges, overcoming *(continued)*
spiritual dimension of suffering and
illness; spiritual healing process;
spiritual laws and ethical
principles; trauma
chants and lyrics: in ceremony, 95, 102;
songbook compilation and CD, 22
chiefship in Ghana: ancestral
veneration as cultural practice,
134–135; as custodian of histories,
120; and history of the Akan and
Guan peoples, 118–120, 122–123; as
inherently spiritual, 106; protocol of
being introduced by others, 128; and
the yam cycle, 128. *See also* Ghana;
Nana Abboa-Offei
children: born already interlaced with
an Obosom, 94; early evidence of
spiritual gifts, 59–60, 75, 94, 142,
150; in Ghana, and police working
with spiritualists, 51; of matrilineal
Akan people, 118; of patrilineal
Guan people, 118–119; of
spiritualists, as belonging to the
Abosom, 74–75; of spiritualists,
resenting the time demands on
their parents, 99–100. *See also*
youth
Christianity: the Black church and the
Holy Ghost, 157; and celebrations
across faiths, 127; Ghana as heavily
Christianized, 134–135, 137;
Okomfokese and, 150; proverbs as
mode of teaching wisdom of, 130,
143; spiritualists also practicing, 118,
137; traditional spirituality used as
term to distinguish from, 120,
174–175n7; upbringing of
spiritualists in, 18, 26, 30–31, 64, 86,
121. *See also* Christian pastors;
misunderstandings of Akan
spirituality
—ANALOGIES OF AKAN SPIRITUALITY
WITH: angels or saints, 16, 70; the
cross as ritual object, 32; grace,

30–31; the Holy Ghost, 157; parable
of the stranger, 130
Christian pastors: adopting elements
of African values and protocols, 10,
20, 48; assassination of Dr. Martin
Luther King, Jr., 151; covertly
seeking assistance from
spiritualists, 52, 53, 137; prohibition
of Abosom practice by, 135, 137
civil rights movement and other
empowerment movements, 4–5,
146–147, 148–152; theopolitics and
intensification of, 163, 164. *See also*
cosmopolitics; post-juristocratic
transition ("after law" moment);
theopolitics
Clarke, Kamari Maxine, 10, 53
clothing: of graduate priestesses, 96; in
professional life of spiritualists, 56;
regalia, 84, 122; traditional cloths,
spiritual significance of, 95; white,
as sign of working in the light, 70,
95, 152. *See also* hairstyles
communication with spirits: ability for,
as limiting oppressors' attempts to
control a person's soul, 136–137; in
ancestor worship as cultural
practice in Ghana, 134; creation of
protected tunnel for, 47; divination
via sacred pot, 43, 96, 136, 143;
dropping into connection at any
time, 47–48, 57, 59; foretelling
events, 136, 156; foretelling events,
free will as limiting, 136; languages
used by spirits, as varying, 98,
143–144; memories of past lives as,
75; putting the ego aside, 46–47;
self-emptying (stepping aside) to
allow, 34, 46–47; spatiotemporal
assemblages and, 135, 136, 156, 167;
transnational modes of, 125–126;
water used in divination, quality of,
62. *See also* dreams; possession; signs
sent by the spirits; visions
compassion, 39

connectedness, the power of positive, 50–51, 54

consciousness of spiritual adepts: permeability of, and spirits communicating via dreams or visions, 44, 45; possession and variation in states of, 34–35, 80, 89–90, 136, 143

constellations of subjectivity: overview, 12–13, 117–118, 148; affective registers and, 10, 53–54, 178–179n18; among the Abosom, 63; challenges and expansion of, 68, 100; conventional understanding of subjectivity as unsettled in, 6–7, 165; copresences and expansion of, 17–18, 19, 48, 54, 165; in copresent jurisdictions, 95; definition of, 8, 161, 164–165, 177n13; as ever-emergent, 161, 166; free will and, 166; Godsister relationships and, 86; graduation of trainees and rebirth/expansion of, 85, 94–95, 100; guidance from the spirits, 110–111; as intersubjective process, 166; multisensorial aspects of, 91, 155, 165; and positive connectedness, 54; the rigors of training and development of, 57–58; the role of high priestess and reconstitution of self, 19; spiritual marriage and other forms of divine union as interlacing in, 54, 56, 93, 94–95, 126; virtual ceremonial spaces and expansion of, 14, 25, 163; as vital affective assemblage, 11, 54, 161, 164–165. *See also* copresent jurisdictions; professional work incorporating spiritual expertise and mastery

—OF INDIVIDUALS: Nana Atei, 55–56, 57, 59, 82; Okomfohema Botwe I, 17–18, 19, 48, 54; Okomfohene Yirenkyi I, 116, 117–118; Okomfokese, 148, 155, 156–157; Osofo Yaw, 107, 114, 115

copresences: Abosom solving problems by working with, 28; as term, 6,

175n8. *See also* constellations of subjectivity; spatiotemporal assemblages of copresences

copresent jurisdictions: overview, 12–13, 160–161; Abosom conversing with or interacting with each other, 112; affective registers and, 10, 53–54, 178–179n18; cogovernance of shrines and the shrine system as, 48; constellations of subjectivity as coursing through, 95; and cooperation without submission, 10; and cosmopolitics, 9–10, 11, 161, 166; definition of, 8–9, 11, 179–180n21; doctors of spirit and, 137–138; dreams as domain for governance of, 126; graduation of trainees and increased subjection to, 85, 94; guidance from spirits working through other spiritualists, 111, 112; and the interconnectedness of all, 10, 127–128; marriage matters, 104; Nana Atei as neuropsychologist and, 55, 56–57, 81–82; Okomfohema Botwe I as clinical social worker and, 20–21; Okomfokese and, 147, 155; Osofo Yaw's work in agriculture and food safety and, 105, 114; and the post-juristocratic transition, 9, 11, 167; and the power of what is not said or shown, 10; and spatiotemporal assemblages, 178n17; theopolitics and, 10, 54, 155, 161, 163–164, 166–167, 178–179n18; and training, taboos and requirements vary among, 84; and virtual ceremonial spaces, 14, 163; as vital affective assemblage, 11–12, 54. *See also* constellations of subjectivity; formal adjudication process for spiritual offenses or violations; professional work incorporating spiritual expertise and mastery; spatiotemporal assemblages of copresences; spiritual laws and ethical principles

cosmopolitics: copresent jurisdictions
and, 9–10, 11, 161, 166; definition of,
176n12; and virtual ceremonial
spaces, 14
Côte d'Ivoire, 126, 131
court systems, expert evaluation and
testimony by Nana Atei, 56, 81. *See
also* justice system and spiritualists
COVID-19 pandemic, and the rise of
virtual ceremonial spaces, 13–14, 24,
117, 162
Coyle Rosen, Lauren, *Fires of Gold*, 41,
62
Crosson, J. Brent, 11–12
crystals, 32
Cuba, 84

dark side: existence of, 69, 70–71; free
will and choice to turn to, 36–37,
70–71; misunderstanding that Akan
spiritualists conduct practices in,
36, 52, 53, 69–70; persons denied
entry to shrine spaces by spirits, 47;
persons harboring jealousies of
those in the light, 34, 47. *See also*
education of people who seek help,
as obligation; Light, the;
misunderstandings of Akan
spirituality; spiritual attacks;
spiritual laws and ethical
principles
de la Cadena, Marisol, 176–177n12
diet: advice from spirits about, 57;
healthy, and requirement to step
aside to allow divine forces to work,
34; as origin of suffering, 39; Osofo
Yaw as nutritionist, 105, 109; yam
cycle, and spiritual festivals, 127–128
divination: on ancestry, 65; quality of
water used in, 62; via sacred pot, 43,
96, 136, 143. *See also* communication
with spirits
DNA tests, 20
Donham, Carolyn Bryant, 149
Douglass, Frederick, 150

dreams: ancestral revelations received
in, 172n5; assistance from spirits in
interpretation of, 44; the call to
serve received via, 23, 65–66, 77–78,
132, 152, 172n5; as central mode of
communication, 44; elders teaching
how to flow through, 45;
enstoolments conveyed via, 18, 23,
132; foretelling events in
spiritualists' lives, 23, 132;
governance instructions received
in, 23, 44, 125–126; of Nana Atei,
65–66, 77–78, 79; needed
information sent by spirits in, 45;
reasons spirits choose to visit via, as
varied, 44–45; spiritualist
appearing in dream, as
manifestation of the Obosom,
125–126; spiritualist appearing with
someone else in dream, 126; of
spiritually gifted children, 59; as
transnational mode of
communication, 125–126; visions
distinguished from, 45; warnings
sent for spiritually unlawful
actions, 30. *See also* communication
with spirits; visions
drums and drumming: function of, 33;
Okomfo Kwabena and, 57, 75, 182n1
Dutch slave trade, 1
dysfunctional patterns, attachment to,
40, 71, 113

education: absence of African
American history in curriculum,
150; importance of teaching positive
view of African spirituality,
147–148. *See also* professional work
incorporating spiritual expertise
and mastery
education of people who seek help, as
obligation: alternatives to desire for
"love spells," 69–70; and discomfort
with hearing the truth, 38–39, 135;
how to turn away from evil or

negativity, 52; refusal to provide services, 36–37, 70; and requests for unethical rituals, 37, 69–70; and requirement not to feed negativity, 113–114. *See also* misunderstandings of Akan spirituality; spiritual laws and ethical principles

ego: as not part of the immortal self, 46; putting it aside, 35, 46–47

elders: advisory board for transnational connectedness, 147; ancestor worship taught to the young by, 134; authority of, and need to respect, 29–30, 154; dream-flow taught by, 45; and enstoolment of chief priestesses and priests, 3, 18, 23, 132, 139; in formal spiritual adjudication process, 30, 112–113; Panyin as title, 95, 140, 171n2; protocol of being introduced by others, 128; the responsibility to help, 28, 112; as spiritual bridge, 157; virtual ceremonial spaces innovated by, 24, 117, 148, 158, 162, 185n1; vital traditions passed down through, 29; wisdom of, 140. *See also* Akan shrine communities

Ellis, Alfred, 149

Elmina Castle (Ghana), 1–2, 172n4

English language: spirits communicating in, 98, 143–144; translation of Twi writings into, 140. *See also* language

enslavement: ancestors who were enslaved, as guides, 50; as ancestral origins of African American spiritualists, 50, 64–65, 67, 107; and Freedom Friday celebration of Great Return/Elmina Castle Akom, 1–2, 160; of priestesses and priests, usual practice of murdering at shipside, 67; slave trade, 1, 18, 67, 172n4; spirituality/religion among the enslaved, 4, 157, 173–174n6; suturing of ruptures due to, the

enstoolment of Okomfohema Botwe I as, 18; tourism to the castle-dungeons, 172n4; trauma of, as ongoing, 50, 149–150, 156–157; as unique trauma, 157

enstoolment, as term, 18

environmental spiritual imprints, 39–40, 46

Escobar, Arturo, 165

ethics. *See* spiritual laws and ethical principles

evil, persistence in the world, 70–71. *See also* dark side

Ewe people, 81, 173–174n6

fainting, 142

family (of origin): support required by, as condition of training, 66–67; support requirement not possible, Okomfohene Yirenkyi I's commitment to work in exchange, 121, 130–131; trainees coming from families of priestesses and priests, 83. *See also* ancestor spirits; ancestral family lines; ancestral worship; children; youth

farming: organic, and knowledge of local resources, 114–115; reciprocity and, 106, 107, 108–109

fasting, 96, 101

fear: experienced during possession, 35, 90; Ghanaians' fear of and prohibitions on Abosom practice, 135, 137; of power of Okomfohema Botwe I, 33–34; resistance to the call due to, 57–58; of the truth, 38–39, 135; of what Akan spirituality involves, 15–16, 17, 52. *See also* misunderstandings of Akan spirituality

feeding the spirits: in ancestral worship as cultural practice in Ghana, 134; food preferences of Abosom, 123; graduation and knowledge of, 94; graduation

feeding the spirits *(continued)*
food-gathering ritual and, 96;
reminders from spirits for, 59; as
routine, and perpetual copresence
of spirits, 59, 115. *See also* ceremonies;
libation pouring
Ferme, Mariane, 178n17
festivals: as key ceremonies for
sustaining transnational
connections, 126, 140, 148; Nana
Kwasi Agyiri Richardson as
working on logistics for, 140; for
Obosom Nana Asuo Gyebi
(January), 23, 24–25, 81, 123, 127, 185n1;
for Obosom Nana Panyin (October),
23, 81, 123, 127; *odwira* (strengthening
of ties with cherished ancestors),
32–33; yam festivals for Abosom,
127–128. *See also* ceremonies; virtual
ceremonial spaces
fire, as spiritual element, 38
Five (pseudonym of husband-to-be of
Ama Baakan), and marriage
blessing ceremony, 101–104, 184n4
flow: dream-flow taught by elders, 45;
surrender and acceptance of, 68. *See
also* spatiotemporal assemblages of
copresences
formal adjudication process for
spiritual offenses or violations:
overview, 30–31; Abosom approval
of resolutions, 113; attempts to
revisit resolutions reached, as
violation of protocol, 113, 114;
consequences for failing to heed
warnings, 30; dreams
communicating information
needed in, 126; elders or council of
elders in, 30, 112–113; and grace,
30–31, 36–37; length of deliberations,
113; the Obaatanpa shrine and, 158;
situations calling for, 112; warnings
prior to, 30–31. *See also* spiritual laws
and ethical principles—offenses or
violations of

foster care, 49
Foucault, Michel, 165
Freedom Friday (Great Return), 1–2,
160
free will: the Abosom as not
superordinate over, 70–71, 136; to
answer the call to serve, 78;
attempts to exercise power over
another's free will as deep violation
of spiritual laws and codes of
conduct, 36, 69–70; and the choice
to turn to the light or the darkness,
36–37, 70–71; constellations of
subjectivity and, 166; education
of those who request unethical
spells of manipulation, as
obligation of spiritualists, 37, 69–70;
foretelling of events by spirits as
limited by, 136; Nyame (God,
Source) as imbuing, 70–71; of
spiritualists, 71, 111

Gandhi, Mahatma, 53
Garvey, Marcus, 150
Gerima, Haile, *Sankofa* (film), 156
gesture, kneeling and finger
placement, 95
Ghana: cultural arts exchange
programs for youth and young
adults, 108–109; Freedom Friday
celebration of Great Return, 1–2,
160; as heavily Christianized,
134–135, 137; history of the Akan and
Guan peoples, 118–120, 122–123, 144;
independence from the British
(1957), 3; infrastructure
improvements of communities in,
132, 145, 158; police working with
spiritualists, 51; President Akufo-
Addo, 1, 160; President Dr. Kwame
Nkrumah, 3, 124. *See also* African
spiritual traditions; Akan people;
Akan spiritual path; ancestral
worship; chiefship in Ghana;
enslavement; Guan people

gift-giving protocols: beaded bracelet for inductions and enstoolments, 141–142; first visit to home of spiritualist, 122; graduation of priestesses and priests, 96, 141–142; marriage dowry gifts, 101, 102–103; positionality of the researcher and, 42, 122, 141–142
Godmother relationship, 87, 92
God. *See* Nyame (God, Source)
Godsister relationship, 86
"going under" (to begin training), 19. *See also* training
Goodale, Mark, 7, 12
grace (chances to change), 30–31, 36–37
graduation of trainees (*akomfowaa*): clearing and leveling processes required for, 100; clothing and beads worn, 95, 96, 101, 141–142; constellations of subjectivity undergoing rebirth and expansion through, 85, 94–95, 100; copresent jurisdictions increasing control after, 85, 94; fasting, 96, 101; final approvals for graduation (Akonnedi shrine), 96; food preparation ritual, 96, 101, 184n2; gift-giving protocols, 96, 141–142; Godsister relationships, 86; medicine given, 101; possession of graduates by Abosom, 96–97, 101; rigors of, and exhaustion of graduates, 95, 96, 100–101; ritual marks given, 101; shrine elder discussions prior to journey to Ghana, 83, 84; welcome ceremony, 95–96; white talcum powder on skin, 96. *See also* Asuo Gyebi shrine (Larteh, Ghana); call to serve; Hill, Eric (videographer and Ifá priest); methodology—research trip to Larteh, Ghana; training
Guan people: the Abosom as welcoming both Akan people and, 145; history of the Akan people and, 118–120, 122–123, 144; Nana Afoah

Baakang's ancestry in, 144; Nana Oparebea's ancestry in, 133, 144–145; and oneness of the supreme God, 128; as patrilineal, 118–119; and spirits that are the children of God, 128. *See also* Ghana
Gyekye, Kwame, 182n7

hairstyles: dreadlocks, 152; *mpese* locks worn during training, 67, 152
Haiti, 84
Hawai'i, spiritual tradition of, 37–38
herbs and herbalism: as amplifiers, 32; lifeforce of herbs, 32; Nana Atei and, 76; Okomfohene Yirenkyi I and, 120; Osofo Yaw and, 105, 106; the spirits as guiding, 57; spiritual baths, 141; training in Ghana, 106. *See also* farming
Hill, Eric (videographer and Ifá priest): as Babalawo, 84; filming graduation trip in Larteh, 84, 90; filming Okomfohene Yirenkyi I, 122, 128, 132
Hindus, and the multicultural Caribbean, 76
honey, 115
hope: as everyday process, 27; fundamental purpose of spiritualists is to give, 38; importance of, 27; ritual objects and, 32; and spiritual purification, 32–33

Ibo people, 173–174n6
Ifá-Orisa religion, 84
intergenerational effects of trauma, 21, 48, 49–50, 71–72, 149–150, 156–157
International African Arts festival (NYC), 158
intuition, as signs from the universe, 69
Ireland, 90
Irish spiritual tradition: ancestor spirits, 60, 79; interrelation of exalted spirits and, 31

Islam: and celebrations across faiths, 76, 127; Nation of Islam (Mosque No. 7), 150; traditional spirituality used as term to distinguish from, 120, 174–175n7. *See also* Muslims

Jamaica, 106–107, 108
Jewish people and Judaism: and celebrations across faiths, 127; and World War II, 77
justice: the fundamental purpose of spiritualists is to bring, 38–39; racism and the search for, 50, 149–151; restorative, Akan spiritualists working for, 20–21, 48–50, 51; social and political transformations of the 1960s and 1970s and search for, 4–5, 146–147, 148–152. *See also* cosmopolitics; post-juristocratic transition ("after law" moment); theopolitics
justice system and spiritualists: court testimony and expert evaluation, 56, 81; probation officers, 73. *See also* police departments, Akan spiritualists working with; youth, incarcerated

Kennedy, Robert, assassination of, 151
King, Dr. Martin Luther, Jr.: assassination of, 151; as cherished ancestor, 102; as inspiration ("I have a dream … "), 15

language: gossip, prohibition of, 114; that which cannot be rendered into, 10, 110, 143; that which must not be uttered, 110; used by spirits during possession, as varying, 98, 143–144. *See also* English language; spiritual laws and ethical principles; Twi language
legal analogies: attorney-client privilege, 52–53; *res judicata*, 114; specialties in practice, 137

libation pouring: in ceremonies, 102–103; in formal openings and closings of conversations, 122, 128; gift protocol for, 122; as routine, and perpetual copresence of spirits, 59, 115; in spiritual consultations, 143; translations of, 140. *See also* feeding the spirits
liberal democratic law: and suffusion by spiritual copresences, 11. *See also* cosmopolitics; legal analogies; post-juristocratic transition ("after law" moment); theopolitics
liberation and empowerment movements: of the 1960s and 1970s, 4–5, 146–147, 148–152; theopolitics and intensification of, 163, 164. *See also* Akan spiritual path; challenges, overcoming
the Light: the Abosom as forces of and aligned with, 16–17; ceremonial request to thank and ask for continued presence of, 103; definition of, 4; free will and choice to turn to, 70–71; spiritual laws and ethical principles as aligned with, 4; white clothing as symbolic of, 70, 95, 152. *See also* Nyame (God, Source); spiritual laws and ethical principles
limitations. *See* challenges, overcoming
"love spells." *See* free will

McAllister, Carlota, 7, 176–177n12
Makeba, Miriam, 88
Malcolm X: assassination of, 151; as cherished ancestor, 102; as cultural icon, 150
Mali, 119
Maroon communities, 107
marriage: blessing ceremony, 101–104; enstooled, 23–24
marriage, spiritual (with Abosom): overview, 28; arrival of Obosom without being called, 99; both

priestesses and priests known as
"wives" to spiritual husbands (for
certain Abosom), 93, 125; calling to
the Obosom, 98–99; dream
communication of Obosom
featuring the spiritualists in,
125–126; as interlacing in
constellations of subjectivity, 54, 56,
93, 94–95, 126; Nana Adade Kofi
and, 93, 98–99, 102, 156; Nana Asuo
Gyebi and, 3, 17, 19, 20, 28, 54, 56, 66,
78, 93, 148, 152–153, 156; Nana Esi
and, 94; patterns of infusion and
modes of interrelation as varying
among, 94; with two Abosom, 56
Mauritania, 119
medical analogies: DNA testing for
biological ancestry, 65; doctor-
patient privacy rules, 52–53; oath to
the profession, 46; operations on
the body, 32; restoring balance, 39;
specialties in practice, 137; violation
of ethics, 36
medical conditions. *See* spiritual
dimension of suffering and illness
medical information: spirits guiding
use of, 57; used in spiritual
consultations, 39
mental health issues: in addition to
spiritual ailments, 66; and
restorative justice, 49
methodology: approval of research by
Akan elders and the Abosom,
41–43, 53, 84–85, 96, 141, 160; as
collaborative engaged ethnography,
3, 8, 12–13, 90, 160–162; interpreters,
187n1; names of interlocutors, 171n2;
sites of, 5; timeframe of research, 5.
See also positionality of the
researcher
—RESEARCH VISIT TO LARTEH, GHANA:
overview, 42–43; affective archives
of the researcher, 97, 184n3;
approval of research collaboration
specified trip to attend priestesses'

graduation, 42–43, 83–85; departing
spaces not clearly meant for
observer, 97; interviews during, 96,
116, 117–118, 122, 141; interviews
following, 97–101; interviews prior
to, 61, 83–95, 107–108; introductions
and welcome ceremony, 95–96
Miami, 106–107, 115
misunderstandings of Akan
spirituality: overview, 4; about the
Abosom, 16–17, 135, 137; belief that
exercise of power over another's
free will is part of Akan practice,
36, 69–70; belief that spiritualists
practice in evil forces and the dark
side, 36, 52, 53, 69–70; desire to
correct, as motivating collaboration
with researcher, 41, 43, 53, 160;
disrespect for priestesses and
priests, 51; fear-based demonizing
and maligning, 17, 52; as fed by
silence of spiritualists due to oath
of confidentiality, 53; importance of
teaching positive view of African
spirituality, 147–148; of spiritual
dimension of medical conditions,
15–16. *See also* dark side; education of
people who seek help; fear
Morris, Rosalind, 52
mpese locks, 67, 152
music: Black music in the 1960s and
1970s, 149; chants and lyrics (and
songbook), 22, 95, 101; drumming
and instruments, 33; importance in
calling forth copresences, 33
Muslims: ancestral veneration and, 134;
celebrations across faith traditions,
76, 127; openness to African
spirituality, 101; seeking assistance
from spiritualists, 137. *See also*
Islam

names and naming. *See* African rites of
passage and naming ceremonies
Nana, as title, 83

Nana Abboa-Offei: on the Abosom of Asuo Gyebi shrine, 140; and Akan spiritual culture, 120, 123, 124; as brother of Okomfohene Yirenkyi I, 117, 118; and the call of Okomfohene Yirenkyi I, 129, 130–131; as chief in Nyambekyere, Ghana, 117, 118; home with his brother in Nyambekyere, 118, 124, 132; on Nana Oparebea's vision to authorize shrines in the US, 123–124; narrative of the history of the Akan and Guan peoples, 118–120, 122–123; on the oneness of the supreme God, 128; as practicing Christian, 118; on the relations among Abosom, 123; on the yam cycle, 128

Nana Adade Kofi (Obosom): overview, 57, 107, 114; and the Akonnedi (Nana Panyin) shrine, 123; and the hierarchy of shrine spirits, 123; human marriage blessing by, 102; *Osofo* relationship to, 106; possession by, 80–81, 93, 98; as spiritual husband, 93, 98–99, 102, 156; travel to the US, 124; as warrior spirit, 94, 99

Nana Adu Richardson, 23–24, 102, 140

Nana Afoah Baakang (Okomfopanyin Nana Afoah Baakang): overview, 139; at Akonnedi shrine, 139, 141, 142; ancestral lineage of akomfo, 144; called as child, and training of, 142; on dreams as communication, 144; as eldest priestess of Asuo Gyebi shrine, 1, 95, 139; and enstoolment of Okomfohema Botwe I as queen mother at Asuo Gyebi shrine, 139; and enstoolment of Okomfohene Yirenkyi I as chief priest at Asuo Gyebi shrine, 139; and the Freedom Friday Akom, 1–2; fundraising in the US, 145; as leader at Asuo Gyebi shrine, 139–140, 142; and Nana Kwasi Agyiri Richardson, 139, 140; Nana Oparebea as teacher, 139, 141,

142, 171n2; Okomfohema Panyin Nana Ama Ansaah as first teacher, 139, 142; Panyin as title of, 95, 140; positionality of the researcher and, 141–142; possession and, 95, 96, 141, 143–144; spiritual consultation process of, 143; as transnational leader, 141, 142, 143, 145; wisdom as elder, 139–140, 141

Nana Agyiri. *See* Nana Kwasi Agyiri Richardson

Nana Asuo Gyebi (Obosom): overview, 55; annual festival for (January), 23, 81, 123, 127; annual festival, virtual opening of, 24–25, 185n1; the call via, 142, 148; the call via physical manifestation of, as stranger, 122, 129–130; details of problem solving not shared with spiritualists, 28; food preferences of, 123; as forerunner of Akan spiritual governance in the US, 22–23, 124; as guide to governance, 22–23; and the hierarchy of shrine spirits, 123, 133, 140; and the history of the Asuo Gyebi shrine in Larteh, 123, 133; and hope, 27; incrementally revealing the path, 27; and marriage blessing ceremony, 102, 103, 104; Nana Oparebea's father as originally bringing to Larteh area, 123, 133; Dr. Kwame Nkrumah and, 124; Okomfokese holding annual public Akom ceremony for, 158; positionality of the researcher and giving of name by (Nyamekye), 43, 96, 141; possession by, 95, 96, 129–130; sacred day of (Sundays), 87; as spiritual husband, 3, 17, 19, 20, 28, 54, 56, 66, 78, 93, 148, 152–153, 156; truth frequency of, matching water element with, 62; water as element of, 38, 55, 61–63, 156

Nana Atei (Ankobeahema Nana Amoabaa Atei Asiedu): overview,

55–57; ancestral origins (enslaved Ghanaian), 59–60, 64–66, 79; ancestral origins (Irish), 60, 79; Ankobeahema, enstoolment as, 23, 55; appearance of, 56; birth brother and sisters of, 77; birth daughters of, 65, 67, 73–75, 86; birth father of, fraught relationship with, 60–61; birth mother of (Pearl), as spiritually gifted, 59–60, 76–77; call, training, and graduation of, 57, 59, 64–68, 77–78; Caribbean island multicultural origins of, 23, 59–60, 64, 65, 67, 76, 77; childhood and young adulthood of, and evidence of spiritual powers, 57, 59–60, 64, 77–78; Christian upbringing of, 64; clothing worn by, 56; constellation of subjectivity of, 55–56, 57, 59, 82; dreams of, 65–66, 77–78, 79; as elder and priestess of the ASUO shrine house and the Asuo Gyebi shrine in Larteh, 23, 55, 78–79, 81, 112; husband of (*See* Okomfo Kwabena); Okomfohema Botwe I as teacher of, 23, 65–66, 78; prebirth trauma experienced by, 60–61; and preparatory interviews for research trip to Ghana, 61, 107–108; and Soul Journey, 56, 78, 87; spiritual age of, 79; spiritual marriage of, 55, 56, 59; as teacher, 86, 87–88; as transnational leader, 23, 81; water as spiritual element and, 61–62

—AS NEUROPSYCHOLOGIST AND UNIVERSITY PROFESSOR: overview, 56; expert evaluations and testimony in court proceedings, 56, 81; as participating in copresent jurisdictions, 55, 56–57, 81–82; private practice of, 56, 81; professional expertise incorporated into spiritual work of, 72, 73; spiritual expertise and mastery incorporated into work of, 56, 72, 81–82

—IN DIALOGUE: on the Abosom, 58; on the Abosom using personal ancestors to send messages, 80; on consequences to spiritualists who break spiritual laws, 69; on the deep knowing of inner truth, 64; on the details of problem solving not being shared by Abosom, 63–64; the existence of the dark side, 69, 70–71; on feeding the spirits, 59; on free will, 70–71, 78; on free will of others as absolutely protected by Akan spiritual law, 69–70; on guidance from other spiritualists, 111; on the healing process, 71–72; on interrelations between the Abosom and exalted spirits from other traditions, 63; on possession, 80–81; on the priestesses and priests as conduits for spirit, 71; on professional and spiritual work as dovetailed with each other, 72–74; on signs and directions from the spirits, 68–69; on spatiotemporal assemblages of copresences, 68; on the spiritual plane of ancestors, 80; on surrender and relinquishing control, 58, 67–69

Nana Baakan. *See* Okomfokese (Okomfokese Nana Baakan Okukuranpon Yirenkyiwa)

Nana Dinizulu. *See* Nana Yao Opare Dinizulu I (Okomfohene Nana Yao Opare Dinizulu I)

Nana Esi (Obosom): overview, 17–18, 55; and the Akonnedi (Nana Panyin) shrine, 123; marriage blessing ceremony and, 102; possession by, 97; specializing in children and the family, 74; in spiritual marriage/bond, 56, 91, 94; travel to the US, 124; water as element for, 61

Nana Kwasi Agyiri Richardson, 24, 102, 121, 139, 140

Nana Oparebea (Okomfohema Nana
Akua Oparebea): Akan influence on
shrine system intensified by,
144–145; authorization and support
for establishment of shrine houses
in the US, 2–3, 20, 123–124, 147, 171n2;
authorization of ASUO shrine
(Maryland), 20, 22; as chief priestess
of the Akonnedi shrine, 2–3,
123–124, 133, 141, 142, 145, 171n2; as
chief priestess of the Asuo Gyebi
shrine, 124, 129–131; and expansion
of Akan shrines within Africa, 126;
family ancestry of, 133, 144–145;
father of, as bringing Obosom Nana
Asuo Gyebi to the Larteh area, 123,
133; grandson of, as enstooled
husband of Okomfohema Botwe I
(Nana Adu Richardson), 24, 102,
140; and Dr. Kwame Nkrumah (first
president of Ghana), 3, 124; and
Okomfohema Botwe I, during life,
20, 22, 120; Okomfohene Yirenkyi I
serving, for eleven years at Asuo
Gyebi shrine, 120, 121, 130–131; and
Okomfokese, 154, 156, 158; passing to
spirit form (1995), 3, 132, 139; and
possession, 129–130; as teacher, 116,
117, 120, 126, 129–131, 134, 139, 141,
142, 171n2; visits to the US, 22,
172n5
—AS REVERED ANCESTOR:
communication in dreams, 23, 44;
guiding governance, 50, 54, 133–134,
145, 156; and interrelation of exalted
spirits with other traditions, 31;
monumental commemorative
statue made for, 22, 124, 158;
museum and library in her old
house, plans for, 158; the Obaatanpa
N'Abosum Fie shrine house (New
York City) named in honor of, 146;
photograph from life as ceremonial
blessing, 104; sending Okomfohene
Yirenkyi I, 23

Nana Panyin (Obosom), a.k.a.
Akonnedi: annual festival for
(October), 123, 127–128; and history
of the two shrines in Larteh, 123, 133;
Obosom Nana Asuo Gyebi
welcomed to the shrine by, 123, 133;
as overall head of Asuo Gyebi
shrine, 140; as principal Obosom of
Akonnedi shrine, 123; as unable to
travel to the US, 124
Nana Panyin Shrine. *See* Akonnedi
Shrine (aka Nana Panyin Shrine)
(Larteh, Ghana)
Nana Yao Opare Dinizulu I
(Okomfohene Nana Yao Opare
Dinizulu I): called to serve, 172n5; as
chief priest of Akan path priestesses
and priests in the US, 20; as
founding the first Akan shrine house
in the US (New York City), 2–3, 19,
147, 172n4; and Okomfokese, 146–147,
152; as teacher of Okomfohema
Botwe I, 2, 3, 19–20, 99; as university
professor, 152; wedding of, 152. *See
also* Bosum Dzemawodzi shrine
house (New York City)
Napolitano, Valentina, 7, 176–177n12
Nation of Islam, 150
nature, lifeforce in nonhuman beings
(*sasa*), 32, 128, 181–182n6. *See also* fire;
water
neoliberalism, precarity of legal and
political legitimacy, 7–8
New Year's celebrations, 127
New York City: African American
culture and music, 149, 151, 152; first
Akan shrine house in (1967), 2–3, 19,
147, 172n4; International African
Arts festival, 158; social and
political transformations of the
1960s and 1970s, 4–5, 146–147,
148–152. *See also* Bosum
Dzemawodzi shrine house (New
York City); Obaatanpa N'Abosum
Fie shrine house (New York City)

Nigeria, 84, 126
9/11 attacks on the World Trade
Center, 78
Nkrumah, Dr. Kwame (first president
of Ghana), 3, 124
Nyambekyere, Ghana: home and
shrine of Okomfohene Yirenkyi I
in, 117, 118, 124, 131, 132; Nana
Abboa-Offei as chief in, 117, 118
Nyame (God, Source): Asase Yaa as
divine feminine counterpart to, 102,
128; communication in any
language, 143; definition of, 16;
divine wisdom beyond language,
10, 110, 143; and evil, persistence in
the world, 71; free will as imbued
by, 70–71; invoked to begin
ceremonies, 102; the *okra* (divine
soul) as domain of, 46; oneness
across traditions and faiths, 17, 109,
180n1; oneness of the supreme
creator, 15, 17, 70, 128, 180n1; service
to man as service to, 128; as source
of spiritual laws, 36; and spiritual
law, violations of, 36; as
unfathomable in its totality, 109, 110,
136–137; the voice of the people as
voice of, 121. *See also* Abosum;
ancestor spirits; Light, the; *okra*
(inner divine flame, divine soul);
spiritual laws and ethical principles

Obaatanpa House of Hope, Inc.,
146, 159
Obaatanpa N'Abosum Fie shrine
house (New York City): and formal
adjudication process for spiritual
offenses or violations, 158; name of,
as honoring memory of Nana
Oparebea, 146; officiating over
life-passage ceremonies, 158;
Okomfokese as founder and chief
priestess of, 146; participation in
the regional Akan spiritual path
community, 146, 159; and

transnational connection, building
of, 158–159; virtual ceremonial
spaces facilitated by, 148. *See also*
Akan shrine communities;
Okomfokese (Okomfokese Nana
Baakan Okukuranpon Yirenkyiwa)
Obama, Barack, 27
odwira festival (strengthening of ties
with cherished ancestors), 32–33
okomfo (graduate priestess or priest), 2,
83
Okomfo Akua Anima Ansa: overview,
91; Ama Baakan as foster child of,
91–92; call to service, 100; as child
of Okomfohema Botwe I,
resentment of the time demands of
service, 99–100; on children in the
Akan sacred culture "playing
Akom," 99; on the clearing and
leveling process in graduation, for
the constellation of subjectivity,
100; marriage blessing ceremony for
Ama Baakan, 101–104; spiritual
bond to Obosom, 91, 94; as teacher,
91–92, 97, 98
Okomfohema Botwe I (Okomfohema
Nana Akua Amoabaa Botwe I):
overview, 2, 15, 17–18, 54; and
approval of the collaboration with
research, 41–43, 84–85, 96; birth
children of (six), 20, 101 (*See also*
Okomfo Akua Anima Ansa); call,
initiation, training, and graduation
of, 3, 19–20, 26–27, 152–153; Christian
upbringing of, 18, 26, 30–31; clothing
worn by, 84; constellation of
subjectivity of, 17–18, 19, 48, 54;
down time, difficulty of obtaining,
37–38, 44, 99–100; enstooled
(enthroned) as chief priestess and
queen mother at Asuo Gyebi shrine
(Ghana), 3, 5, 18, 19, 22, 23, 121, 139;
enstooled husband (Nana Adu
Richardson), 23–24, 102, 140;
Nana Dinizulu as teacher of, 2, 3,

Okomfohema Botwe I *(continued)*
19–20, 99; and Nana Dinizulu's
shrine house, 19, 146–147; and Nana
Oparebea during life, 20, 22, 120;
and Okomfohene Yirenkyi I,
120–121, 132, 139; and Okomfokese,
146–147, 152–153, 154–155; Okres, as
driver and *okyeame* (spokesperson)
in Ghana, 122, 124; praying for a
foster child, 92; and shrine
governance and expansion, 20;
songbook compilation and CD of
sacred lyrics and chants, 22;
spiritual marriage of, 17, 28, 54, 66;
as teacher, 20, 23, 57, 65–66, 78,
105–106, 146, 154–155; as
transnational leader, 3, 22, 54, 120;
water as spiritual element and, 38;
Yoruba spirituality and, 19–20. *See
also* Akan Spiritual Order (ASUO)
shrine (Maryland); Soul Journey,
Inc. (Washington, DC)
—AS LICENSED CLINICAL SOCIAL
WORKER: participating in copresent
jurisdictions, 20–21; praying for a
psychologist to help her (Nana
Atei), 66, 78; spiritual expertise
and mastery incorporated into
work of, 20
—IN DIALOGUE: on the Abosom as
positive forces aligned with the
laws of Light, 16–17; on the
authority of elders and the need to
respect, 29–30; on the call to serve,
26–27; on the challenges of being
born into human form, 29; on
connectedness, the power of
positive, 50–51; on the details of
problem solving not being shared
by Abosom, 28–29, 41; on disrespect
for Akan priestesses and priests, 51;
on dreams, 45; on drumming and
music, 33; on educating those who
ask for unethical rituals, 37; on the
ego, keeping in check, 35, 46–47; on

fears people have of herself, 33–34;
on formal adjudication process and
warnings for wrongdoing or
spiritually unlawful actions, 30–31;
on the Freedom Friday celebration
of return, 2; on the group effort
required to expand Akan culture,
23; on Hawai'ian spiritual tradition,
38; on her ancestral line, 26; on
hope, 27, 38; on incremental
revelation of the path by Abosom,
27; on interrelations between the
Abosom and exalted spirits from
other traditions, 31; on the
inviolable sanctity of the *okra*
(divine soul), 46; on justice, 38–39;
on the justice system, 48–50; on
nonattachment, 28–29; on oath of
confidentiality, 52–53; on the
omnipotence of spirit to choose a
spiritualist, 19; on the oneness of
God, 15, 17; on past lives, 25–26; on
police consultations with
spiritualists, 51; on possession,
31–32, 34–35; on prevention of
misunderstandings and expansion
of Akan path as motivating
collaboration with researcher, 41,
43, 53; on protected shrine spaces,
47; on the responsibility to help
others, 27–28; on ritual objects and
hope, 32; on seeking peace and
balance within herself, 38, 44; on
Soul Journey, 21; on the spirits
keeping her on a fast track, 27, 44;
on spiritual age, 79; on spiritual
attacks on herself, 34; on spiritual
attacks, refusal of requests to
perform, 36–37; on the spiritual
basis of suffering and illness, 15–16,
39–40; on spiritual purification as
seeking hope, 32–33
Okomfohema Panyin Nana Ama
Ansaah, 139, 142
Okomfohene, as title (chief priest), 116

Okomfohene Yirenkyi I (Okomfohene
Nana Yaw Yirenkyi Opare Gyebi
I): overview, 116–117; and Asuo
Gyebi shrine, enstooled as chief
priest, 23, 116, 121, 132, 139; and Asuo
Gyebi shrine, serving Nana
Oparebea for eleven years, 120, 121,
130–131; brother of (*See* Nana
Abboa-Offei); call, training, and
graduation of, 117, 121–122, 128–131;
Christian upbringing of, 121;
constellation of subjectivity of, 116,
117–118; copresent jurisdictions
taught to spiritualists in the US, 116;
as doctor of the spirit, 137–138;
dreams foretelling his enstoolment,
23, 132; dual residencies in Ghana
and DC, 23, 116, 117, 121, 126, 132;
family of, lack of support for
calling, 121, 130–131; film of (by Eric
Hill), 122, 128, 132; Ghanaian
upbringing of, 116; home, shrine,
and community in Nyambekyere,
Ghana, 117, 118, 124, 131, 132; as Larteh
lineage's first male priest, 117, 130,
132; mother of, 129; Nana Oparebea
as teacher, 116, 117, 129–131;
Okomfohema Botwe I and, 120–121,
132, 139; shrine in Washington, DC,
117; as teacher in the DC area, 116,
117; as transnational leader, 116, 117,
120, 138; trophy given to by group of
American okomfo, 132–133; virtual
ceremony innovation and, 117; wife
of, 23, 116, 121, 126, 131–132
—IN DIALOGUE: on ancestral worship
as Ghanaian cultural practice,
134–135; on ancestral worship by
spiritualists as imperative, 135; on
Christian pastors covertly seeking
assistance from spiritualists, 137; on
expansion of Akan tradition within
Africa, 126; on Ghanaians'
simultaneous fear and respect for
the Abosom, 135, 137; on the

hierarchy of shrine Abosom, 140; on
the history of the two shrines in
Larteh, 123, 133; on the life of Nana
Oparebea, 133–134; on transnational
modes of spiritual communication,
125–126; on the yam festivals,
127–128
Okomfokese (Okomfokese Nana
Baakan Okukuranpon Yirenkyiwa):
overview, 146; and African and
African American music and
culture, 149, 151, 152; Baakan as title,
146; birth mother of, 152; and the
broader African traditional
spiritual culture, 152, 153, 157; call,
training, and graduation of, 148,
152–155; children of, 153, 155–156;
constellation of subjectivity of, 148,
155, 156–157; and copresent
jurisdictions, 147, 155; dreams of, 152,
153; early sense of the divine and
baptism in a Christian church, 150;
as elder, 147, 155; as first lieutenant
of ASUO shrine house, 146; as
founder and chief priestess of
Obaatanpa shrine house, 146;
husband as supportive of her
training, 153–154; leadership in high
school and college, 151–152; and
Nana Dinizulu, 146–147, 152; and
Nana Oparebea, 154, 156, 158; New
York City origins of, and political
and social transformations, 146–147,
148–152; Okomfohema Botwe I and
the call to, 146–147, 152–153;
Okomfohema Botwe I as teacher,
146, 154–155; as public school
teacher, 147; and regional
promotion of the Akan spiritual
order, 146, 147, 159; spiritual
marriage of, 148, 152–153, 156; as
teacher of priestesses and priests,
148, 155; as transnational leader, 147,
148, 158–159; and virtual
ceremonies, facilitation of, 148. *See*

Okomfokese (continued)
also Obaatanpa N'Abosum Fie
shrine house (New York City)
—IN DIALOGUE: on the bridge to
spirituality, 157; on the call to serve,
meaningfulness of, 155, 157; on
education, absence of African
American history in, 150; on
education, importance of, 147–148;
on family life, 150; on making things
right in this lifetime, 157–158; on
miracles, 155–156; on the MLK and
other assassinations, 151; on the
political and social transformations
of the 1960s and 1970s and the search
for justice and liberation, 148–152;
on racism, experience of, 149–151; on
spatiotemporal assemblages of
copresences, 156; on the spiritual
aspects of physical healing, 156–157;
on spiritual marriage, 156; on the
trauma of enslavement as unique
and ongoing, 156–157
Okomfo Kwabena (Okomfo Kwabena
Duku) (husband of Nana Atei):
ancestry of, 79; call, training, and
graduation of, 57–58; as drummer,
57, 75, 182n1; marriage and, 61; as
physical therapist, incorporating
spiritual expertise and mastery,
72–73; and possession, 80–81;
support for Nana Atei to train, 67
Okomfopanyin, as title, 140
okomfowaa (trainee), 83. See also
graduation of trainees (akomfowaa);
training
Okomfowaa (then Okomfo) Abena
Baakan: overview, 85–86; call to
serve, 86–88; Caribbean origins of,
86; Christian upbringing of, 86;
graduation to okomfo in Larteh,
Ghana, 86, 100–101; and Miriam
Makeba, 88; Nana Atei as teacher,
86, 87–88; possession experiences
of, 88, 89–90

Okomfowaa (then Okomfo) Ama
Baakan: early exposure to Akan
sacred culture, 91–92, 93, 97–98; as
foster child of Okomfo Akua Anima
Ansa, 91–92; graduation to okomfo
in Larteh, Ghana, 91, 97, 101;
initiation of, 92; marriage blessing
ceremony for, 101–104; Okomfo
Akua Anima Ansa as teacher, 91–92,
97, 98, 101–104; as okyeame
(spokesperson and interpreter of
the spirits), 92, 97–98; and
possession, 93, 97, 98; spiritual
marriage of, 93–94, 98–99, 102
okra (inner divine flame, divine soul):
oath of spiritualists not to step into
the domain of, 46; oppressors
seeking to control, the ability to
communicate with spirits as
preventing, 136–137; reconnect to
Akan path and connection to, 52; as
the reincarnating part of the
person, 46; as remaining after
passing to pure spirit, 46. See also
Akan spiritual path; Nyame (God,
Source); reincarnation
Okres, as driver and okyeame
(spokesperson) in Ghana, 122, 124
okyeame (spokesperson and interpreter
of the spirits): definition of, 92; for
Nana Afoah Baakang coming out of
possession, 143; Okomfo Ama
Baakan as, 92, 97–98; Okres (for
Okomfohema Botwe I in Ghana),
122, 124
optimism. See hope
Orisha: Ifá divination, 84;
interrelations of exalted spirits and,
31, 63, 93; as more well-known than
the Akan path in the US, 4;
possession and, 93. See also Yoruba
people
Osofo, as title, 106
Osofo Yaw (Nana Osofo Yaw
Nkrumah): overview, 105; Budd

Boyz, Inc. a.k.a. BBiBrotherhood Stool (nonprofit for rites-of-passage mentorship), 105; call and training of, 105–106, 108; chiefship calling of, 106; clothing worn by, 84; constellation of subjectivity of, 107, 114, 115; cultural arts exchange programs for youth and young adults, 105, 108–109; efficiency and timekeeping by, 107; father of, as ancestor, 106–107; father of, as organic farmer and herbalist, 106, 107, 108, 114–115; Jamaican ancestry of, 106–107, 108; mother of, 109; Okomfohema Botwe I as teacher, 105–106; *Osofo* as title and function, 106; pouring libations, 115; and preparation for the graduation trip to Larteh, 84, 107–108
—IN DIALOGUE: on discerning the path of right action for making things right, 110–111, 113–114; on the formal adjudication of spiritual law violations, 113; on knowledge of local resources, importance of, 115; on the oneness of Source, 109; on organic farming, 114–115; on refusing to feed negativity, 113–114; on responsibility to care and respect, 112; on Source as unfathomable in absolute essence, 110; on the totality of correlations and connections as elusive, 109
—PROFESSIONAL LIFE OF: alternative medicine practice and herbalism, 105, 106; food safety and security consultancy and workshops, 105, 114; as participating in copresent jurisdictions, 105, 114; spiritual expertise and mastery incorporated into work of, 109, 114

Pan-Africanist movement, 149, 150
Panyin, as title, 95, 140, 171n2
past lives. *See* reincarnation

physical therapists, 72–73
Pierre, Jemima, 172n4
pluriversal futures-making, 9–10, 165
police departments, Akan spiritualists working with: to assist specific clients, 49; to facilitate higher understandings, 9, 21, 49–50; in Ghana, 51; informal consultations requested by police, 51
pollution, physical and spiritual, 62–63, 125
popular consciousness. *See* misunderstandings of Akan spirituality
Portuguese slave trade, 1
positionality of the researcher: affective archives, 97, 184n3; approval of the research by the Akan elders and the Abosom, 41–43, 84–85, 96, 141; attended a graduation ceremony for Akan path priestesses (for research), 95–96; clothing worn by, 95; and customary gift-giving, 42, 122, 141–142; name given (Nyamekye), 43, 96, 141; and Nana Afoah Baakang, 141–142; and Obosom Nana Asuo Gyebi, 43, 96, 141; participation in yearlong Soul Journey program, 21, 42; protocols and procedures required by Akan rules, 96, 128; virtual ceremonial spaces and, 24. *See also* methodology; methodology—research visit to Larteh
positivity. *See* hope
possession by spirits: and affective archives of the researcher, 97, 184n3; appearance of persons in, 80–81, 96–97; Christian pastors covertly seeking assistance from spiritualists for problems of, 137; cleanliness of the body for, 125; consciousness of the possessed as taking different forms in, 34–35, 80, 89–90, 136, 143;

possession by spirits *(continued)*
    crying as response to, 98; ease of, as
    validation of the call to serve, 88,
    89; fatigue and soreness in the
    aftermath of, 89–90; fears
    experienced by the possessed, 35,
    90; and the Freedom Friday
    celebration of Great Return, 2; of
    graduates in ceremonies, 96–97;
    information obtained through,
    nonspiritualists as trusting of, 136;
    by nature spirits, 128; negotiation
    with spirits about, 80–81, 90; *okyeame*
    (spokesperson and interpreter of
    the spirits) for, 143; *Osofo* function
    distinguished from, 106; out-of-
    body experiences of the possessed,
    35, 89; protocols of verbal
    interactions and spiritual
    permission for, 32, 80; self-
    emptying (stepping aside) to allow,
    34, 46–47; spatiotemporal
    assemblages and, 89–90, 135, 136,
    144; specific movements and songs
    to summon certain spirits, 90;
    spirits communicating amongst
    themselves during, 112, 144; in
    spiritual consultations, 136, 143, 144;
    surrender to, 80; training as
    preparation for, 125; as transnational
    mode of communication, 125;
    uncertainty of whether it will
    occur, 89; by wandering spirits,
    31–32; in the Yoruba Orisha
    tradition, 93. *See also*
    communication with spirits
post-juristocratic transition ("after
    law" moment): copresent
    jurisdictions and, 9, 11, 167; as
    theoretical framework for
    analyzing social responses to
    neoliberal precarity of legal and
    political legitimacy, 7–8, 161, 164
poverty, 150
prebirth trauma, 60–61

probation officers, 73
professional work incorporating
    spiritual expertise and mastery:
    Nana Atei as neuropsychologist, 56,
    72, 81–82; Okomfohema Botwe I as
    licensed clinical social worker, 20;
    Okomfo Kwabena as physical
    therapist, 72–73; Osofo Yaw as
    nutritionist and food safety
    consultant, 105, 114; probation
    officers, 73; spiritual work benefiting
    from professional expertise, 72–73;
    teachers, 74, 91–92, 93, 147;
    university professors, 124, 152. *See
    also* copresent jurisdictions

Quayson, Ato, 182n7
queen mothers (enstooled): ancestral
    worship as imperative for, 134, 135;
    elders and spirits in choice of, 3, 18,
    132, 139; enstooled marriage, 23–24;
    enstoolment as term, 18; sacred gift
    of beaded bracelet given at
    enstoolment, 141–142. *See also*
    Okomfohema Botwe I;
    Okomfohema Panyin Nana Ama
    Ansaah

Raboteau, Albert, 173–174n6, 180n1
racism, and the search for justice, 50,
    149–151. *See also* enslavement; justice
Rattray, R. Sutherland, 119
reciprocity: cultural arts exchange
    programs for youth and young
    adults, 108–109; farming and, 106,
    107, 108–109; spiritual, and cycles of
    the soul's reincarnations, 157–158;
    and understanding of the answers
    as within, 40; and working with
    police departments to raise
    understanding, 49
reincarnation: accepting spiritual
    lessons in a future life, 37; Akan
    focus on making things right and
    good in this lifetime, 110–111, 113–114,

157–158; and cycles of spiritual reciprocity, 157–158; of the *okra* (divine soul), 46; spiritual age and, 79
—PAST LIVES: children revealing knowledge of, 75; lines of priestesses and priests from, 83; memories of, as communication with spirits, 75; traumas and sensitivities inherited from, 21, 49
religion. *See* spirituality and religion
restorative justice, Akan spiritualists working for, 20–21, 48–50, 51. *See also* justice
Rhodesia, 88
Richards, Sandra, 172n4
Richland, Justin, 10
ritual objects, 32, 134, 181–182n6
Roman Catholic church, 64
Rosen, Jeffrey, 117, 118, 122

Sankofa (film, dir. Haile Gerima), 156
Santería, 4, 6
sasa as lifeforce in ritual objects and nonhuman beings, 32, 128, 181–182n6
shrine elders. *See* elders
signs sent by the spirits: for call to serve, 64, 86–89, 92, 130, 142; as intuition, 69; surrender and recognition of, 68–69
social justice movements: intensification of, 163, 164; social and political transformations of the 1960s and 1970s and, 4–5, 146–147, 148–152. *See also* cosmopolitics; justice; post-juristocratic transition ("after law" moment); theopolitics
Soul Journey, Inc. (Washington, DC): overview, 9–10, 21; leveling of everyone to a safe middle ground, 50; mission of, 21; Nana Atei and, 56, 78, 87; Okomfohema Botwe I as founder and CEO, 21; in the path to initiation, 87; and programs for restorative justice, 48–50; and understanding of the answers as

coming from within, 40; yearlong program, 21–22; yearlong program of, researcher participation in, 21, 42
soul. *See okra* (inner divine flame, divine soul)
Source. *See* Nyame (God, Source)
sovereignty from below. *See* theopolitics
spatiotemporal assemblages of copresences: the Abosom accessing information via, 135, 136, 156, 167; copresent jurisdictions and, 178n17; definition of, 6; possession by spirits and, 89–90, 135, 136, 144; and surrender to cocreation with the spirits, 68; transnational modes of communication and, 136; virtual ceremonial spaces and, 14
spiritual attacks: the Abosom as protecting from, 16–17, 34, 47; jealousies harbored by people in the dark, 34, 47; refusal of requests to perform, 36–37, 70; on spiritualists, due to the need to move around in unprotected spaces, 33–34; as violation of Akan sacred spiritual laws, 36, 69–70. *See also* dark side; misunderstandings of Akan spirituality; spiritual purification
spiritual consultations: Christian pastors covertly seeking, 52, 53, 137; divination in, 136, 143; for fainting, 142; for family problems, 74; information obtained by possession, trust of people for, 136; libation pouring and, 143; medical information used in, 39; narrative of process of, 143; police seeking assistance with case, 51; possession in, 136, 143, 144; refusal of requests, 36–37, 70; and truth, discomfort with, 38–39, 135. *See also* education of people who seek help, as obligation; misunderstandings of Akan spirituality

spiritual dimension of suffering and
illness: ability of the individual to
make changes, 40; addressing issues
prior to medical interventions, vs.
afterwards, 15–16; answers as
coming from within, 40;
attachment to dysfunctional
patterns, 40, 71; delivery of
information by the spirits, as
varying, 40; environmental
spiritual imprints and, 39–40;
fainting, 142; medical information
used to identify, 39; origin of the
issue, identifying, 39, 40, 71–72;
prebirth trauma and, 60–61; and the
trauma of enslavement as unique
and ongoing, 156–157. *See also*
challenges, overcoming; spiritual
healing process
spiritual healing medicine: given at
graduation, 101; pollution of
elements used in, 63; water used in,
62, 63
spiritual healing process: faithfulness
to the process, 71–72; professional
expertise as dovetailing with,
72–73; self-awareness and insight as
ultimate goals of, 36. *See also*
challenges, overcoming; hope;
justice; medical analogies; spiritual
dimension of suffering and illness
spirituality and religion: celebrations
across faiths, 76, 127; children of
God as the messengers and helpers
for humans, 128; the divine
feminine and the divine masculine,
128; and oneness of God/Source/
Nyame across faiths, 17, 109, 180n1;
traditional, as term used by Akan
spiritualists, 120, 174–175n7; use
of term, 171n1, 180n23. *See also*
African spiritual traditions; Akan
spiritual path; Christianity; Islam;
Nyame (God, Source); *other specific
faiths*

spiritual laws and ethical principles: as
aligned with the Light, 4; and the
call to serve, resistance to, 57–58;
challenges in life may only be
understood in retrospect, 58, 68;
education of people who ask for
unethical rituals, 37, 69–70; forms of
spiritual-physical interweaving
and, 5–6; gossip, prohibition of, 114;
healing elements must resonate
with truth frequency of Obosom,
62; lessons replicated until the
person learns, 111, 113; negativity,
avoidance of feeding, 113–114;
Nyame (God) as source of, 36; oath
of confidentiality, 52–53; oath to
allow Nyame the domain of *okra*
(divine soul), 46; proverbs and
other indirect methods used to
teach, 4, 110, 143; responsibility to
each other in relationships, 112;
responsibility to help others, 27–28,
112; that which must not be uttered,
110. *See also* analogies with Akan
spirituality; copresent jurisdictions;
education of people who seek help,
as obligation; free will; reciprocity;
reincarnation; spiritual purification
—OFFENSES OR VIOLATIONS OF:
breaking the oath of confidentiality,
52–53; chances to change (grace)
given to trainees or spiritualists
who break, 30–31, 36–37;
consequences of, loss of spiritual
healing gifts or of one's life, 69;
consequences of, misfortune, 30;
consequences of, self-haunting, 37;
cultural taboos, 182n7; free will of
others, attempts to exercise power
over, 36, 69–70; *musuo* (harms that
afflict the soul), 182n7; Nyame
(God) and, 36; warnings given,
30–31. *See also* formal adjudication
process for spiritual offenses or
violations

spiritual purification: Akan shrine
spaces as protected, 47; asceticism,
125; baths, 47, 88, 141; centering and
grounding, 34, 35; cleanliness is
next to godliness, 125; diet and, 34;
of drum makers, 33; hope and, 32–33;
odwira festivals and, 32–33; as
operations on the body, 32;
positionality of the researcher and,
141; respect for elders and, 29–30;
self-emptying (stepping aside) to
allow divine forces to work, 34,
46–47; the spirits denying entry of
some people to shrine, 47. *See also*
clothing; hairstyles; pollution
state institutions: neoliberalism and
the precarity of legal and political
legitimacy, 7–8; theopolitical
engagement of Akan spiritualists
with, 48–50. *See also* copresent
jurisdictions; justice system and
spiritualists; professional work
incorporating spiritual expertise
and mastery; theopolitics
Stewart, Kathleen, 178–179n18
subjectivity. *See* constellations of
subjectivity
surrender: to the call, 58, 67; to the
guidance of the spirits, 110–111, 113,
156; *mpese* locks (hairstyle) and, 67;
of parents, to the separate life paths
of their children, 74–75; to
possession by spirits, 80;
spatiotemporal assemblages and,
68; to that which cannot be
rendered in language, 110; training
and learning of, 67–69, 154; to the
unknown, 109

Tano (Obosom), 63
Tegare (Obosom), 73
Temple of Nyame (Washington, DC),
124
theopolitics: anthropology and,
176–177n12; copresent jurisdictions

and, 10, 54, 155, 161, 163–164, 166–167,
178–179n18; definition of, 7, 163–164;
engagement of Akan spiritualists
with state institutions, 48–50; and
the power of what is not said or
shown, 10; as theoretical framework
for analyzing social responses to
neoliberal precarity of legal and
political legitimacy, 7–8; and
virtual ceremonial spaces, 14; as
vital affective assemblage, 11
"thinking justice beyond law," 7. *See
also* post-juristocratic transition
("after law" moment)
Thomas, Deborah, 184n3
Till, Emmett, 149
Togo, 126
traditional spirituality, defined by
Akan spiritualists, 120, 174–175n7
training: family support required to
allow, 66–67; family unable to
support, Okomfohene Yirenkyi I's
commitment to work in exchange,
121, 130–131; fear of the rigors and
requirements of, 57–58; "going
under" as phrase used to denote
beginning of, 19; humility and, 154;
mpese locks (hairstyle) worn during,
67, 152; for possession, 125; as
rigorous, 57–58, 154; surrender and
relinquishing control learned in,
67–69, 154; taboos and requirements
during, as varying with location,
84; trainees (*akomfowaa*; sing.,
okomfowaa), 83; violations of spiritual
law during, and chances to change,
30–31, 36–37. *See also* call to serve;
graduation of trainees (*akomfowaa*)
transnational connection of Akan
spiritual community: annual
festivals as key ceremonies for
continuation of, 126, 140, 148;
authorization and support in
starting Akan shrine houses in the
US, 2–3, 20, 22, 123–124, 147, 171n2;

transnational connection *(continued)*
commemorative statue of Nana
Oparebea, 22, 124, 158; copresent
jurisdictions and, 167; enstooled
marriages and, 23–24; expansion
within Africa, 126; fundraising, 22,
24–25, 145; improvements to
community infrastructure in
Ghana, 145, 158; modes of spiritual
communication to facilitate,
125–126, 136; Nana Afoah Baakang
and, 141, 142, 143, 145; Nana Atei
and, 23, 55, 81; Nana Kwasi Agyiri
Richardson and, 140; Okomfohema
Botwe I as vital link in, 3, 22, 54,
120; Okomfohene Yirenkyi I and,
116, 117, 120, 138; Okomfokese and,
147, 148, 158–159; spatiotemporal
assemblages of copresences and,
136; Dr. Walker and, 122, 124. *See also*
virtual ceremonial spaces
transnational connections of African
spiritual traditions, generally, 84
trauma: of enslavement, 50, 149–150,
156–157; intergenerational, 21, 48,
49–50, 71–72, 149–150, 156–157; from
past lives, 21, 49; of racism, 149, 151;
spatiotemporal assemblages and,
178n17. *See also* challenges,
overcoming; enslavement
Truth, Sojourner, 150
Tubman, Harriet, 150
Twi (Akan) language: italicized terms
in, 171n3; spirits communicating in,
98, 143–144; translation of writings
from, 140; understood by some
spiritualists without having studied
it, 98. *See also* language

US Department of Health and Human
Services, 105

village, "it takes a village," 21, 36–37, 48
violent racism, and search for justice,
149–151

virtual ceremonial spaces: Akom
ceremonies, 24; and constellations
of subjectivity, expansion of, 14, 25,
163; and copresent jurisdictions,
expansion of, 14, 163; COVID-19
and the rise of, 13–14, 24, 117, 162;
devices and audiovisual media as
conduits for copresences, 6; elders
and innovation of, 24, 117, 148, 158,
162, 185n1; expansion of access to
Akan spiritual path facilitated by,
148, 162–163, 185n1; fundraising and,
24–25; Nana Asuo Gyebi festival,
24–25, 185n1; positionality of the
researcher and, 24; possible
expansion to realm of healing and
spiritual readings, 14; real time
nature of, as lessening mediation
effects, 25; spatiotemporal
assemblages and, 14. *See also*
ceremonies; festivals
visions: distinguished from dreams, 45;
of Nana Oparebea for expansion of
Akan tradition, 123; as one central
mode of communication, 44;
permeability of consciousness in,
and choice of spirits to use, 44; as
portals or amplification spaces for
communication, 45. *See also*
communication with spirits;
dreams
vital matter, 32, 181–182n6
Voudun, 4, 84

Wakanda movement (*Black Panther*
film), 32–33
Walker, Dr., 122, 124
Washington, DC, police department
culture and diversity training
with Okomfohema Botwe I,
49–50
water: pollution of, 62–63; as spiritual
element, 38, 55, 61–62; used in
divination, 62; used in medicine,
62, 63

Whisper from the Mountains (sacred songbook and CD), 22
World War II, 77

yam festivals, 127–128
Yoruba Ifá-Orisa religion, 84
Yoruba people: Okomfohema Botwe I's early involvement with spiritual tradition of, 19–20; and religion among the enslaved, 173–174n6. *See also* Orisha
youth: Budd Boyz, Inc. a.k.a. BBiBrotherhood Stool (nonprofit

for rites-of-passage mentorship), 105; cultural arts exchange programs for young adults and, 105, 108–109; and disrespect for elders, 29–30; in foster care, 49
youth, incarcerated: Akan spiritualists working with, 21, 49–50; probation officers who are spiritualists, 73

Zenker, Olaf, 7
Zoom. *See* virtual ceremonial spaces

Founded in 1893,
UNIVERSITY OF CALIFORNIA PRESS
publishes bold, progressive books and journals
on topics in the arts, humanities, social sciences,
and natural sciences—with a focus on social
justice issues—that inspire thought and action
among readers worldwide.

The UC PRESS FOUNDATION
raises funds to uphold the press's vital role
as an independent, nonprofit publisher, and
receives philanthropic support from a wide
range of individuals and institutions—and from
committed readers like you. To learn more, visit
ucpress.edu/supportus.

www.ingramcontent.com/pod-product-compliance
Lightning Source LLC
Chambersburg PA
CBHW020855270326
41928CB00006B/716